A Map of the Mind

Plate 64 from the *Arcano del Mare* by Robert Dudley, published by Giuseppe Cocchini in Florence, 1661. Map Division, The New York Public Library, Astor, Lenox, and Tilden Foundations. Used by permission.

A Map of the Mind

Toward a Science of Psychotherapy

Richard Brockman, M.D.

PSYCHOSOCIAL PRESS
Madison, Connecticut

In order to protect the anonymity of patients quoted in this text, changes as to sex, race, profession, family structure and background have been freely made. Material from different patients has been combined. All specific references to names, places, and events were invented.

Library of Congress Cataloging-in-Publication Data

Brockman, Richard.
    A map of the mind : toward a science of psychotherapy / Richard Brockman.
        p.   cm.
    Includes bibliographical references and index.
    ISBN 1-887841-14-8
    1. Psychotherapy—Research—Methodology.   2. Psychotherapy—Research—Methodology.   I. Title.
    RC337.B75   1998
    616.89'14—dc21   98-11890
                                                                                    CIP

Manufactured in the United States of America

For my patients.
For my teachers.
For Mirra.

Contents

Introduction

I am deep in the dream book, am writing it fluently. I shall report on the first crude map of this territory.
(Freud in Masson, 1985, pp. 298–299)

Let us start with feeling as a prediction of behavior, partly because it is squarely within the realm of the testable and partly because it has tended to be neglected.
(Bowlby, 1969, p. 121)

How are the data of clinical psychiatry gathered and then shaped from the first crude map of unknown territory into a working formulation? The clinical formulation is not only the first organizing principle of therapy but also consists of a series of hypotheses that inform the entire course of a treatment. The clinical formulation is the central aspect of the psychotherapeutic process, establishing direction, but it is also a process that must itself be given direction. How one finds one's bearings and maintains one's course in clinical work—in short how to use a map and compass in clinical work—is the main goal of this book.

The book begins with a theoretical hypothesis of how interpersonal psychodynamics are structured. From that brief theoretical beginning, it demonstrates the techniques of data gathering, observation, and interview techniques necessary to move from tentative hypotheses to working formulations. I seek to demonstrate that the data of formulation are often encountered in unexpected ways, and that they must be appreciated and sought. Once the data have been identified, hypotheses must be made, and once made, tested, and once tested, refined or discarded, augmented, and used to help define the search for more precise data.

The construction of hypotheses begins with data about the patient and not necessarily with the first meeting with the patient. The data might be in the form of a referral from another clinician, a letter, the clinical chart, a telephone call. The first encounter with data must generate the first hypothesis against which to measure and test subsequent data and subsequent hypotheses. The first data and tentative hypotheses together serve as the therapist's first bearings in the search for meaning on these otherwise uncharted waters. No data can be accepted passively or at face value. Data must be compared and measured against data from other sources within the patient, within the history, within the therapist. There must be this constant back-and-forth assessment of all clinical data against multiple reference points without which there is no tension; without tension there is no movement; and without movement there can be no direction.

The therapist must be active in every step of this uncovering process. The therapist not only receives and records data, but actively guides the patient toward data. As the patient describes the landscape of the unknown, the therapist through the active construction of hypotheses begins to understand and anticipate the topography of the journey. By beginning to understand what to anticipate in the landscape, the therapist comes to have a clearer sense both of what is and is not being shown. As the data are gathered little by little, the practice of making tentative hypotheses will be demonstrated and developed. Each step provides new information that will either support or weaken the tentative formulations already constructed. Depending on the nature of the data, the hypothetical formulations will be supplemented, modified, or discarded. This leads to the practice of constantly making and challenging one's clinical hypotheses. Constant tension exists between data and hypothesis which in turn generate movement and direction.

It would be an error to rely on the patient for direction, for the patient is an unreliable navigator in the early stages of any evaluation. If one relies on the patient's understanding for direction, the formulation will be based on generalized wisdom and passive truths, and the journey will end in much the same place that it began without new or specific meaning, based as it was on hypotheses that were generated from within the illness. But the journey guided by data and hypothesis does lead to more and more specific data and more specific hypotheses in dynamic interaction. The formulation itself becomes from the very beginning of the journey the compass that the patient cannot be. The clinical formulation is not something that is formulated at the end when all the data is in. The formulation is an evolutionary process.

I also propose that psychotherapy is appropriately a prospective science that can and should be practiced in accordance with scientific procedure where psychological and biological data are combined into a dynamic unity. The book shows how and why this approach is crucial to a science of psychotherapy. The process is less the receptive unfolding of layers, as in traditional psychotherapy, than it is an active search for data and the construction of multiple hypotheses, leading to validation through the generation of new meaning.

The book proceeds from the discovery of data and the construction of interpersonal hypotheses to the biological impact of affect. As the motive force of attachment behavior, affect is core to the understanding of self and object. From the data, multiple hypotheses are generated about the level of affect, the quality of affect, and the psychobiological freedom of affect. These more biologically based hypotheses are actively integrated with interpersonal hypotheses to result in a clinical formulation that has evolved and been tested at every step of the way.

Part I provides background to the theories that are addressed in this book. Clinical presentation begins with Part II. Discussions of the psychological and neurobiological centrality of affect are the focus of Part III.

Acknowledgments

There are always people one wants to thank for helping one in the creative process. In this instance there are many such people, but most of them will have to remain nameless because of the nature of this book. Thus I am first and foremost indebted to the patients I have had the privilege to work with directly as a clinician and indirectly as teacher and supervisor of residents and medical students at the New York State Psychiatric Institute and at Columbia University, College of Physicians and Surgeons.

There are, however, several people whom I can identify and to whom I am very grateful. To Eric Marcus, M.D., for encouraging me to write this book, to Lyle Rosnick, M.D., for his enthusiasm and support, to David Lindy, M.D., for his careful reading of an early version of the text, and to Ethel Person, M.D., for her creative presence and encouragement. I am also grateful to present and past editors at the Psychosocial Press including Margaret Emery, Ph.D., George Zimmar, Ph.D., and Eunice Petrini who helped improve the clarity and focus of the book.

Greatful acknowledgment is made to the following publishers for permission to reprint material.

Excerpt from *Angels in America, Part One: Millennium Approaches* by Tony Kushner. Copyright © 1992, 1993, by Tony Kushner. Used by permission of Theatre Communications Group.

PART I

Background

Travelling backwards into the patient's past, step by step . . . I finally reached the starting-point of the pathological process.
(Freud, 1896, p. 151)

1.

Traveling Backwards

Freud had some interesting ideas about how to formulate a case. He felt that the best way to work was from the present into the past, beginning with what could not be questioned, the symptom, and moving from there to the etiologic factor, which he argued had to be associatively connected to the symptom and which lay buried somewhere in the unconscious. "Hence the chain of causation can always be recognized with certainty if we follow the line of analysis, whereas to predict it along the line of synthesis is impossible" (1920, p. 168).

Proof was reconstructive. Prognosis was rarely argued. What was going to happen was not the issue because the symptom was connected to an etiology in the past. The argument was persuasive and was based on certain "facts": that symptom and etiology were connected, and that they were connected by "psychic determinism." Freud's theory of psychic determinism held that nothing in the course of human thought or behavior occurred by chance. Since nothing mental occurred by chance, everything was determined by antecedents that lay in the mind—conscious, preconscious, or most significantly unconscious. Because they were factors in the mind, they could be discovered by the retrospective science of psychoanalysis.

Another core aspect of Freud's theory was memory, and in particular the notion that forgotten memories accounted for the gaps in the associative link between symptom and cause. "That this state of affairs [amnesia] should exist in regard to the memories relating to the history of the illness is *a necessary correlate of the symptoms and one which is theoretically requisite"* (1905, pp. 17–18). Pathogenic memories were repressed memories of events (the seduction theory) or of wishes and affects (the drive theory) that were too painful or shameful to be recalled. Neurotic symptoms were caused by memories that could not be recalled, and if these memories were uncovered by psychoanalysis then the symptoms would be relieved.

Thus Freud argued that these etiologic factors had to have happened and had to be unknown to the subject. They had to have happened because of the fact of the symptom and because of psychic determinism. They had to be unknown because if they had been known they would not have caused the symptoms in the first place. Freud argued that these "unacceptable" memories—of events, wishes, affects, or historical memory (species memory)—were present in mind, but because they were repellent, were buried under a blanket of repression. "To put it crudely," Freud wrote in a letter to his German colleague Wilhelm Fliess, "the current memory stinks just as an actual object may stink; and just as we turn away our sense organ . . . in disgust, so do the preconscious and our conscious turn away from the memory. This is *repression"* (Freud in Masson, 1985, p. 80). Repression took the distressing memory and buried it in the unconscious—". . . the ostrich policy . . . " (Freud 1900, p. 600).

Thus in the search for meaning, the symptom was the place where one started. Psychic determinism established the direction of the search. Repression was the barrier that had to be crossed. Memory was what was being sought.

These memories, however, also might include experiences that in the normal state could never be recaptured but which existed as a primitive form of memory in what Freud labeled "primary process." This was a way of thinking which existed at birth, but which was overlaid by the "secondary process" that occurred with maturation and development and established more normal memory. Where and how memory was stored was a developmental factor in Freud's theory. The earlier and more primitive the memory the more likely it was to be stored in and be acted on by the more primitive "primary" apparatus of mind. This was another factor that had a huge influence on Freud's concept of mind and direction of his formulation.

Freud argued that when the infant was born, the mind existed in a state that he called "primary narcissism," a state comparable to the mental state of primary process. This state he felt represented an undifferentiated id–ego matrix and that this was the only psychical structure that existed at birth. The argument was that the baby lived for a very real period of time in a homogeneous perceptual world, and while in it, the baby could not distinguish between self and other, between internal and external, between wish and reality. "An infant at the breast does not as yet distinguish his ego from the external world" (1930, pp. 66–67). In other words, within this id–ego matrix, the outside world did not exist, and all of existence was represented by a sense of internal space because there was no experience of external space. "At birth no object existed . . . " (1926a, p. 170).

The baby seemed to function in his own universe, as his own god, at least briefly. Outward interest was nonexistent because hallucinatory gratification satisfied all needs, according to Freud's pleasure principle. Only when perfect satisfaction was interfered with too severely and too repetitively, did the infant give up the pleasure principle and begrudgingly accept reality. Frustration lead to reality, and it was only with time, development, and frustration, that the ego emerged from the id and was differentiated from it.

Freud thus came to see the autonomy of the ego and the id as on a continuum from total merger in the id–ego matrix of the healthy infant, to relative independence in the healthy adult. Because of this developmental time line, the unhealthy adult was seen as behaving more like a normal infant than like a sick adult. In this way Freud established the theoretical underpinnings for what he defined regression and fixation.

Fixation was a state when the ego's developing separation from the id got stuck or fixated at some infantile point. Regression similarly was a state when the ego slid back and merged once again, more or less, with the id. These two concepts, fixation and regression, became extremely important by establishing psychic growth along a continuum where the relative mix of id and ego determined health.

It is important to recognize that by creating a theory based on the notion of a continuum, Freud established a specific and rather singular use for data. Data were used to éstablish where repression had to have intervened, where memory had to have failed, and where reality testing had to have broken down, and on the basis of those deficits locate where the patient had to have been functioning along the continuum of development between id and ego, between regression and health. In a sense Freud constructed the hypotheses of memory and repression and then used the hypotheses of psychic determinism and the continuum as validation. It was a brilliant argument where one set of hypotheses was being used to validate another—it was brilliant, and wrong.

> If psychopathological theory is to fulfill its own function of doing full justice to its empirical data and at the same time to formulate theory in a form that is truly scientific, nothing is more important than that it draws, and rigorously maintains, the distinction between the causes of behavior and its function. All too often they are inextricably confused. (Bowlby, 1969, p. 126)

John Bowlby, writing after the Second World War, took particular exception to Freud's confusion of hypothesis and data in his theory of attachment behavior. Bowlby had observed young animals and infants, and on the basis of his observations, came to the conclusion that attachment behavior was a primary mammalian characteristic. "One of the first behaviors that are seen in man and animal are behaviors directed towards attaching to an object, towards a mother or mother figure" (Bowlby, 1969, p. 155).

For Bowlby attachment behavior was not secondary ("anaclitic" as Freud called it) to some other instinct; it was basic. Bowlby had observed that the focus of the newborn was outward, that the first biologic direction was toward mother. The perception of reality, he observed, began with birth. The shift in orientation was dramatic from internal, self, and past to external, object, and present.

But if a neonate is instinctively primed to attach to objects in its environment, what is the "stuff" of that behavior, what is the "glue" of attachment? The answer is complex. Freud argued that the "stuff" of the behavior was the experience of pain and the abandonment of the pleasure principle and the acceptance of the reality principle. What now seems clear is that attachment behavior is biologically driven, is environmentally sensitive, is sui generis, and in higher mammals is related to the broader concept of affect.

2.

Affect and Attachment

The current understanding of affect began, though not without a long Freudian detour, with Darwin. "The movements of expression in the face and body whatever their origin may have been, are in themselves of much importance for our welfare," Darwin wrote in *The Expression of the Emotions in Man and Animals.* "I attended to this point in my first-born infant, who could not have learnt anything by association with other children, and I was convinced that he understood a smile and received pleasure from seeing one, answering it by another, at much too early an age to have learnt anything by experience" (1872, p. 358). Subsequent research into the nature of affect has supported Darwin's position that affects exist from birth, and serve an outward, communicative purpose.

In their work, Robert Emde and collaborators have noted a smiling response in the infant that appears "within minutes after birth" and that investigation showed to be linked to rapid eye movement (REM) states. "The conclusion that forced itself upon us was that REM smiling is mediated by midbrain and lower diencephalic structures" (Emde, 1991, p. 9). In other words, the autonomous smiling response was controlled by areas of the brain that also regulated such basic responses as the beating of the heart and breathing. Smiling is essential neonatal behavior. Darwin's observations were correct. What he was observing in his son were not learned behaviors; they were innate. "It has become increasingly clear that human infants are born with a broader range of complex abilities than had been previously thought. Infants, for instance, are born with considerable competence in communicating with their mother in nonverbal ways: they can recognize and discriminate between different facial expressions of affect within the first few days of life" (Amini et al., 1996, p. 219).

The drive to communicate and to attach to an object is biologically innate. With the newborn's first breath, comes what may be considered the newborn's first "thought." Who is the object? How do I identify her? How do I assure that she will not leave me? Questions addressed at the level of the midbrain and diencephalon and crucial for survival. These are not dilemmas that the baby, calf, puppy, or chick registers consciously, but they are dilemmas that each newborn engages behaviorally and expresses outwardly through affect.

Affect connects the self to the object and it does so not only by orienting toward the object but also by effectively communicating to the object. Stated in another way: The "activation of the neurobiological affect generators reliably triggers motor stereotypies—like facial expression, posture, and tone of voice—which in turn transmit the physical data underlying empathy and emotional communication" (Schwartz, 1987, p. 469). The midbrain and higher centers of emotional and neuromuscular control generate smiles intended for the object's reception and delight. Affect is not just an internal assessment, it is simultaneously a communication. Affect connects the internal state of the one who is generating the experience to the internal state of the one who is registering it. It is not sufficient to just make the assessment: "I am hungry," "I am alone,"

"I am frightened." The neonate must also communicate the assessment to an object. Survival depends on it.

By communicating to the environment, affect also prepares for action on it. "The neurologic data fit most closely a hypothesis that defines affect as neurally generated and introspectively perceived signals that generally . . . induce action" (Schwartz, 1987, p. 475). Thus affects are not passive receptors. By initiating neurohormonal changes within the organism, affect prepares for action. By acting on the environment, affect influences the environment. By reacting to the environment, affect molds learning and development. Affect provides both an assessment of and a motive for behavior. Affect is not just a feeling; it is a reinforcer to learning, to behavior, and to choice. One does not have a perception of mother that can be separated from neurobiological interactions with her, nor separated from affectively based learning (memories) about her, nor free of action directed at her, nor free of biological affect genetically received from her. Affective interactions are biological, genetic, interpersonal, and operational—and should not be interpreted from any one level alone. Therefore, affect must be assessed from the many levels of communication that it serves and from the many etiologies from which it may be derived. This requires data from many sources and at many levels of integration received from the past (memory and genetic), the present (action), and the future (intent and effect).

By understanding affect as an internal experience that prepares one for action, one has created the potential of an experimental situation where affect can be tested. "To ascribe feeling is usually to make a prediction about subsequent behavior. Thus to describe a person (or an animal) as amorous, angry, or afraid is to predict that during the coming minutes certain behavior is much more likely than any other sort" (Bowlby, 1969, p. 121).

To ascribe feeling, however, is rarely a simple task, and indeed the prediction of behavior is not easy, even conceptually. Affects may be consciously or unconsciously registered. One may do something unconsciously, nibble on a piece of bread out of loneliness, when the awareness of hunger is low or nonexistent. Or one may do something unconsciously when the affective component is quite high, such as steal a loaf of bread when driven by hunger without thought to the consequences of the act. Further one state may block the experience of another. Such as one might steal a loaf of bread that mother had just baked because one felt hungry, but under that was the fact that one was furious with her for refusing permission to watch cartoons that morning. Thus hunger covered anger. Or perhaps one was hungry and angry, and stealing the bread represented multiple-determined behavior. Affects are complex, contain input from many sources, and may not always manifest clearly in a single interaction, communication, or piece of behavior. Do not rush to conclusion.

"Now I know your motive," Freud told his 18-year-old patient Dora in his "Fragment of an Analysis of a Case of Hysteria." It was a premature statement that Freud came to regret. He went on, "It was not that you were offended at his [amorous] suggestions; you were actuated by jealousy and revenge" (1905, p. 106). Dora, a girl "in the first bloom of youth," had been sexually approached by an older man, and was subsequently presented to Freud for treatment with various psychosomatic symptoms, conversion reactions, and depression. Dora listened to Freud's interpretation of her motive, argued with him, and then at the end of the session, quit the treatment never to return again. Freud may have been right about her motive and about the affects in question, "jealousy and revenge." But his argument was closed-ended and sought to emotionally define her. Dora refused to be pinned down by his hypothesis of "jealousy and revenge." Freud recognized that her behavior was more complex than he had given credit.

Labeling affects too rigidly, reifying the motives of behavior, moves quickly to closure and removes complexity. There is usually a heavy price to be paid for such an error. Freud, knowing the difficulty of the work, and the ever-present potential for failure, added, "No one who, like me, conjures up the most evil of those half-tamed demons that inhabit the human breast, and seeks to wrestle with them, can expect to come through the struggle unscathed" (1905, p. 109).

In wrestling with "half-tamed demons" to find the meaning in another's or one's own affect, it is crucial that one respect the complexity of human behavior and never rush to end confusion by ascribing conclusive and definitive motives when one's understanding of the demons is still incomplete. Hypotheses are not definitive; they are tentative as their goal is not to pin the diagnosis so much as to encourage more data. Move slowly; investigate from as many perspectives as possible. One needs a sense of the past, present, and the future before one can say, "Now I know your motive," and even then it may be incorrect. Gather data. The purpose of the hypothesis is not only to figure out where affects have come from, but also where they are going. What thoughts and behavior, what data, to expect.

The patient–therapist setting is in many respects an excellent one for this purpose. The subject and observer are constant, data can be gathered, affect can be observed, hypotheses constructed, predictions made, interventions initiated, outcome measured, more data gathered. The goal is not the generation of hypotheses; the goal is the discovery of data that can be used to test hypotheses.

PART II

Data and Hypothesis

> *Hamlet.* Slanders, sir; for the satirical
> rogue says here that old men have
> gray beards, that their faces are
> wrinkled, their eyes purging thick
> amber and plum-tree gum, and
> that they have a plentiful lack of
> wit, together with most weak
> hams. All which, sir, though I most
> powerfully and potently believe, yet
> I hold it not honesty to have it thus
> set down; for you yourself, sir,
> should be old as I am if, like a crab,
> you could go backward.
>
> *Polonius.* Though this be madness, yet there
> is method in't.
>   (Shakespeare, Hamlet, II, ii)

3.

First Data

Now, sir, spare not your skill
In bird lore or whatever other arts
Of prophecy you profess. It is for
  yourself,
It is for all Thebes. It is for me. Come,
  save us all.
                    (*Sophocles,* Oedipus Rex)

This chapter will outline an aspect of clinical work that is often underappreciated and underused—the information that is available to the clinician and which is gathered before the patient is actually seen. These data provide the clinician with the *first* opportunity to think about the patient and to establish reference points. It is also the first opportunity to draw the tentative map for the journey on which the therapist and patient are embarking.

This approach provides a reasonable response to the question, how does one know where one is headed when the journey is into the unknown, by asserting that one cannot know until the first step has been defined and figured. The first contact, in whatever form, must be used and the data from this contact must generate hypotheses as to where one is located. If one fails to actively use the initial data to generate hypotheses and to establish points of reference, then one risks remaining in the infinity of possibilities that any clinical investigation offers, without a sense of place and without a clear sense of direction.

One makes hypotheses about the direction of the data from within a specific frame. The theoretical frame is that of affect and attachment behavior. A human being seeks to attach to another human being through an affectively mediated bond. Because of the fundamental nature of affect, one attempts to understand the direction of another's interpersonal relations, their intrapsychic world, and their psychobiology from within the context of affect and attachment.

One attempts to make these determinations not at the end of the evaluation but at each step of the evaluation. Only in that way can the clinician look for more data and test his or her ideas with some expectation of what should be found, rather than trying to induce what must have once existed. One is attempting to formulate what will happen and not just explain why something had to have happened.

Although the clinician is operating with a minimum amount of data at this early stage of the evaluation, hypotheses are certainly possible. Many hypotheses should be anticipated whilst at the same time the clinician knows that most or all may be invalidated by subsequent data.

There is obviously manifest information in every referral, such as, "I would like you to see this 50-year-old woman with depression." This information may be written on the chart or expressed verbally by the referring clinician. If this is all the data available on a patient one should not hesitate to make hypotheses about the patient and about the nature of the relationship with the referral source. But this is rarely all the material available. Often there is other, latent material that needs to be integrated into what is already known. Very often the manifest reason for the referral conceals underlying motivation or unconscious conflict—in the patient, in the referring doctor, or in an aspect of their interpersonal dynamics. In any referral there is an already existing object relation and transference between the patient and the person who is making the referral. This provides one with a preview of the transference and countertransference within which one will soon be engaged.

For example, I received a call from an internist. He stated that he wanted to refer a patient to me, 'She's a 40-year-old woman, married. Very patient husband. They're trying to have a child. She's very nice but, well, she's really too much." There was a pause, a self-conscious laugh. Then he went on, "There's always something wrong with her. Her head, her stomach—pains in her joints aren't pains; they're sarcomas. There's always an emergency and yet there's nothing wrong with her ever—except her. Always calling night and day. She really needs to see a psychiatrist. Like I said, Jackie's just too much."

From this description, one can and should make predictions and formulations about whom it is one expects to meet. One can make diagnostic impressions: somatization disorder; dependent personality disorder; possible history of abuse (the association of somatization and a history of child abuse); bipolar disorder; atypical depression.

The internist referred to her as "Jackie." He liked her, felt protective, perhaps a bit paternal, and at the same time overwhelmed, she's "too much." Speculate that this woman is attractive enough to get others involved with her and then once they are "hooked," the problems begin. Her expectations grow and her demands overwhelm. In the referral there was the sense that he was trying to fend her off—defense mechanisms of projection and projective identification should be anticipated. One might wonder that his pushing her away may have exacerbated her need to maintain contact with him.

Did she not only experience her doctor this way, but others too—were her parents also seen as too distant? Explore this theory in the history. Was she flirtatious in an attempt to engage men, thus enraging women, perhaps her mother? Was there a history of hypersexuality? Was there a history of impulsivity—"Always calling"? Was there poor frustration tolerance, possible drug or alcohol abuse, frequent fights, affective instability? If the referring doctor was saying that he felt overwhelmed and invaded, anticipate that experience from this patient (transference and countertransference), and consider that limit setting might be necessary in dealing with her (treatment plan). These are boundary issues.

Was this too much to read into a 5-minute conversation with an internist I barely knew and a patient I had never met? No, this kind of formulation and speculation is crucial because it predicts behaviors—which either will or will not occur. On meeting the patient one can begin to test whether some, any, all, or none of one's hypotheses are valid. With new data form new hypotheses to be tested, retested, and shaped into more specific hypotheses to be further elaborated and tested against behavior. Because affect motivates behavior, one's observations are a way of validating one's hypotheses about the underlying affect.

Written communications are no less valuable. A patient was referred to the psychiatry clinic from the emergency room. On the chart there were the patient's name, address—she had come a long way and had traveled past many good hospitals to be seen—her age, 34, and her sex. The rest of the page was blank except for one line from the triage nurse: "Says she's depressed."

What are the data and how does one begin to analyze them? The woman had traveled far to get to this hospital. Had she been to the four other hospitals along the way? Did she have treatment refractory depression, or was she manipulating the system by going from hospital to hospital? If so, was she seeking attention—and/or drugs? Since this is the largest hospital in the area, perhaps she felt entitled to the "biggest" care available. "Says she's depressed." The words were potent. The triage nurse doubted her credibility. She was warning me to be careful of the patient. She may have felt that the woman was pushy and asked for more than she was entitled.

On the basis of this brief but potent comment, one should anticipate meeting a woman with depression, perhaps treatment resistant depression. It may be hypothesized that she is manipulative, perhaps sociopathic. She should be asked about drug abuse. Speculate also that the triage nurse felt offended by the patient (i.e., didn't like her) and hypothesize that the patient was pushy, entitled, offensive—narcissistic issues. These are some of the things the clinician has in mind, on the way to the waiting room. One should be watchful too of disliking the patient—countertransference. One needs to get some sense of the patient and of her relationship with the triage nurse, neither of whom one has ever met. By all means formulate these hypotheses but invest in none of them because more data are obviously needed and the hypotheses are guides not goals. One should have a sense of where one is going with a patient, however, before one has ever met him or her.

Preliminary formulations can and should be made. Formulations of who you feel the patient is (sense of self, identity, history, transference); what you feel the patient will expect of you (transference, affect, object relation); and what you anticipate you will feel toward the patient (object relation, countertransference). All of these formulations would have been made before the patient was seen, so they are tentative. But they are very important because they are one's first bearings and first compass as one approaches an unknown interpersonal world.

Sometimes the data of the referral are minimal, seemingly too little to provide anything to speculate about. But this is in fact never the case because it is possible and necessary to speculate with whatever data are available. It is necessary to make a hypothesis, establish a reference point, that may be kept or may be discarded, but it is crucial to formulate. It would be an error to passively note the referral, think no more about it, and wait for the patient. Such an error maintains the unknown beyond the point when definitions and limits could have been drawn. From the very first data, in whatever form they are presented, hypotheses should be made against which all subsequent data must be measured. The interaction between data and hypotheses must be constant, active, and ongoing.

The data of the referral are vital for one other reason. The clinician has not yet seen the patient, so the relationship is as yet uncontaminated—a clean slate. It is at this stage that one has the greatest freedom to think about this human being one is soon to meet because one knows the least about the person and because the interpersonal influences (transference, countertransference) have not yet had a chance to come into play. This is the point when hypotheses must not only be made, but written down. These original ideas should be referred to in the course of the evaluation. It is important to play with the data at every stage of the formulation, and at every stage of the treatment because it is often in play that the most unexpected and therefore most important insights are found.

Therefore the written referral, "I would like you to see this 50-year-old woman with depression," contains abundant data with which to work. What are the data? How does one play with them?

This is a very polite and orderly referral. There is no particular urgency, no particular excitement. I would anticipate a polite, somewhat sad woman, not too attractive, and not in crisis. I would expect her to be uncomplaining, orderly, and therefore I would be careful lest I underestimate the level of her depression. She is someone whose life has been lived so as not to cause trouble. She is a martyr, and perhaps obsessional. Therefore I would be worried lest she underestimate or conceal her pain and suffering. Obviously I would be sure to ask her carefully about her depression and suffering. But I would also be certain to ask her about suicidality, for in addition to depression, I would hypothesize that this is the kind of woman who in an effort not to cause anyone any bother, might take her life sooner than ask for help. She is someone who keeps things to herself, and thus might be too polite and too proud to appear needy. I formulate all this not knowing the patient and knowing I could be all wrong.

A hospitalized patient was presented by a group of students. The student stated that the man was 30 years old, a successful pianist, with bipolar disorder. He had been hospitalized five times for mania in the past 2 years. He was currently being treated with lithium. The patient was aware of the interview, indeed he had eagerly volunteered for it. The student went out to get the patient at the appointed time, returning a minute later to tell us that we would have to wait as the patient had to "take a leak." What are the data?

A man with bipolar disorder needed to take a leak. What hypotheses can be generated? Coincidence: his need to urinate and the start of the conference happened to coincide. Anxiety: he has something like stage fright before interviews. Iatrogenic: he had polyuria secondary to lithium. He could have diabetes insipidus, again secondary to lithium. Interpersonal, intrapsychic: he could have wanted to establish dominance, "You doctors think you're so important? You're not. You wait for me." It could have been one, several, all, or none of the above.

There were, however, more data with which to speculate. Five hospitalizations in 2 years for bipolar disorder would seem

to indicate either very poor control (possibly due to rapid cy-
cling bipolar disorder), or an issue of compliance—he was stop-
ping the medication as if to say, "I am in control, not the illness
and not you, doctor." If this last hypothesis had merit, then
the bipolar disorder and medication adjustment (to add to or
adjust the mood stabilizer) was less the issue than addressing
interpersonal and intrapsychic issues of what it meant for this
man to be ill, to have to take medication daily, to have to depend on someone else for care, and in this case, for him to be
in the care of another man. All this can and should be considered from his behavioral statement that he had to "take a
leak."

The formulation of these hypotheses did lead to an exploration in the interview of the issues described, gathering more
data, and the discovery that he had deliberately stopped his
medication which had led to each of the five hospitalizations.
This then pointed the interview toward the exploration of new
data and to the generation of new hypotheses—of an even
more speculative nature. Thus I wanted to know more about
his relationship with his doctor (past psychiatric history, past
history, transference); his feelings about taking medication
(history, dependency issues, narcissistic issues); and sexual issues (object relations, sexual identity). This last is the most
speculative. Why is it included?

If a competent patient is hospitalized five times because
of noncompliance, then the patient has some *very* powerful
feelings about the treatment. One highly speculative hypothesis
that I would consider would be that the patient felt forced to
comply, forced to take something into his mouth (a pill) that
was the doctor's. One further hypothesis to consider but not
to explore at this time with the patient, would be the patient's
unconscious experience of equating taking the doctor's medicine with forced fellatio or rape. This would indeed be a hypothesis that one might choose never to explore as the
exploration might lead to further anxiety (resistance), refusal
to take the medication at all (acting out), and flight from the
treatment altogether (acting out). Were this issue forced on
the patient, it could well recreate an intrapsychic issue in the
interpersonal context of the treatment.

Of interest, however, was that according to the medical student, several days after entering the hospital, the patient had reported having read an article about sexual dysfunction and lithium and had the following dream: "I was reading the label on a bottle of medicine. It said the pill may be painful to swallow when you first take it but that it would get easier over time if you just 'took it'." There then are additional data as to his feelings about having to "take it," data that would seem to corroborate the complex issues involved in the patient's non-compliance.

Another type of referral is in the context of treatment failure or impasse. I received a phone call from a therapist, a psychologist. She had been given my name by a colleague. "Do you have any time for a new patient?" she asked, and then added before I had time to answer,

> I hope you do. I've been treating this woman for 4 years. She's really very sick. Depressed and suicidal. She's always threatened to kill herself—and lately she has been threatening again. She acts out, drinks. I am very worried for her. She's been very difficult to treat. A psychopharmacologist has been seeing her as well. Her depressions don't respond to psychotherapy. She really needs more medication and more time than I can give her right now. Do you think you could treat her?

The patient seemed to be in crisis and the therapist seemed to want to transfer her, urgently. I hesitated. To change therapists and treatment in the midst of a crisis seemed like bad timing. I asked her, "Have you thought about getting any supervision to help you deal with someone who sounds like a very difficult patient?"

There was a brief silence and then the therapist said, "She really needs more than I can give her right now. I've got other things on my mind. . . . I'm ill. It was just diagnosed about a month ago. I have to take care of myself right now. I will have to go into the hospital. . . . It may be cancer. . . . Please will you take her?"

I had doubts about the referral, even though it seemed that the therapist's concerns were justified. I felt some obligation to help a colleague who had her own personal crisis to deal with. I agreed to the transfer of the patient's care. There was a great sigh of relief from the other end of the phone line. I was eager to get more information about this patient whom I had just accepted, but it seemed that once I had agreed to take the patient the therapist was eager to hang up.

I called the psychopharmacologist. He told me that the patient suffered from depression. He had tried her on a host of medications and hospitalized her twice in the past 18 months. "Her depression has been refractory to whatever we try. I'm sure this is not just affective illness. She's a severe borderline and needs more psychotherapy." He said that he was more than willing to have me take over the management of the patient's psychopharmacology.

I was struck that both the therapist and the psychopharmacologist were eager to refer the patient elsewhere. The therapist felt that psychotherapy was ineffective, and that the patient needed more medication. The psychopharmacologist recommended more psychotherapy. Both seemed to agree that someone else other than themselves should be treating this woman.

I formed several hypotheses. The patient suffered from major affective disorder, depression or dysthymia. She drank. Could she be hypomanic? An atypical or mixed bipolar? Did she suffer from character pathology? She engendered feelings of helplessness and repulsion. No one liked her. Her sense of herself reflected this feeling of unworthiness and disgust. Split treatment had not worked; indeed both treatment providers seemed to be subtly complaining about each other. I anticipated primitive defense mechanisms, splitting, and projection. Should I agree to do both the psychotherapy and the psychopharmacology? I had still not seen or spoken to the patient. Yet I was already formulating a treatment plan. Was I getting way ahead of myself, locking myself into preconceived notions and doing her a disservice?

Although I had no direct knowledge of the patient, I had a lot of information about her. I tried to use that information as freely and as honestly as I could, knowing that every thought I had was highly speculative, based on fantasy as much as on fact. I did not hold firmly to any of these preconceived notions.

They were possible indicators, awaiting substantiation, without which they would be discarded. One must ask questions of the data and as much from the questions as from the data, form hypotheses. Having data and not "playing" with them (thinking and fantasizing in a creative way) is to shortchange the material, one's work, the formulation, and ultimately the patient.

I was also struck that I had gotten so little data from the therapist about the patient she was referring to me. She had flooded me with information about her own life and her own possible illness, cancer, but I had been unable to direct the communication away from this understandably charged material back to where our focus should have been—the patient. Was this interpersonal observation about the therapist, about me, or about the patient? Why had I been rendered so passive by her need to successfully "complete" this referral (projective identification)? I would need to be mindful of this in my interventions with the patient (transference and countertransference), and also parallel process.

When discussing a patient with a colleague, especially in the context of a treatment impasse and therefore when affect is raw, observe the interaction between you and your colleague. More often than not this interaction, called parallel process, holds some clue as to what is going on in the treatment itself. But in order to do this one must be open and reflective not just about one's colleagues but also about one's self.

Two days later the patient called, "Hello doctor, this is Mary Smith. I was referred to you by Susan Doe and by Dr. Jones." She was cordial and to the point. She asked if I had talked to her two doctors. She sounded gentler than I had expected. The anxiety that I had been feeling abated. We set up a first meeting. I suddenly found myself looking forward to meeting this patient whose arrival I had only just before been dreading. Data: affective lability, but in me (countertransference). I wasn't sure why.

The first contact obviously modifies, shapes, and changes earlier hypotheses, and leads to new ones. The data and hypotheses from one source must be compared and tested against the data and hypotheses from other sources. Data about one person come from multiple sources within that person. We should expect tension within the data themselves.

And thus despite the desire to find consistency, sometimes meaning is not consistent, coherent, integrated, or unitary. Meaning is complex and the desire to find an all-encompassing theory may do the patient and the "truth" more harm than good. Indeed many therapeutic traps come from an attempt to find a unitary truth or to accept (via projection, projective identification) the patient's version of "the simple truth."

The generation of multiple hypotheses may be the necessary consequence of diverse data. When this is so, the therapist must guard against the patient's and his own very human desire for order. The tolerance of inconsistency and paradox is crucial—and it is a capacity that many patients cannot tolerate and therefore attack (transference).

On the basis of inconsistency, the conflicting emotions her doctors and the patient had been able to generate in me, I considered primitive defense mechanisms, splitting, projection, projective identification, denial. I also wondered about affective lability, bipolar disorder, or cyclothymic disorder. I was considering these various possibilities in a patient whom I still hadn't met.

4.

First Meeting

Freud attached tremendous significance to "first things": "The patient's first symptoms or chance actions, like his first resistance, may possess a special interest and may betray a complex which governs his neurosis" (1913, p. 138). In his case reports, he was meticulous in his descriptions of first encounters with patients; for example, Frau Emmy von N., age 40 from Livonia,

> This lady, when I first saw her, was lying on a sofa with her head resting on a leather cushion. She still looked young and had finely-cut features, full of character. Her face bore a strained and painful expression, her eyelids were drawn together and her eyes cast down; there was a heavy frown on her forehead and the naso-labial folds were deep. (Breuer & Freud, 1893–1895, p. 48)

From this description, one knows a great deal about the woman, about her affective condition, about Freud's attitude toward her. This attention to detail is crucial. The first face-to-face encounter with the patient provides a wealth of data. First impressions in whatever form must be taken quite seriously and held in one's mind until they can be understood. They are never without meaning.

One should not approach the patient, even to say one's first "hello," without a very specific hypothesis about whom one expects to meet. And even before one does introduce oneself to the patient, one should be observing his or her behavior, manner, dress, etc. One does not wait for the first words to be spoken to begin listening for meaning—"There's language in her eye, her cheek, her lip—Nay her foot speaks" (Shake-speare, *Troilis and Cressida,* IV, 5.55).

Take, for example, the first meeting with the patient with multiple pains who had been referred to me by her internist. I had anticipated that she would be late, disorganized, and in a crisis. She arrived on time. Thus far I had been wrong. I added new hypotheses: despite her disorganization, she valued doctors greatly (defense mechanism—primitive idealization), and would therefore idealize me as her newfound Prince Charming until I failed her, at which time I would be devalued. She was punctual, and despite her somatization and histrionic traits, she had obsessional strengths.

I went out to greet her. She was a petite, neatly made-up, slender woman loaded down with shopping bags from several department stores. She was searching in her purse for lipstick. I was impressed with the amount of "baggage" that she had brought with her. I was impressed with the amount of activity she generated around herself. As I had hypothesized from the referral, this was a woman who was prone to action. Before I could speak, and as she still searched in her purse as though something were missing, she began: "Oh you must be the doctor. Am I late? I hate to be late. I'm not am I?" I began to say that "No, you are not at all—" when she interrupted me, and said, "Good. My husband promised to bring me here. But well—something. Do you have any idea what it is like finding a cab in this city? And they're so rude. How do you do?"

Other patients in the waiting area were watching to see what I would do. In the face of her rush of language (hypoma-nia, anxiety, histrionic behavior?), I felt a little awkward (coun-tertransference, and defense mechanism, projection; I was already feeling emotions and inhibitions that belonged to her, and superego projections; I was feeling embarrassed for her). I nodded and said, "How do you do, I'm Dr. Brockman." She smiled, "Yes of course," as if the obvious, like me, were beneath her. Devaluation and primitive idealization, both. And then as I asked her to come into my office, I was thinking also about boundaries, limit setting, lithium. As she reached for one of her shopping bags, coins fell out of her open purse. Thoughts were flying through my head. I felt a little hypomanic myself (projective identification). I thought more seriously about lithium.

First impressions: appearance, behavior, gestures, words, complaints. First words: The words may be the patient's statement of the chief complaint, but very often they are not. The opening comments may be extremely important precisely because they "don't count" and are unguarded. It is important to recognize that the first words often contain vital information that may be poorly understood at the time, but that the therapist must register and return to later. One should not be looking for *the* correct hypothesis, one should entertain many.

In addition to the possibility of bipolar disorder, I was thinking how she had made it difficult to answer as if she were afraid, unwilling, unable to allow me space. Biological issues: bipolar disorder, cyclothymia. Psychological issues: fear of rejection, control. Issues of enmeshment with her husband: she controlled, he disappointed. Were these prefiguring the transference? Everyone ran from her: was this prefiguring the countertransference? Did she make people want to flee from her and then hold onto them for fear of being abandoned (countertransference, transference)?

Another example: A woman with depression presented for her first appointment. She sat, looked around, smiled politely. Her first words: "Excuse me doctor, where is the box of Kleenex?" One can organize this data in many ways. First hypothesis: "I am depressed; I expect to cry; I want to be ready." I hypothesized that this woman maintained appearances. She was doing her best with obsessional defenses, order, planning, and neatness, to deal with biological depression. Therefore I would want to take a very careful history, get specific data about the depression itself and any family history of depression, as I hypothesized that this woman was stoical and would be inclined to minimize her illness.

Second hypothesis: "There is no Kleenex, Doctor. You have failed me already." She was enraged with the illness perhaps, but certainly with me. She attacked first to put me on the defensive because she felt very vulnerable and needy and would rather make me be the one who must retreat. I wondered about her defense mechanisms, projection, and projective identification—was she trying to make me experience what she was experiencing? Was she attacking me because she feared dependency? I recognized that I must be careful not to reject her (countertransference), in response to her rejection (transference). There was also a paradoxical relationship between her polite demeanor and her criticism of the way I arranged my office—between the data of the mental status and the data of the first words.

Third hypothesis: "I expected to cry even before I got here. I didn't bring Kleenex with me. I expected you to provide them for me." She did not want to take care of herself. She wanted me to take care of her. She was comfortable with the sick role (ego syntonic), so long as there was someone around to take care of her. I wondered about the quality of her object relations, her sense of self and object. In the history I would listen carefully to how dependency issues were handled with her parents, with other doctors, with her husband. What was comforting to this woman about being sick?

I did not know which if any of these hypotheses were valid—perhaps all, perhaps none. But the hypotheses would direct the search for data and would also warn me of potential transference and countertransference interactions before they had been deeply established. There would be indications where to look, as well as of the difficulties that might be encountered in the search for more data.

It is extremely important as the doctor and patient are sitting down for the first meeting, that all the data be reviewed, organized, and formulated. It is extremely valuable that hypotheses made at this point in the treatment be noted and compared with later versions of the formulation, when the more regressive aspects of the transference, countertransference, and defense mechanisms would have most likely been introduced. As the therapist and patient are sitting down for their first session, when seemingly only "polite" introductions and comments have been exchanged, the journey has actually begun and the unknown has been revealed, at least to some degree. Reference points have been established, a map has been outlined. A compass is in the therapist's hand.

At least three perspectives exist at this point in the evaluation:

1. The referral should give the therapist some sense of another treatment, of someone else's attitudes toward the patient, and the problems and challenges this patient may present.
2. The first contact should offer a whole other set of data and hypotheses of the first transferences and first countertransferences and about attitudes toward treatment, either in contrast to or in support of the information in the referral.
3. The waiting room encounter and first words offer the opportunity to weigh which of either impression was valid. This first face-to-face encounter, because it is less influenced by regressive transference than subsequent meetings, offers a unique glimpse of the patient that will have to be compared carefully with subsequent impressions as well as with those already generated.

A great deal should be formulated about the patient before much has been said. The next stage of the evaluation clarifies whether any of the early hypotheses are true, untrue, or a mixture of truth and error. But however "true" they are does not change the fact that these early hypotheses are crucial to the formulation and to the progression toward meaning. Because the data and hypotheses are in active interaction, there is tension and thus direction. The mental status exam is the next general source of data, although they begin to accumulate from the first moment one has direct contact with the patient.

To return to the woman who had been referred by her ailing therapist and her psychopharmacologist. The mental status exam had begun once the patient first called. Assessment of the doctor–patient relationship, past history of her relationships with doctors, and the medical history itself had also been started. I had made diagnostic impressions. Certain defense mechanisms were being considered: splitting, projection, denial. I anticipated intense affect: her therapist had felt overwhelmed by her and had rather abruptly handed over the patient's treatment to me. I expected the patient to be angry either at the therapist, at me (displacement), or at both of us, or I would expect to find defenses against anger; self-recriminations. I also expected someone with treatment resistant affective illness, a condition that can be frustrating to both doctor and patient.

I hypothesized that part of the reason the treatment was failing was that no one wanted to be near this patient. After all, the therapist who was entering the hospital was not referring away all her patients, only this one. The patient seemed to incur rejection. I anticipated therefore meeting someone who in one way or another was unattractive and would repel me.

The doorbell rang at 5 minutes before the appointed hour. A few minutes later, I went to the waiting area. A woman sat alone reading a magazine. She was slender, dressed in dark colors, very neat, and elegant. She kept reading as I approached her, and did not look up until I asked, "Ms. Smith?" She put down the magazine and stood up without ever really looking at me. She was taller than I had imagined, with long auburn hair hanging straight down her back. Her shirt was buttoned to the collar. She wore a short skirt, and black stockings, not much jewelry, a large watch. She was carefully made up, with dark lipstick, and wore perfume. She said nothing.

I introduced myself and offered my hand in greeting that she accepted after the slightest pause. I indicated, "Please come in." She walked ahead of me. She sat right down, placed her large purse beside the chair, adjusted her skirt, and crossed her legs. She had long legs, which the short skirt made longer. There was something both sexual and asexual about her. I asked her, "What brings you to see me?"

She looked at me, looked away. She was quite attractive; I hadn't expected that. "Didn't you talk to Dr. Jones and to Susan?" she asked. The therapist's first name was Susan. The patient's tone indicated dissatisfaction with Dr. Jones, with Susan, and it seemed most of all with me. There was impatience in her voice and the implication that I hadn't done my homework. Criticism was the order of the day. I felt drawn into a place where I wasn't welcome. I felt a little put off.

My impression of her first words then were that she was disappointed in me already. She was extremely critical and demanding. She drove people away. Was this because she could not tolerate need or envy, because no one was good enough for her, because no one could help her—not Susan, not the psychopharmacologist, and in anticipation, certainly not me? Was it devaluation or hopelessness, or both? I would have to be careful lest I return her devaluations of me (defense mechanism) by being defensively remote (countertransference). I would have to be careful lest her sense of futility became infectiously mine. Attachment was clearly conflicted: an attractive and visually alluring woman who in her tone was critical, remote, and impatient.

Perhaps she anticipated that I would be disappointed in her—after all she had been "sent away" by her therapist. She was someone who anticipated rejection and met it defensively with anger (transference). She projected disappointment into me (defense mechanism). Sadomasochistic issues: attack those whom you need because they will fail you. Affects: anger in anticipation of rejection, futility in anticipation of failure.

She referred to her psychopharmacologist as "Dr. Jones" and to her therapist by her first name. Splitting. Without both of them how would she deal with the just one of me, I wondered. I told her that I had talked to them both, but that I wanted to hear the details of her life and her treatment from her. She went into her purse and took out a packet of tissue. "I've been depressed for years. I've tried just about everything. Nothing seems to work. The depression is awful. There's nothing in my life that makes me think it will ever end." She was not crying so much as the fact that tears were running down her face. She blotted under her eyes, fastidious about the makeup. "I get suicidal. . . . I'm suicidal all the time. Sometimes it's worse, sometimes it's better. But the thoughts are there always."

She wadded the tissue up, put it into her purse, took another tissue. There was a waste bin, but she was careful not to leave the tissue in it. I was struck as she was telling me that she was chronically suicidal, that she was being so fastidious with the tissue. What was this neatness about? Why was she so afraid to leave anything behind? It was as if she didn't want to leave anything with me, and thus despite the fact that she was crying, it was as if she were withholding emotion.

I asked her about her suicidal thoughts—was she having them then? She told me that she had been having thoughts about cutting her wrists, putting her head in a plastic bag, asphyxiating herself in the oven. Indeed suicidal ideation had been a constant in her life for "5, 10 years—maybe forever." I thought of major affective disorder, chronic dysthmia, hypothyroidism, any current medical conditions? No. I wanted to know if her suicidal thoughts were more acute of late especially in view of the switch of therapists. I began to worry about the chronicity of her illness, or was it illnesses?

She told me she had been seeing Susan for 4 years and that nothing ever changed. Criticism continued; failure continued. She added that Susan was chronically late to session. "I always felt worse after seeing her. Losing her is no loss." I was impressed with how unemotional she had become. Four years with Susan seemed to mean nothing to her. "I always felt worse," she repeated looking at me, then looking away. Both patient and therapist seemed to share the desire to be rid of one another (projective identification). The patient had seemed angry with her illness, and with care providers. The care providers had seemed relieved to be free of their charge. Hatred, almost.

She added that she had recently bought a book describing ways to suicide. She was no longer tearful. As she talked about suicide she seemed to grow calm, which made me anxious. She took the tissue, folded it up, and put it back in her purse. The latch snapped shut. *"Final Exit,"* she said. "What?" I asked. "The name of the book," she said, *"Final Exit."* I thought for an instant of the referral and the urgency that the therapist had communicated. For the first time I felt that urgency. There was something calculating and dangerous about this woman. I both liked and disliked her. I was also beginning to feel a little annoyed with "Susan" and her cancer. I was feeling ungenerous. I was dealing in my mind with two people both of whom were facing the threat of death—one by suicide, the other by cancer—and I was feeling annoyed with the one and burdened by the other. I was impressed at how quickly I wanted nothing to do with either. I wanted distance (countertransference), providing data and some validation to an earlier hypothesis—that the patient was extremely ambivalent about attachment and would find a way to push away needed people.

My anxiety remained. I thought of defense mechanisms that I had tentatively identified which helped me to realize that the anxiety I was feeling was probably the patient's as well as mine; that the patient might be in very significant danger and that I had to assess that danger. Action might be required of me (I might have to hospitalize this woman). This might be one of those patients who dare you to try to help them and then act in one way or another in an attempt to paralyze all effective action. It was as if her lack of movement and fixed stare were rendering me passive (Stone, 1991).

I had to assess the danger of her suicidality. I had to think calmly even as, and especially as I was containing the patient's anxiety. That pressure was the pressure of the patient's primitive affect communicated to me by projection and projective identification. I was feeling a mixture of concern for the patient and anger at the therapist for having "dumped" her on me. I was surprised by the intensity of the affect as it seemed to spread over me like a net. I was impressed at how in less than 10 minutes this patient had been able to make me want to run away from her as she had done with her other doctors over the course of 4 years. A question followed, What was in her that I wanted to run away from?

I expressed my concern about her suidical ideation. "It's always there," she said as if to reassure me (or to brush away my concern). I added that I needed to know more about her and about her suicidal urges before we decided on a course of action. "What do you want to know?" she asked. I asked her to tell me more about her depression, when it began, its course, and more about her suicidal ideation and behavior. She opened her purse, took out another tissue, then looked up at me—stared for an instant as if she were refusing to cry, as if she were daring me to get involved with her. When I realized that I felt less distant, less anxious, and better able to assess her despair, her affect, her suicidal intent, which is to say, her mental status. I began to sense that what everyone, including myself, had been repelled by was this woman's deep conviction of hopelessness.

5.

The Mental Status Exam

> My "splendid isolation" was not
> without its advantages and charms. I
> did not have to read any publications,
> nor listen to any ill-informed opponents;
> I was not subject to influence from any
> quarter; there was nothing to hustle
> me. I learnt to restrain speculative
> tendencies and to follow the unforgotten
> advice of my master, Charcot: to look at
> the same things again and again until
> they themselves begin to speak.
> (Freud, 1914a, p. 22)

While each aspect of the clinical evaluation, including the mental status, will be examined separately, it should be obvious that the data obtained from any one part must be examined and compared with the data from each other part.

The mental status provides valuable early, as well as ongoing data for the dynamic formulation. First, this chapter will examine how to use the mental status to begin to identify dominant patterns of attachment behavior, affect, object relations, and transference. Second, it will demonstrate how themes emerge in the way someone tells a story as well as in the story itself (the form of the communication as well as the content of the communication). Third, issues of psychobiology must be considered when dealing with the phenomenological–descriptive data of the mental status. These aspects of the mental status must be kept in constant interaction through the generation of multiple hypotheses.

The mental status exam includes a formal assessment of various parameters of clinical function such as memory, judgment, affect, cognition, the content and processes of thought, suicidal ideation, and homicidal ideation. In addition, the mental status includes extremely useful information for the early identification of defense mechanisms or patterns of resistance that can help to identify where the patient habitually feels safe. The mental status, by identifying the affects, forms of communication, and forms of attachment with which the patient is comfortable, thereby helps in identifying, by their absence, those forms with which the patient does not feel safe.

"All the defensive measures of the ego against the id," wrote Anna Freud, "are carried out silently and invisibly. . . . The ego knows nothing of it; we are aware of it only subsequently when it becomes apparent that something is missing" (1966, p. 8). The mental status helps to identify not only where the patient wants to go, but where the patient does not want to go.

From the outset, Ms. Smith, the patient referred by her therapist and the psychopharmacologist, had tremendous difficulty looking at me. The first thing that she did on meeting me was avoid my gaze. By itself this "first" behavior might be considered a component of depression, paranoia, or shyness. One would need to examine this aspect of the mental status, a behavioral component, with other aspects. Indeed, and not surprisingly, in her verbal interaction with me, connections seemed to be avoided. When I would comment in particular on an aspect of the transference, that is, on an aspect of our relationship, she would usually avoid my comment just as her gaze had studiously avoided mine. An issue seemingly as inconsequential as using her own tissue to wipe her tears, and then taking the tissue out with her, became meaningful in the context of avoidance of contact. Joining me on any level was unsafe.

It was of course unclear as to why contact had to be avoided. The mental status does not answer questions. It identifies questions that need answers. Behavior—avoidance of my gaze, not leaving anything behind—is observed in the mental status and held until it can be understood when amplified by data from other sources. To ask the patient, "Why are you so afraid to look at me?" would be wrong. It would be wrong because the patient most likely does not know the answer, and because the question would increase the patient's resistance (see chapter 8). In general it is best not to ask the patient, "Why?" with regard to conflicted behavior until you yourself have a fairly good sense of what the answer may be. Do not ask until the behaviors "begin to speak."

A young man with an advanced degree in physics from M.I.T. presented for treatment with the chief complaint that he wasn't sure whether he wanted to be a physicist and therefore wasn't sure where his life was headed. He felt lost and adrift. Periodically during the evaluation, he would ask broad, quasi-philosophical questions about "life" and the process of "self-awareness": "How do you know when you know who you are?" "What is identity?" "What is the real meaning of friendship?" "How can you tell when you're on the right path?" These vague, in some ways unanswerable questions, were asked in context, but were very much out of character given his structured background and education.

As I thought about this aspect of the mental status, I felt like a parent with a young son who kept asking, "Daddy, why is the sky blue?" I hypothesized about the transference, the countertransference, and the defense mechanisms; I felt that this extremely bright and articulate young man was idealizing me (defense mechanism) in order to maintain a very immature and dependent relationship with me (transference). With this hypothesis in mind, I learned in the history that the patient's father had abandoned the family when the patient was 7. With this added data, I hypothesized more specifically that he maintained this regressed pattern of behavior and thought in order to preserve a time when he and his father were still together. This was obviously one aspect of the past.

I anticipated that his mood would change if this regressed pattern of communication were challenged. He might become depressed at the loss of the ideal, or he might become enraged, and thus this idealization of me in the transference might have been an attempt to defend me and himself from devaluation.

I hypothesized that he was attempting to maintain attachment in the context of underlying disappointment, and that his style of relating was in the service of this desire. I also hypothesized that this pattern, if left unchallenged, would leave the patient feeling very attached to me and very confused about himself. That is to say, it was a pattern that was comfortable for the patient, and if allowed to remain, would lead nowhere. I would have to test these hypotheses.

Mental status behaviors and communications, if placed in the frame of attachment and affect, help to identify patterns of interaction within which the patient desires to stay (resistance). It becomes a clinical decision whether to challenge or accept the patient's view that this pattern of communication is the one that is most reasonable or is the only one allowed the patient neurobiologically, and whether the safety of these limitations are indeed safe.

A patient who I was scheduled to see for the first time, after having been in the waiting area for a few minutes, knocked at my office door. I opened the door to encounter a very attractive Asian woman dressed in a black evening dress, and wearing a great deal of jewelry. I looked at my watch (countertransference). She asked about our appointment and I informed her that she was early, and that I would see her shortly. She apologized for disturbing me and sat down again.

Approximately 10 minutes later I went out to greet the new patient. I introduced myself. She was sitting on the couch, slouching; one leg was crossed over the other; it was rocking. She stood slowly, greeted me warmly, and then entered my office. There were two chairs facing each other, one with a pad of paper, prescription blanks, and a telephone alongside. To every other patient, that chair was obviously mine. She pointed to it and asked, "Is this where you want me to sit?" I indicated no, and asked her to take the chair opposite.

What did I know about this woman? What was the mental status communicating? What should I expect in the history, the transference, the countertransference, the psychobiology? What was this woman's view of safety, danger, attachment? Interpersonally I had found myself in the presence of a very attractive elegant woman appearing like some fantasy of Oriental royalty who in her first encounter with me was invading my space. Psychobiologically this behavior suggested the possibility of hypomania. In the history I would need to establish or exclude affective disorder.

From an intrapsychic perspective, there were other hypotheses to consider: she was someone who acted first and thought later; someone who was consistently dominant in defiance of the submissive; a woman who would try to control the treatment rather than be a party to it; a woman who had learned that she who hesitates is lost. "What brings you to see me?" I asked her. "These are lovely rugs," she said looking around the office. "Tell me doctor, do you collect rugs?" Her first words were consistent with both initial hypotheses: that she wanted to be the active agent as a defense against introspection; that there was the possibility of underlying affective disorder, or attention deficit disorder.

By clearly observing the mental status, one is in a better position to know when a patient is moving along a defensive pathway and therefore staying within a parameter of what is safe, and when the patient is exploring issues that are not well known, less secure, and therefore less safe. The mental status, because it defines the surface, the phenomenologically accessible, shows not only what someone wants to show but also the patterns of how someone avoids showing what he or she does not want exposed. Identifying these patterns is crucial if one is to avoid going over and over the same path.

This young woman then had come to my office, knocked on the door interrupting a session, assumed that my chair was hers, and responded to an open question by referring one back to me. "Thank you," I replied. "Do you have an interest in Oriental rugs?" She started telling me how her life had been spent traveling and collecting. She had been a buyer, she told me, for a chain of Thai hotels. "You are from Thailand?" I asked. She looked at me, then smiled, "Of course." As she talked she stretched up catlike, looked around the office, at one point stood up to inspect a picture on the wall. I felt that she was examining me, a countertransference impression reinforcing the sense that she did not want to examine herself too closely which was worth noting since she had presumably come

to see me for help with some problem. I suggested that she
sit back down which she did cooperatively. Her behavior was
controlled and contained. There was none of the biological
pressure of mania or hypomania. There was none of the dis-
tractibility of attention deficit disorder. She stretched again.

I still had no idea why she had come to see me but I found
myself both enjoying and dreading being in the company of
this very attractive, shapely, Asian woman whom I saw at this
point as something of a cross between a call girl and a princess.
When she ran her hands over the arms of the chair I felt as if
I were being touched. I asked her if she could be more specific
about what had brought her to treatment.

She looked at me, sat forward, smiled as if whatever I had
asked was irrelevant, and then sat back and shrugged. She admitted that she had been having trouble in her marriage of 8
years, and except for the well-being of her two young daughters,
would have left her American husband long ago. She emphasized "American," and then added, "That's it." "That's it?"
I repeated.

It had taken her only a few minutes to dispatch her husband, her marriage, her daughters. She again looked at me
fixedly and inquired, "So what do you want to talk about, doctor?" And again I felt her eyes, her sexuality, and the treatment
thrown back on me. I thought about Freud's "Observations
on Transference-Love" and his advice to those dealing with
powerful positive transferences,

> The psycho-analyst knows that he is working with highly explosive
> forces and that he needs to proceed with as much caution and
> conscientiousness as a chemist. But when have chemists ever been
> forbidden, because of the danger, from handling explosive sub-
> stances, which are indispensable, on account of their effects?
> (1915b, pp. 170–171)

I felt the explosive nature of the session. Afterwards I
read more,

> To urge the patient to suppress, renounce or sublimate her in-
> stincts the moment she had admitted her erotic transference

would be, not an analytic way of dealing with them, but a senseless one. It would be just as though, after summoning up a spirit from the underworld by cunning spells, one were to send him down again without having asked him a single question. (1915b, p. 164)

And then in thinking about this patient and the mental status, I realized that whatever questions I did ask were answered so long as they were specific structured questions. But that if I removed the structure by asking a more open-ended question, "Tell me a little more about your relationship with your husband," she would refuse to answer and turn the question on me; for example, "This isn't fair. You know so much about me, but I know so little about you. Are you married, doctor?"

As I thought about this, I realized that her responses had less to do with "a spirit summoned from the underworld," the transference, than they did with the mental status and a pattern of resistance. I realized that this pattern had been there from the very first. And indeed this was a style of relating with which she seemed perfectly comfortable. It was my discomfort (countertransference) that made me believe that her forwardness and need for information about me was not the real issue, that this was not from a "spirit from the underworld."

The patient had been refocusing the treatment onto me, my rugs, my person, onto sexuality—as a way of avoiding psychological exploration. Acting out was her resistance to thought; thus the mental status was helping to define the parameters within which this patient felt safe. She had to know where she was going before setting out. If she had defined the route, "Do you collect rugs, doctor?" or if I did, "What kind of work does your husband do?" mattered little so long as a specific path had been defined before it was embarked on. She did not seem to need to know where the treatment was going so much as how it was going to get there. These issues were about safety and the resistance more than about the transference. This "spirit" then, was not really from the underworld. It was a spirit of the resistance; it was a decoy.

I decided to ask historical questions, which she was comfortable answering. Having identified what was safe for this patient, I decided to structure the evaluation and remain within

that confine until I had a better sense that the patient was ready
to deal with what lay beyond. Obviously I could have challenged
her pattern of relating by asking, "The way you frequently turn
questions back on me as if I am the focus of this treatment and
not you, makes me wonder whether there isn't some other issue
that we still haven't identified." But it is equally important to
know when it is right to challenge behavior and defenses, and
when it is best to leave them—timing. Gather data, generate
hypotheses, gather more data. There are few situations in medicine, psychotherapy, or life that require immediate action.

These hypotheses, formulated on the basis of data from
the first meeting, from the mental status, were primarily about
the patient's defensive structure. Again, interpersonal patterns
that are identified in the mental status are rarely about the
substance of psychological, intrapsychic conflict. They are usually about the structured *defenses* and repetitive patterns that
prevent the identification and exploration of these very issues.
To fail to recognize this is to allow the resistance to become
the "guide" of a treatment. Thus if I had asked the patient
why she had knocked on my office door, why she had wanted
to sit in my seat, why she was interested in my rugs, or even
why she was interested in so much information about me, any
of these questions would have led deeper into the resistance
and would have led the treatment nowhere.

Use the mental status to help identify the resistance and
from that generate hypotheses about what is being resisted. If
that is impossible, then identify the forms of the resistance, the
cognitive style, the interpersonal style, the defense mechanisms
that are being used for resistance. This can be found in a careful observation of the mental status. One follows the path set
by the patterns of the mental status, until one understands its
function and until one feels the time is right to confront the
patient with the specific information that something is being
concealed or is not understood, that something is missing or
contradictory.

The data of the mental status provide understanding of
the habituated patterns that are controlled by psychological
defenses, biological forces, or both. With this woman, there was
from the very first moment evidence of acting out behavior,

impulsivity, and the inability to accept a self-reflective attitude. There was the hypothesis that she did this in order to avoid letting the interviewer or herself know what her underlying thoughts were. There was also evidence of projection. Her assertive, sexual provocativeness made me feel both excited and uncomfortable (countertransference). She remained the calm, seductive temptress who waited (transference), which established me and not her as the focus of the evaluation. The patient's own anxiety seemed nonexistent even as she faced divorce, financial uncertainty, living halfway around the world from her family of origin, and the sole care of two young children. That she seemed so calm, and that she had made me feel so anxious (projection), made me feel more certain that there was something quite significant that was missing.

During the course of this extended evaluation, this patient presented faithfully, answered questions, and reported superficially about her husband and two daughters. It was only over time and with the handling of issues that emerged in the mental status, basically by avoiding directly challenging her resistant behavior until I felt she would be able to deal with it, that she gradually began to allow the structure of the sessions to change. She began to show interest in herself, and in the process of therapy. And finally confided something that I had in no way anticipated. The mental status does not indicate what is missing; it only helps to identify a pattern of avoidance. "An evil spirit," she said. "I'm not sure I know what you mean," I said. She was convinced that she had been possessed by an evil spirit. It was this spirit she was certain that had made her depressed, at times tearful, and made her lose sleep.

Now that some "real" data were coming in, I began to wonder whether she suffered from a major affective disorder with psychotic features. I felt the urge in me to act, to ask a list of questions that could cinch the diagnosis, lead to a treatment plan with medication and possible hospitalization, with me in other words reestablished in control as the doctor. I realized that this was my countertransference reaction to her having "forced" my passivity and that there was a certain punitive aspect in it directed at her for having made me feel both so sexually aroused and uncomfortable. I realized that she had been functioning for years with this depression, this delusion, this overvalued idea, this alternative view of psychic energy, this alternative cultural belief, this—? I wasn't sure what. She was not suicidal. There was no need to rush.

I asked for more information about the spirit. She told me that she was convinced that the spirit had been sent by her sister-in-law who disapproved of her brother's marriage to a woman who was not American. When they were youngsters, the sister-in-law had been incestuously involved with him. "She's resented me from the moment we met," she said. "She'll never give him up." She was looking straight at me to gauge my reaction. There was none of the seductive quality to her behavior that had once been so pronounced. "She's particularly jealous of my youngest child because she looks just like him. I'm afraid she'll try to kidnap Zia."

The patient was aware that her thoughts about spirits were not "normal—at least not in this society," that she had to be careful to whom she spoke about them, and was afraid that I would think her crazy and hospitalize or medicate her. She said that she had to be certain that she could trust me before she could risk confiding this information in me, trust that I was someone who would be able to understand this as a problem of energy, not an illness, and that she did not require medication. Indeed she made it quite clear that medication was "out of the question." I realized that I would have to weigh issues of the therapeutic alliance, diagnosis, safety, current functioning, cultural belief.

The hypothesis from the mental status, that something crucial was missing, had indeed been an accurate guide during the times when the patient's attempts to avoid her mind were strongest. Not surprisingly, once the patient felt safe enough to be open with me, her acting-out behavior, in the form of her need to control both the session and me with her seductiveness, abated, and not surprisingly as she became more interested in her intrapsychic life, I started to feel more comfortable in my role as her doctor. Indeed her mood improved considerably just in the telling of the tale.

The patient first had to find a path that enabled her to feel safe. It is almost always a valid assumption that if you, the therapist, feel anxious with a patient (countertransference), the patient also feels unsafe either consciously or unconsciously with you. When this is so, the task is to gather the data that allow one to understand the patient's safety and how she maintains it. Had her assertiveness and sexuality, her "phallic narcissism," become the focus of the treatment rather than accepted as a piece of the mental status and resistance, I am not sure that the treatment would have progressed.

A young lawyer was referred for evaluation because of difficulties at work. I listened over several sessions as he explained the problems he was having with clients, colleagues, friends. I found that I had tremendous difficulty following his stories. They would each begin simply enough and then grow in complexity, roping in one issue after another (tangentiality, circumstantiality), until despite my best efforts to listen, I found myself confused and lost. When I tried to get him to clarify certain points, he would add more details that confused me further. I considered hypomania and attention deficit disorder but neither diagnosis was substantiated. Soon he added that there was one other aspect to his problem. He stated how he dreaded warm, sunny days. I was in the midst of asking what he dreaded about them when he cut me off to tell me the answer to the question that I was asking.

He dreaded sunny days because women wore less clothing, and he would be "captured" by the sight of a woman on the street and would then be forced to go home to masturbate. I asked him for a detail about which women tended to excite him most, and instead of listening to my question, he again sped up his narrative (pressured speech). At another point I tried to interrupt him. He allowed the interruption, apologized, and then after I had asked a question, he went on as if my question had never been asked (avoidance).

This behavioral interaction continued. I realized that just as he tried to avoid the sight of a pretty woman on a warm sunny day by averting his eyes (content of communication), so too he was trying to avoid me by talking in a way that made it hard for me to follow him (form of communication). In this context I began to realize how in listening to him, I felt both trapped and excluded. I realized that I was not allowed real understanding, that the patient wanted me to witness but not to participate in what he was telling me (transference and countertransference). By virtue of how he told a story and how he maintained control of its details and boundaries, he was refusing me any meaningful connection not only to the story but also to him. I hypothesized that just as it was dangerous for him to see a woman on the street, it was dangerous for him to "see" me for fear that he would lose the control that he felt he needed in order to feel safe with another human being. That safety included behavior where emotional bonds were either avoided (on the street) or controlled (in the transference). Attachment was a prison, and one was either its master or its slave. There was no experience of freedom in any situation where attachment was recognized. Affect, or more specifically, the experience of affect, was for him extremely unsafe because by attaching self to object, affect was creating what was for him the most dangerous state. By combining the data from these various sources, the content of the narrative, the mental status, the transference and countertransference, a more complete perspective emerged even or perhaps especially in this instance where the destruction of meaningful narrative (mental status) seemed to be one of the patient's unconscious goals.

There were two broad, interrelated hypotheses that emerged from the data. One was that attachment was dangerous and had to be countered with obsessive, schizoidal, and narcissistic defenses. And the other was that attachment could be made safe by "inflicting" it on someone else. That is, others could be held in a bond that excluded meaning or emotion. But in no case did human attachment involve freedom. He felt trapped by the women on the street; I felt trapped by the style of his speech and his refusal to allow me to be a part of the dialogue.

But as I sat trying to understand him, I realized that his communication was not in the content of his speech. I realized that he was not trying to tell me what his day was like, he was instead forcing me to experience what it was like (countertransference and projective identification). Direct communication was through the experience and not the content of his words.

And thus to merely describe this man as bizarre, with obsessional, narcissistic, and schizotypal features, was phenomenologically correct but not a sufficient use of the data. Through the inclusion of data from the narrative, the transference, the countertransference, and the phenomenological diagnosis, a tension was developing which indicated direction toward safety and danger. I hypothesized that the open communication of affect was dangerous, because it led to attachment, and attachment meant being in the control of a foreign despot. I did not know who the despot was or why he was felt to be so dangerous. I would listen to the history for more data.

The mental status then sets up certain problems, certain ways the patient has of listening and not listening. It provides if you will the unvoiced "chief complaint," that ailment the patient isn't so much aware of at a conscious level but which he lives with day to day. The mental status presents the problem that is so familiar it is practically unrecognized: "A clever young philosopher with exquisite aesthetic sensibilities will hasten to put the creases of his trousers straight before . . . [the] first hour. . . . A young girl will at the same juncture hurriedly pull the hem of her skirt over her exposed ankles . . ." (Freud, 1913, p. 138).

A woman will knock at the closed door, a man will ask questions but then be unable to wait for answers, a woman will spill coins over the floor. The mental status defines the paths by which someone has gotten to his or her safe place. But safe places are not always easy to find, nor are they always safe. One rarely wants to go to unsafe places alone.

During any evaluation, it is crucial that one hypothesize about the nature of a patient's versions of safety and fear. These evaluations must be specific to that patient at that time. This is not the same as the question of the patient's physical safety or potential for suicide. The question has to do with someone's psychologically and biologically structured sense of safety. It has to do with the relationship between safety and affect.

The mental status often provides clues by showing what a patient wants and accepts. The transference on the other hand shows what someone wants and fears.

The imagination. That's our out. Our imagination teaches us our limits and then how to grow beyond those limits. The imagination says listen to me. I am your darkest voice. I am your 4 a.m. voice. I am the voice that wakes you up and says this is what I'm afraid of. Do not listen to me at your peril. (Guare, 1990, p. 37)

6.

Transference and Safety

What are transferences? They are new editions or facsimiles. . . . To put it another way: a whole series of psychological experiences are revived, not as belonging to the past, but as applying to the person of the physician at the present moment.
(Freud, 1905, p. 116)

As I feel closer to you, I feel like a frog in a pot of water. The temperature goes up slowly so the frog never realizes that it's being boiled alive.
(Patient, Columbia Presbyterian Medical Center, evaluation clinic)

Freud's discovery of the transference was a huge one in the history of psychiatry. He argued that he had discovered in the transference a window into the patient's unconscious and into the nature of what he referred to as the infantile wish, "The core of our being, consisting of unconscious wishful impulses, remains inaccessible to [our] understanding. . . . These unconscious wishes exercise a compelling force upon all later mental trends. . . . [These] wishful impulses [are] derived from infancy, which can neither be destroyed nor inhibited . . ." (1900, pp. 603–604).

These "wishful impulses," Freud believed, were sexual, potentially dangerous (oedipal), and primarily for that reason were repressed and therefore forgotten. He argued that the transference, like the dream, was one of those factors that opened the amnesia of childhood to investigation.

> The transference thus creates an intermediate region between illness and real life through which the transition from the one to the other is made. The new condition has taken over all the features of the illness; but it represents an artificial illness which is at every point accessible to our intervention. . . . From the repetitive reactions which are exhibited in the transference we are led along the familiar paths to the awakening of memories, which appear without difficulty. . . . (1914b, pp. 154–155)

Because his theoretical position argued that the transference was retrospective, it was reasonable to assume that the data of the transference were about past relationships. Therefore, the science of psychoanalysis was the study of pathology generated by and continuing because of past relationships and especially sexual aspects of those past relationships.

Transference does provide data about the unconscious past, but it provides more. By recognizing the basic, psychobiological position of attachment behavior in animals and in man, another aspect of transference emerges. The study of transference in the context of attachment behavior is the study of how someone connects to another human being. It is the study of essential, *ongoing* biopsychological behavior, and not, as it was in the analytic framework, the study of how the infantile sexual wish was frustrated.

The study of attachment includes research on psychobiology, the observation of animal species, and infant observation. Thus in the context of attachment, the study of transference is the study of one of the most primal psychobiological behaviors. In this context transference is not a recreation of past frustrations, it is a vector force that is influenced by the past, by the present, by psychobiology, by affect, by expectation, by resistance, by anticipation, by trauma, by stress. All of these factors operate through the transference to emerge in the form of a relationship created by the patient with the therapist. It is true that transference includes a repetition of the past frustrations and past relationships, especially of close intimate relationships from the past, for example, with a parent. But this is a reductionistic view of transference that limits its usefulness and makes it into a caricature of what it could be. Through the transference one is able to observe the external, observable representation of what had been internal, biologic, and intrapsychic. Transference brings to the surface the data of another human being's attachment behavior, that is to say behavior that includes very primitive and basic biologic forces.

To return to the example of the lawyer whose talk was rambling and who seemed not to allow my questions into his consciousness. I expressed how difficult it was sometimes for me to understand him (the content of the narrative) or to stay close to him emotionally (affect). I was thus using data from the mental status and the countertransference to try to better locate where we were (transference) and where meaning might lie. He seemed to both ignore and accept what I had said. He came to the next evaluation session having spent the weekend with a couple who had a 3-year-old son, Jimmy. He felt it was important that he relate a little about what had happened. He began in his somewhat pressured style (mental status),

> We were driving to the city. I was in the back seat with Jimmy. He was playing with a group of toy figures. He had to line them up in just a certain way. There was an order that they had to be in and this was very important to him. And I was just there watching him play with the toys. And watching him drool.

He looked at me the way he might look at any object in the room, and then went on,

> The feeling was Jimmy was comfortable enough drooling backwards down his throat without coughing. I just watched the saliva slide down his throat. He didn't recognize that he's drooling backwards because he's got his mind on something else. It doesn't concern him that saliva was leaving his mouth. It doesn't concern him that he's drooling. It wasn't something that he was particularly attached to.

What are the data here? The content of the narrative was about a boy playing a game. But there was more. The patient

had in the course of our meetings seemed to find it very difficult to listen to anything that I might ask or say. His speech
was a monologue addressed, it seemed, to no one but himself.
I had been confronting him, as best I could, with how difficult
it sometimes was to understand him, and he brought in material about a boy who played intently and drooled. Was he talking about his own boyhood? About an infantile wish? About his
relationship with his mother 30 years ago? Perhaps he was talking about aspects of all of them, but not exclusively so.

The data of the mental status had established that this man
had trouble allowing the other person into a dialogue. For
example, he used words to hold and imprison but not to include me. The mental status provided a framework within
which to listen. So while the content of the story was about a
boy who spilled fluid from his mouth, the data of the mental
status had to do with a man whose mouth also spilled—words
not saliva. I hypothesized that this data provided a bearing as
to the location of the transference. I said to him,

> Jimmy wasn't particularly attached to his saliva as it left his mouth.
> I wonder if you haven't become somewhat more aware of the fact
> that you too aren't that attached to things leaving your
> mouth—not saliva as with Jimmy but words with me.

He paused, smiled. We were both a little surprised that he
had let me finish my thought. Then he said,

> I've always been incontinent. I'm not sure what psychic continence
> is, but whatever it is, I've always assumed it was not having to
> release everything onto the world. I guess I do feel strangled by
> my own secretions. I'm not comfortable with my own productions.
> If I write something down, I have to scratch it out. If I say some-
> thing, even before I give you the chance to say you understand it, I
> have to add to it. Jimmy was comfortable enough drooling without
> coughing. He's going through toilet training. It's a developmental
> issue. He must be thinking about other things. He doesn't care
> about drooling. It might be my fantasy to be totally incontinent. I
> think I am incontinent. All the talking and not letting someone
> else talk.

The data of the mental status had also supported the idea that he feared attachment to me, that he feared the communicative aspect of affect, and that words therefore were spilled out without affect, without thought, without any meaning attached. I asked, "Incontinence, having something pass unformed. Just letting a word or a thought pass through?" "Yeah something like that," he said.

The data that were from multiple sources—the mental status, the countertransference, and the content of the story—reinforced and helped to locate what was going on between us in the transference and in the affect. His response to my interventions added support that emotional connection was both feared and desired and that he was aware to a degree that he used language not so much to communicate as to control his ambivalence about communication.

To return then to the question, "What is transference?" It is a distortion of a relationship. "Psychoanalytic treatment does not create transferences; it merely brings them to light like so many other hidden psychological forces" (Freud, 1905, p. 117). In particular, transference is a distortion of attachment behavior between the therapist and the patient. Why is this relationship special in this regard? It isn't, it just sometimes seems that way.

The woman who was referred for chronic suicidal ideation by her therapist and psychopharmacologist, who wouldn't look at me, brought her own tissue to the session, and left with it as if cleaning up after herself (data from the mental status), described her relationship with me as follows:

It's one of two things. I'm really unhappy when I talk to you. That's the basis of "us." And if I don't start to feel better one of these days, well, I'll just end it. Disappear. Suicide's been a part of me ever since I can remember. But if I do get things straightened out, I won't ever talk to you again. If I get worse or better, it's temporary. I'll lose you. It makes me anxious that I can't talk to anyone but you. . . . It's pathetic. You're the only person I can talk to, and I have this whole other fantasy about you—if I were happy we wouldn't be talking. This isn't a real relationship.

The transference relationship included her conviction

that I, like other people she cared about, would abandon her. Her internalized sense of attachment was that involvement on any level with another human being was certain to lead to loss and pain. "If I get worse or better, it's temporary. I'll lose you." I said to her, "I think it attests to your bravery that you have let me be a part of your solitude. It would be much easier for you not to let anyone in, not to answer the phone, to be alone, to hide." In saying this I was attempting to support her ambivalent movement from solitude to attachment, from a safe place to a feared place. It was support that I hoped I was offering and that she was receiving. She said to me, "This morning before I came here, I got very anxious. I dreaded coming to see you. I was alone this weekend; the sun was out. I didn't want to see anyone. I feel worse with people. When I'm with someone it just gets worse."

The data from the mental status, from the content of the session, and from the transference supported the hypothesis that the slightest evidence of attachment to another person was ambivalent and dangerous and had to be denied even as it was desired.

Transference distortions can and do exist in any interpersonal context. But the doctor–patient relationship incorporates a regressive component which tends to increase the stress of the relationship and consequently increases the potential for distortion (exposing the form, not the etiology of pathologically unsafe affect and attachment). Because a patient comes to a doctor in pain, issues of danger and safety are immediate in the doctor–patient relationship. This is furthered by the fact that the patient knows little about the therapist to whom he is entrusting his well-being. The intensity of the suffering heightens the danger; and the relative anonymity of the therapist allows for distortions of the safety.

The therapist maintains a certain "neutrality." That is not to say that the doctor operates without feeling or without empathy. "Neutrality has to be conceived of as a principle of handling the transference and not as a description of the actual emotional behavior of the analyst" (Killingmo, 1989, p. 77). The therapist needs the data of the transference in order to better understand the workings of his patient's mind, but must

remain empathic and human. Nor does the principle of neutrality mean that all of the patient's "transference demands"
should be ignored. There is a balance.

The patient's demands for immediate comfort and reassurance may be gratified or not. Questions addressed to the
therapist may be answered—or not. In either case the patient
rarely knows the doctor as well as he is convinced that he needs
to know him, and rarely feels as comforted and protected by
him as he feels he needs to be in order to feel safe. Because
of these needs and desires, there are projections that become
misperceptions about the doctor. As the patient continues to
distort, the distortions become larger. An interpersonal interaction can become more and more distorted by the patient's
world of self and object representations; that is, by his internally
held view of who he is in relation to who he feels the doctor
must be in order to feel safe, in order to feel comforted, in
order to attach. This is not a repetition of past relationships,
rather it is a creation, in the interpersonal sphere, of a complex,
multiply determined intrapsychic and psychobiologic aspect of
the patient through the medium of affect.

Before the conclusion of any evaluation, it is important to
allow something of that relationship, of that distortion, to develop and be observed. To do this, it may at times be necessary
to allow stressful interactions to occur, and this is usually done
through the transference. In this way the fuller quality of affect
can be assessed from both a psychological as well as from a
biological perspective.

Consider the following: A 39-year-old biochemist presented to a male therapist with the overt complaint that he had
not been in a relationship with a woman for over 7 years. He
felt hopeless about ever being in a loving relationship and felt
chronically suicidal because of this conviction. Data supporting
the phenomenological diagnoses of chronic dysthymia and
avoidant and schizotypal personality disorder emerged over the
course of the first two sessions. (Because the phenomenological
diagnosis is usually more evident, that data should be used to
help anticipate the distortions of transference and affect.)

There was the expectation that he would be anxious whenever he felt in any way emotionally close to his therapist. There

was the hypothesis that if intimacy were to become a more conscious issue of the transference, the patient would be placed in a very unsafe place and would need to react in some way in order to protect himself from that experience. Just how he would do this was uncertain.

At the end of the fourth evaluation session and the end of the month, the therapist handed him his bill. The patient looked at the bill, smiled from some deep inward place, and then tore the bill up, tossing the bits to the floor. His only comment, "You're just like all the rest." He sat back, folded his arms and waited comfortably for a response. What are the data, and how do they apply to transference and diagnosis? The patient's act seemed to say that he had discovered some truth about the therapist. What truth? "Just like all the rest"— that the therapist like all the other people, but especially the women in his life, did not love him enough. One could surmise further that the patient's need for absolute comfort and care was placing an impossible burden on the therapist (counter-transference), and probably on all the nonexistent relationships that he longed for. "All the rest"—the other women in his life probably did not exist (data confirmed more from the phenomenological diagnoses than from the history).

A possible hypothesis was that no other relationships existed because, just as he placed impossible demands on his therapist for proof of his love, so too he must have placed impossible demands on "all the rest." The transference distortion then led to data about attachment, about the prerequisites that had made attachment impossible.

This hypothesis was supported by the emptiness of the man's life (avoidant personality disorder—diagnosis and content of the narrative) and the transference. The transference added further data as to why this might be so and to a further hypothesis: when the impossible demands were not met, he had to devalue the object. He had to do this perhaps to lessen his need for the object, to lessen his fear of the object, and perhaps to communicate how insulted he had felt for having received something so unloving as a bill. The transference data added an element of meaning to the underlying affects that the patient was struggling with interpersonally and biologically, and thus: "This will be a very difficult treatment for you," the therapist said as he looked up from the pieces of paper on the floor,

It will be difficult because all the while that you are wanting me to care for you in a way that you feel no one else has ever been able to love you, you will at the very same time see me as failing to care for you enough. I have a feeling that those two thoughts will be with you together both at once. And they will, I believe, cause you a lot of pain [prediction of the affect with which he is struggling and which he is concealing]. But dealing with those two issues and with the pain that they cause you will be very much a part of what this treatment will be about [a supportive statement that the patient's rejection had not caused the therapist to reject in retaliation].

There was a pause. The patient nodded, shrugged, said nothing. The therapist went on, "We have to stop now. I will give you another bill next time we meet."

The validation of one or more hypotheses might have to wait for quite some time but the possibility of validation came from the hypothesis that he could experience the sadness of his isolation, and that in time he would be able to confide in the therapist that he had indeed been right about the underlying affect, which was still too intimate for the patient to risk sharing with him.

Transference is about distortion and about the kinds of distortions that are necessary in order to make it safe enough for attachment. Attachment involves an aspect of love, and love at this level of affect is driven by deep psychological and biological forces. These multiple factors often add an enduring, illogical, and sadomasochistic quality to "love." Consider the following exchange with the patient who had been referred by her internist because of symptoms of chronic somatization and frequent negative workups and "emergency" phone visits. It had become clear that the patient's emergencies were interpersonally determined but beyond that generalized insight, her crises were poorly understood and uncontained. She entered the session after another shopping trip.

This time my father brought me here. Drove me here I should say. He picked me up at Saks. He saw me on the street and started honking. Once, twice, three, five times. I fucking saw him. I waved for Christ's sake. He knows how sensitive I am to noise! And what does he do? Honk! Honk! What's wrong with him? Shit. I can hear. But he just keeps on honking, honking, honking. Oh that reminds me, can I use your phone?

I felt a little confused and a little overwhelmed. I asked, "Why do you want to use my phone?"

Well the phones around your neighborhood are mostly broken and the others, well there are so many street people just coughing and drooling onto the phones, I'm sure I'll get some horrible disease—AIDS or Gods knows what. I've got to use the phone. I saw my internist; he took some blood tests, you know, to see if I have leukemia.

She glanced at me as she took out a lipstick from her purse. She was applying it looking at herself in a mirror as she said, "I may not have leukemia but his office closes at 4 and it's what, 3:45 now? By the time I get out of here, his office will be closed. So can I use the phone?" She put her lipstick away.

I wasn't sure what the significant data were except that she had just described a powerful affective response to her father who had disappointed her. She had also indicated how I could gratify or frustrate her in the transference. I decided that non-gratification was more consistent with the material and that it would lead to further distortions. Distortion in the direction of the content of the material (disappointment) was the direction of greatest potential. For those and other reasons (limit setting in a woman with a history of acting out behavior and affective illness, hypomania), I said, "No. If you want to leave early to make the call of course you can do that, but I can't let you use the phone." She was incredulous:

What? Why not? What's wrong with you? I mean shit, whose side are you on? Fuck it all. I don't get it. I'll give you the fucking quarter. Here. You're such an uptight jerk. My internist said you were smart. He was wrong. You're an idiot. God I hate you. I mean what if I'm sick? What if I really do have leukemia—hunh?"

"That would be unfortunate," I said. She looked at me, "Unfortunate? Unfortunate! Shit I think I'm gonna get sick just to spite you." She was showing in the distortion a perverse, sadomasochistic aspect of her attachment behavior and exposing her definition of love: if anyone disappoints me in any way, I can do anything to them or to myself to redress that wrong. It was a definition with both biologic (hypomania) and psychologic sources. And so I said, "I think that's the point. I think it shows how far you're willing to go to get what you feel is your just revenge." "What the hell is that supposed to mean?" she said.

That when someone disappoints you, your father, your husband, your internist, me—however big, however small, you feel that you have the right to do anything to them, and if that doesn't work, to yourself in order to show them just how hurt you feel. Well I don't think that you are entitled to get leukemia because I, for whatever peculiar reasons of my own, don't want you to use my phone. You can't do that to me, to them, and most importantly to yourself.

One listens for the transference in the context of nontransference data, in the context of working hypotheses about attachment, in the context of affect.

But just because the data is transferential, it should not be argued that therefore, the *etiology* of the distortion is interpersonal. Just because someone establishes a dependent relationship with his therapist does not in and of itself mean that he was recreating the dependent relationship that he once had with his father. The phenomenology of the transference is interpersonal. The etiology of that distortion, however, is multiply determined and the sources of it must be sought out, compared, formulated. (The patient's hypomanic behavior was more compelling as etiologic. However, the fact that she and her husband were actively trying to conceive, limited any pharmacologic intervention.)

Transference is a rich source of new data. By listening to the transference, one can hear more than the patient knows he is sharing. And again Freud's genius in this regard: "In confession the sinner tells what he knows; in analysis the neurotic has to tell more" (1926b, p. 189). But what does transference look like? Where does one locate it? To identify the transference one must listen to a patient tell his story from multiple perspectives. One listens to the content of the narrative from the perspective of the person telling the story; that is, one enters the story and allows it to become one's own. One also listens to the content as if one were the object of the narrative: as the patient is describing his love, hate, pity for someone, one becomes that someone. In both instances one listens in oneself for the affective response of the subject and of the object. One also listens to the form of the overall story, "This is a story about betrayal"; or "This is a story about discovery," and apply that overall frame to the present interaction. And then one holds all of the narratives, all of the stories, all of the affects, and in the context of the present interaction, searches for all of the data of agreement, of disagreement, and of meaning.

One must have access to all this in oneself in order to locate the transference. To focus on one perspective at the expense of the others is to narrow the focus and limit the data that one may find.

The following clinical vignette may serve as an example. The patient was a 43-year-old single woman who was an only child raised in a strict Catholic home. She had been hospitalized for refractory depression and persistent suicidal ideation. She had returned to New York one year ago after the breakup of a relationship with a man in Sweden. She had wondered whether the failure was due at least in part to the fact that she had never been sexually responsive to him. Indeed she wondered about her sexual attraction to any man. She had never discussed sexual attraction to women other than to dismiss homosexuality as—"not something I think about."

Pharmacologically she had responded well to antidepressant medication. On admission she had been briefly treated with a neuroleptic (Trilafon) because of intense anxiety of near psychotic proportions that abated as her depression cleared. Her therapist was a 28-year-old woman to whom the patient felt extremely close. This, their fourth meeting, was after a holiday weekend and during the last week of the therapist's rotation.

Therapist: Do you have any thoughts about last Thursday's session?

Patient: It went well. I do feel different now. But they took away the Trilafon. I've had more dreams, more anxiety. If I'd have had a session with a nurse over the weekend I'd have felt better, but I didn't have one. She wasn't available. I asked for more meds but they wouldn't give me that either.

Therapist: Can you describe how you did feel after our last session?

Patient: I felt more confident about the future. Now I feel more disorganized.

Therapist: Why?

Patient: This is a lousy way to start a week. I feel like I'll fall apart without the Trilafon. I know it's ridiculous. But I'm missing it. I felt it helped me keep my thoughts together. Maybe it did, maybe it didn't. I don't know. I feel like crying. . . . It's only been a couple of weeks. . . . Easy for me to cry.

What is the context of the session? What is the affect? What is being described? She identifies losses: of what? What is the frame of the session? The therapist asked, "Last time you mentioned going to Sweden and your relationship with Edgar. You cried a lot then. I was curious what made it so difficult?" The patient said,

I knew it wasn't a good relationship but I never admitted it. I had trouble finding work. I was too dependent on him. I spent a lot of time alone. I didn't feel he gave me enough time or support—how could he? He had a job. He had friends. What did I have? Time—I hated the dark winters—dark for so long. I'd blame Edgar. If he wanted to relax on the weekend, I'd be really angry if he didn't want to do what I wanted to do. I felt I couldn't continue feeling that way—always so alone. I knew I needed help. You couldn't talk about getting help, psychotherapy, over there, not even amongst friends. And the language, that was a problem.

I felt people couldn't understand me. Some kind of communication was missing. I didn't feel I was understood at all—I forgot
what your question was.

The content of the session concerned a woman with refractory depression recently taken off a low dose of Trilafon who
was complaining about the loss of the medication. There was
a long weekend and a nurse was unavailable. She went on to
describe other losses. The affect was sadness; the frame of that
affect was abandonment, things that had been taken away. In
the content of the narrative losses included: medication, time
with a nurse, time with Edgar, companionship, people who
spoke English, understanding. It seemed both painful and easy,
safe, for this woman to talk about people, places, things that
had passed out of her life.

The affect is then tested not just against the content of the
story but also in the context of attachment between the patient
and the therapist. So, as the therapist is listening to the patient
tell her story, she is reformulating the story using the data of
the story itself, and also using the data of transference, history,
extratransference, mental status in order to arrive at more specific understanding of the affect. And thus the story might be
told as a story between the therapist and the patient and understood as follows,

I am leaving you (They took away the Trilafon. There was no
nurse.). In fact even though I am still here, I am already gone (I
asked for more meds; they wouldn't give me any. I'm falling
apart.). And that is part of the reason why you are so sad (I feel
like crying because after only a few weeks what I had come to value
and need is being taken away.). But more than sad, it makes you
afraid because you want me to comfort you (It held me together.).
But you have never been able to ask for comfort from anyone,
including me (No one asks for help in this country.), and you are
afraid of what would happen if you did ask (I'm too dependent.
No one speaks the language. No one would respond even if
asked.). That's why you are feeling so lost (I forgot the question.).

Data from outside of the content of the narrative were
applied to the context of the session: the therapist was unavailable to the patient for the long weekend; she was about to

leave the patient; the patient had a history of few and failed heterosexual relationships; she had been raised in a stern religious setting; she suffered chronically from intense loneliness and longings for greater intimacy; she had intense ambivalence about homosexuality; she had been taken off Trilafon 2 weeks ago, and there may have been biological (affective instability) and psychological (transitional object) ramifications to that.

Transference involved the clarification of attachment behavior beginning with the clarification of the affect in the original story, the generation of multiple stories guided by the affect, the reconfiguration of the characters in the new stories, and then the comparison of the different stories. By virtue of witnessing and containing the multiple stories and data within the psychobiological context, one is able to establish the direction of the transference.

A question that the therapist might have asked, a question that might have helped her to get more information about the transference, the state of the affective illness, whether to have restarted the medication, and to have brought the patient closer to what she was most afraid of, was simply, "Are you feeling sad now?" That is bringing the patient closer to the emotions she was feeling in that moment. And perhaps later she might have added, "Are you sad about my leaving?" This could bring the patient not only closer to the affect but to the intensely felt affect she was experiencing toward the therapist and would thus identify the affect within an object relation (self, object, affect). A more provocative question might have been, "I wonder if you are afraid to feel the sadness about my leaving because you are afraid of feeling such intense and intimate feelings toward me, a woman?"

But this degree of intensity would have been inappropriate given the situation and given the fact that it would have probably led to increased anxiety, resistance, and therefore to less self-awareness. Questions are framed within a context that includes an assessment of where the patient feels safe and where the patient feels at risk, and how far to push from safety toward risk. One must decide how far to push the patient toward the edge of the perceived limit of the transference. What is crucial in any evaluation is that at some point one does either "push" the transference, or decide why it would be unwise to do so. The transference should be considered a tool with which to test a patient's internal psychobiological position of safety. It should be used, but used cautiously because of the power that it contains.

Another example: The patient was a 40-year-old woman being seen in the follow-up clinic after being discharged from the hospital for a suicide attempt in the context of major affective disorder, depressed type. She was discharged much improved. This was the third meeting with her therapist, a young man. He began by asking her,

Therapist:	How are things going?
Patient:	Good. But I have this job interview today. I'm a little nervous about it. Is it okay if we talk about it?
Therapist:	Sure.
Patient:	You know I haven't worked in 4 years. Not since my first hospitalization. Before that I once tried to work as a baker. All bakers are crazy. I failed at that. Then I went to secretarial school. When it came time for the job interview, I panicked. I went to bed.
Therapist:	Did you go to any interviews?
Patient:	No I went to the day hospital. So this is really a big step.
Therapist:	Tell me about the interview.
Patient:	Well it's for a doctor here at the hospital. I've never been able to see myself as separate. My husband takes care of things. I want to become financially independent. Start things for myself.
Therapist:	Does your husband know about your job interview?
Patient:	He says he's very supportive. Says he understands. But I don't think he does.
Therapist:	How is he unsupportive?
Patient:	He doesn't want me to be independent. He prefers that I'm at home. That he controls things. He won't let me have my own checkbook or my own money. But this interview today, when I see the

doctor and he asks me what I've done the past year, do I tell him I've been a mental patient in the day hospital or do I lie? I mean would a doctor hire me if he knew the truth about me? I mean you're a doctor, what should I do?

What are the issues? What are the stories? On one level the story was about a woman meeting her outpatient doctor, a man she has met twice before. She was preoccupied with a job interview. Past attempts to work had failed; she desired independence from a domineering husband. She saw her husband as standing in the way of her autonomy. The literal story was about the woman's desire for independence and the desire to be less attached.

The emotional action of the story, the affect, however, had to do with a woman asking a man for advice. She knew little about him except that he was a doctor and on the basis of that she wanted him to tell her what to do. The therapist asked her, "How will you decide what to do?" This was a valuable question and one that addressed a third story, namely, the fact of contradiction. The literal story was moving the listener in one direction, she wanted independence; while the affect pulled in another, she wanted to be told what to do, dependence.

Patients' narratives can and must be listened to on as many levels as they are told. This introduces the possibility for contradiction and inconsistency, a possibility which must be accepted, for it is often in the exploration of such contradictions that new meaning and new direction can be found. Contradictions between stories must be identified, contained, and worked through. The exploration of the transference accepts contradiction. The very human desire for attachment is often fraught with fear and illogic, and it is crucial to allow this illogic if one is going to understand another's confusion, pain, and multiple levels of attachment and transference.

Another example of the layering of transference is the following session involving a 45-year-old, single woman, who had been in treatment for 8 months. She worked as a regional sales director for a pharmaceutical company that was among

other things one of the world's leading manufacturers of nicotine patches. She had presented with the chief complaint that
her life was barren and empty. While she functioned well at
work and had a successful career, she was without intimacy on
any level. She described herself as having no friends. Acquain-
tances were as much as she could handle. She stated that after
an intensely promiscuous adolescence, she had been asexual,
and for the past 20 years was unable to contemplate the idea
of close friends, let alone a lover, both of which she wanted in
her life. Yet the very thought of sex disturbed her, whether
with a man, a woman, or masturbatory.

She was an only child, raised in rural Texas. Her mother
had been a dressmaker; her father was the town banker. She
hated her father and adored her mother. Indeed she saw her
mother as the only significant person in her world, the only
person with whom she could tolerate intimacy. She had often
stated that if her mother died, she would suicide. Safety was
being alone with her mother. She recognized that there was
significant pathology in what she was describing and indeed
had consulted therapists throughout her life, but always found
something wrong with the therapist and quit after a few visits.

This session took place in the context of her parents' visit
from Texas, and the patient's attempt to stop smoking, a habit
that she felt unable to control and which left her feeling deeply
humiliated. Her company after all was the world's leading manufacturer of nicotine patches. She entered, sat down, took out
a container of coffee and a cigarette. She did not light the
cigarette. She didn't look at me. Her finger tapped nervously
against the arm of the chair. Her spike-heeled shoe clicked
against the floor and her crossed leg nervously rocked. "I feel
awful. I feel like dying. If life is going to work, going home,
watching TV, not being able to sleep—and the only pleasure
is having a cigarette, then I'd rather be dead." She put the
cigarette back in the pack and continued, "It's just not worth
it. Smoking is the only thought that gives me any pleasure. That
and the thought of seeing myself splattered on the street. Of
course then I'd be dead but the thought of that feels good."

She went on describing how miserable she was feeling. I
was concerned about the level of her depression and asked,

"Are you feeling suicidal?" "I'm not going to kill myself—I just wish it would happen. I can't stand this. I can't stand anything. Sally was in town. I couldn't wait for her to leave. Then my father called. I told you what happened at the wedding didn't I?" She didn't expect or wait for an answer. "He's so disgusting. He embarrasses me. He's so greedy. I mean before dinner, he's stuffing himself with hors d'oeuvres. Just stands there and eats. And he just keeps picking one thing after another. Never puts the fork down. He uses it like a fucking shovel. And then we sit down at dinner. Does he wait for others? No. Just starts right in—eating. Can't wait 2 minutes for the others to sit down."

As she spoke, I assessed the level of her depression, her suicidality. She seemed involved, almost animated. I had identified no other neurovegetative signs of depression. As I began to listen to the content, I realized that she was telling a story about someone who consumed everything in sight. Was I consuming her or was she consuming me? She went on about her father, "He started complaining because he was ready for more before anyone else had even started. He's just so fucking disgusting. I hate him. Never hated anyone more." She stared at me then shrugged as if what she was about to confess didn't matter, "And you want to know something—I'm just like him. I'm just as greedy and controlling as he is. Everything has to be my way or not at all. . . ."

She identified part of her self-hatred as stemming from the fact that she identified with her father. She was someone who consumed.

Patient: Sometimes I feel like I'm full of maggots and at any moment they'll just start oozing out of me. I feel nothing. I feel like shit. I hate it.
Therapist: Do you feel you will be safe outside of a hospital?
Patient: I'm not going into a hospital. Maybe it feels like a safe place for you, but it's a terror for me. I'm not suicidal. I just hate my life.

I felt concern for her safety and further concern that we seemed to share no common understanding of what was going

on. She seemed to be in one place, despairing about her identification with her father, and I in another, concerned about
her suicidality. I thought, in error, that I could establish some
common ground by going to an extratransference topic that I
thought we could both agree on.

Therapist:	You continue to make a faulty equation. You see your father's greed and control over your mother as the same as your desperate desire to be close to her. Your faulty equation is that you can't be close to her because if you are close, you will harm her with your ravenous hunger.
Patient:	I don't know what you're talking about. Can you repeat it? [I could tell she hadn't really heard any of what I had said.]
Therapist:	What are you thinking? (She looked around the room, took a sip of coffee.)
Patient:	The more I think about it, the more I see me and my father as alike. I hate him. I've always hated him. I've spent my whole life making sure that his genes didn't get out, stayed quiet, but I can feel them. They're inside me eating like maggots. I've always had to be real careful or else I'd be like him. I do miss my mother. She's the only one that ever mattered to me. I'm terrified she'll die. She's the only reason I don't kill myself, what it'd do to her—but I know I'm like him. I'm just like him.
Therapist:	How do you feel?
Patient:	I hate this depression. I really hate it.
Therapist:	Do you feel safe enough to go home?
Patient:	I feel safe. I don't feel safe. I don't know.

It was near the end of the session. I felt that I knew her
well enough and that there was a reasonably strong bond between the two of us. I felt safe letting her leave the office. I
added, "If you start to feel really bad and suicidal overnight, I
want to know that you'll call me." She said she would. She
didn't move, thought for a moment, and then she said, "I feel
guilty already." Guilt. It seemed like a odd emotion given the

context of the session, so I asked, "Guilty?" "That you'll be up all night now. Unable to sleep with worry about me."

I realized that she had been describing not only her sense of herself, as ravenous and devouring like her father, but that she had also unconsciously experienced her relationship with me in that context. That she was the glutton with the fork, and I was the object, the food being steadily devoured, and that one of the dangers of connection was that it aroused so much greed and hunger that someone would be devoured. I said to her, "You see me as wasting away with insomnia. There is this conviction in you that you will destroy those whom you care about, whether it be your mother or me." She looked at me, and said, "Funny—when you said 'wasting away' I pictured you as that, unable to eat or sleep with worry, all night long." "I'll see you tomorrow." She said, "I feel a little better. I don't know why. Yeah, I'll see you tomorrow."

Attachment, transference, affect: When listening to a patient relate a story, identify the emotion, recognize and conceptualize it as the bond existing between you and the patient. Then reformulate the story in the context of the affect and the transference. Begin with affect. To return to Freud, "The affects are the constituent which is least influenced [by repression] and which alone can give us a pointer as to how we should fill in the missing thoughts" (1900, p. 461).

Pay attention to affect because affect is the compass. Not just the affect that the patient identifies, but the affect that one experiences as one identifies with the patient, with the objects, with the story. Beginning with despair, greed, and ravenous appetite, the task had been to understand how those feelings were contributing to her suicidality. Consider psychobiological and psychopharmacological issues and interventions—including hospitalization, but also consider the transference. Make the assumption that the affect in the transference is powerful enough to influence some if not all of what the patient is telling you. Then test that assumption against other data, other hypotheses, other questions.

Questions: Why was this woman depressed and suicidal now (affect)? Why was she feeling that she was dangerous to her mother (attachment behavior in the context of the narrative, extratransference)? Why was she feeling that she was dangerous to me (attachment behavior in the context of the transference)? Why was identifying with her father (attachment to a man) so dreaded?

Biology: She had stopped smoking. Nicotine withdrawal causes an intensification of depression among other things (Glassman, 1993). The deterioration of her mood may have intensified her need for comfort from others leaving her feeling more vulnerable.

Sexuality: For this woman to want greater closeness from anyone other than her mother was the most dangerous desire of all, especially if that desire were directed toward a man.

Her parents' visit: The fact that her mother was nearby but unavailable because of the overriding needs of her husband.

Oedipal issues: The competitive feelings aroused toward her father and the fully conscious wish that she had had ever since she was little, that he die.

Transference: Her increased feelings of attachment to me.

Affect: All these factors combined in the transference to increase this woman's need for me.

Common to all of these was the fact that her safety—the capacity to preserve the object by isolating herself from it—was threatened.

Hypotheses included: (1) She uses caffeinated beverages and nicotine as a way of treating her mood. (2) She may need more medication and therefore check the blood level of the antidepressant to see that it is therapeutic. (3) She works for a pharmaceutical company and therefore is someone who may have access to medications. She may take some of her "samples" to self-medicate her moods. (4) Her parents' visit is destabilizing on many accounts and her mood will improve when they leave. (5) The intensity of the transference is frightening to her and leaves her feeling less safe. She will need to distance herself from me. (6) Since she is a woman who uses primitive defense mechanisms (splitting, projection, acting out, denial), anticipate that in subsequent sessions she may need to see me as the dangerous and greedy devourer (projection) that she had herself identified with. (7) Anticipate the affect of anger instead of sadness as she will need to increase distance between us (resistance). (8) Return to the history to reexamine the data of intimacy (operant conditioning). (9) Given the dangerousness she sees in any attachment, reconsider the issues of abuse or trauma in childhood.

The story had multiple levels. It contained many affects: sadness, despair, greed, suicidality. A full assessment of the acuteness of affect and suicidality was an obvious priority.

Once accomplished, there was a specific historical context to the story. We heard that a woman became depressed when her parents come to visit. Watching her father eat made her think of his greed. It made her think that she too was just like him—full of hungry maggots that would consume everything. The story also had an immediate context. As the patient told a story about a wedding banquet, I identified the immediate context by identifying with the characters in the story and with the storyteller. As the patient described two people—one eating and the other watching him eat—I identified with someone enjoying a meal, someone watching another eat, and someone being eaten. By applying the affect of the story to the immediate context, a new hypothesis emerged: the patient was terrified of closeness because of her conviction that intimacy led to sadomasochistic greed. With this hypothesis other data were examined.

She had always maintained physical distance from me as she entered or exited the office. She always knew to the minute when the 50 minutes were over, "I have to leave now." Once at the end of a session, the door had been a little difficult to open. She panicked. Another hypothesis: she had to have an immediate and foolproof way out of a room, a relationship, an office. She was convinced that intimacy would have devastating consequences. The story about her hunger and greed was not just a story about the interpersonal past. It was a story about the intrapsychic present that could have been precipitated by multiple factors—nicotine withdrawal, the affective pressure of dysthymia, the visit by her parents, the flood of memories from the past, the experience of beginning to feel comfortable with me, and of the (almost) conscious experience of wanting more of me. All these as well as other unknown factors, could have led to an intensification of her need for the object, leading to her increased experience of terror because this placed her in the very situation that for her was least safe, the situation where she was no longer confident that she could find her way out, the possibility that these stresses were leading to more and more primitive affect experienced in the transference (see chapter 11).

A distortion was emerging both inside and outside of the transference. Intensification of affect from whatever psychological or biological source was dangerous. It was dangerous because the patient was convinced that intense affect would lead to attachment, and in consequence she would be in a position to devour or be devoured by those whom she valued. This was a hypothesis that could be tested. It could be tested by extending the session a few minutes longer; by observing what happened when the patient needed more from me; by unstructuring the session; by specifically addressing the transference perhaps later at a time when she felt safer, "After you told me how angry and frightened you had been with your father, you seemed in such a hurry to run from me. I'm not sure if it was because you were more afraid of me or because you were more in need of me."

Transference transforms the doctor–patient relationship in accordance with intrapsychic and psychobiologic versions of safety. Because of the integration of transference and safety, one can test the validity of one's hypotheses by moving the interaction away from or toward the transferentially determined edge of safety.

7.

Safety

Psychotherapy takes place in the overlap of two areas of playing, that of the patient and that of the therapist. Psychotherapy has to do with two people playing together. The corollary of this is that where playing is not possible then the work done by the therapist is directed towards bringing the patient from a state of not being able to play into a state of being able to play.
(Winnicott, 1971, p. 38)

Transference and safety are related. Because of this, one's hypotheses about transference and safety can be tested one against the other. A very simple way to challenge issues of safety (and to increase the pressure of the transference) is to decrease the structure of the interview. This is a valuable manipulation especially early on in the evaluation. Thus in their first meeting a therapist began by asking, "Can you tell me a little about yourself?" The patient, a man in his thirties, shook his head. "Tell you about myself? How can I? It's such a general. . . . I can't. I hate it when a doctor does that to me. It's too general. I don't know where to start."

One can and should generate many hypotheses from this reaction. Included among them would be the hypothesis that this man was threatened by lack of direction and that one might periodically return to that "edge" during the evaluation to see how over time he would deal with the loss of structure. But this question was perhaps too open to begin an evaluation.

It is better to begin an evaluation with fairly structured questions, and only later, remove the structure, that is, to increase the stress of the interview by removing the safety of the structured question. In this way one has a better sense of how the patient deals with stress, and also allows for the unexpected. A woman hospitalized with an eating disorder was being seen for an extended evaluation by a therapist. They were both in their midtwenties.

Therapist: How are things going today?
Patient: Okay. I'm getting used to the routine.
Therapist: Tell me about your urges to binge and purge. What's happened since you've been on the ward?
Patient: Well, they're not too hard to understand. I get very hungry and then I eat. But I hate it when I gain weight. So bingeing and purging made sense. It still does—just harder to do when you're locked up.
Therapist: What about what you're doing to yourself?
Patient: Well, I don't look forward to wearing dentures by the time I'm 30, but I try not to think about that.
Therapist: Is that your only worry?
Patient: No. Could I have children? I sometimes think about that.
Therapist: What else?
Patient: Well, what this whole process is doing to my insides. My body can take just so much.
Therapist: Your insides?
Patient: My digestive system.
Therapist: What about what it's doing to your mind?

The therapist was trying to get his patient to be more reasonable about her behavior, a reasonable approach when dealing with rational behavior. But he wasn't dealing with rational behavior.

Patient:	Yeah that too. I don't really know. I mean the only thing I've ever seemed to enjoy has been bingeing and purging.
Therapist:	Do you enjoy bingeing and purging?
Patient:	No, I don't enjoy it. It's just that it's the thing I always do.
Therapist:	If it weren't for bingeing and purging, what things might you do?
Patient:	Traveling, going out, music. I used to love to go to concerts.
Therapist:	How does it make you feel that you don't do any of that anymore?
Patient:	Hopeless. My life has been nothing but failures. Being so caught up in this. Everything. It's all hopeless.
Therapist:	Can you give me an example?

The patient looked at the therapist. She seemed confused, almost lost, and asked, "What do you want to know?" "Whatever you feel would be helpful," he said.

After a series of "leap frogged" questions, this was a significant change. The patient looked around as if searching for guidance. The therapist just waited, which was not an easy thing to do given the patient's level of discomfort. She shrugged, then said, "I don't know what to tell you." The therapist remained silent. In other words, by not asking any questions he removed the structure and safety that the questions had been providing. It also allowed for the unexpected, a crucial allowance when dealing with the irrational. Another moment passed in silence before the patient stated:

| Patient: | I don't know. I got a job once in Chelsea with these book publishers. They picked me over a hundred people. It was a great achievement. When the day came for me to begin, I called in sick. They had high hopes for me. Instead of a good impression, I made a terrible impression. After 3 weeks I quit. . . . |

She fell into silence. He said nothing. She added, "I don't know why I'm telling you this. It's weird." She picked at a scab on her arm.

Patient: I was accepted in an honors program at Montrose Community College. You know in Jersey. It was real special—small classes, the professors holding your hand the whole way. It was a great opportunity. I went for 3 weeks and then I just stopped going. I ended up with all incompletes.

By increasing the stress of the interview, that is by removing structure, something quite unexpected emerged. The patient told two rather interesting stories. In both she had been accepted to programs where she was given special attention and where hope had been held by others for her success. And in both instances she destroyed their hope. This unexpected data when applied to the transference were of particular interest in that she had just that week been admitted to a special eating disorders unit where again hope for her recovery was held high. She had, perhaps, been warning the therapist not to show her too much hope because in the past hope in others' eyes had become something of a target for her to destroy. One hypothesis would be that a resistance to her improvement was the sadomasochistic pleasure, sense of well-being and perverse safety, that she derived from denying success to others.

Withdrawing the structure of the interview is an important way to challenge the patient with the loss of safety; unexpected data or resistance often result. One can evaluate these data by applying them to the multiple perspectives of the narrative itself, the transference, and safety. During any evaluation it is important to challenge the patient in this way in an attempt to uncover data. It would be an error to "support" the patient automatically, without having ascertained that she actually needed the support.

The following interview took place between a therapist and a patient with character disorder on a long term inpatient unit. The patient was an attractive woman in her twenties. The therapist was also in his twenties. She entered with a newsletter for a publication that she had been working on. This was their third meeting. She began, "I'm supposed to write for it, an editorial or something. But I just don't . . . I can't. I thought I would but I can't. I got confused. I don't know why. Now I don't know what I want to write." He asked if there was a topic. "Was that the problem, that you didn't have a topic?" "No," she said, "Stupid of me to volunteer to do it. Just lots of problems. I don't know why I haven't been able to write." The patient was saying that she was frightened of not knowing what to say, in the newsletter or in the evaluation. The therapist had the choice of helping her either by directing or not directing a question to her. He chose to provide structure,

Therapist: What did you write about last time?
Patient: Something about how, when I was in Israel. My impressions of living there. How that compared to being here.
Therapist: Sounds interesting.
Patient: No. It wasn't. How that kind of life—I wrote it but this time I just—I was too embarrassed. Sounds like I knew what I was talking about but I didn't. I don't know very much. Sounds pretentious. It felt like a school paper.

She was talking about what was going on in their interaction as well as about the newsletter. He was listening solely to the content of the narrative and thus the tension between the narratives was lost, and with that loss went any hope of establishing bearings or direction. He said, "Sounds like you were thinking about things but didn't put them in the paper," which indicated that he was following along with her on the surface, following the content of the session and the resistance (ignoring the transference).

Patient: I take little things and make it a bigger deal than it is. I spend time worrying about it.
Therapist: About the content?
Patient: Yeah.

Therapist: You edit your own stuff. You're very hard on
              yourself.
Patient: I guess in a way. But nothing gets thought out.

Yes. Nothing was getting thought out. The problem with
the interview was not that the therapist was supportive. The
problem was that the interviewer never established that the
patient needed that kind of support in the first place. He just
became the wise healer without ever having addressed the issue
of whether his patient needed a wise healer, or was she like
him just more comfortable with this dependent transference–countertransference enactment? Helping a patient feel
safe by following along and gratifying the resistance may in the
long run be an extremely dangerous course because it establishes a treatment where over a short or a long period of time
nothing happens.

Safety is a complex issue. It is made more so by the fact
that for someone who is ill, what feels safe may indeed be based
on emotions that are volatile and dangerous, ambivalently held
hatred, envy, revenge, lust, rage, dependency. The definition
of safety is not a general one. Rather it is specific, and must be
defined specifically in each evaluation before it can be used as
a counterpart to and test of transference. Safety and transference are specific to the individual and can be inconsistent by
virtue of their ambivalent affective base,

> This fact of transference soon proves to be a factor of undreamt-
> of-importance, on the one hand an instrument of irreplaceable
> value and on the other hand a source of serious dangers. This
> transference is *ambivalent:* it comprises positive (affectionate) as
> well as negative (hostile) attitudes. . . . (Freud, 1940, pp. 174–175)

The "irreplaceable value" and "serious danger" have to
do with the underlying affects on which safety is built and on
how the interpersonal bonds that rest on them are maintained
or broken.

The following is an example of a patient whose interpersonal safety was founded on exceedingly ambivalent, hostile,
dependent, and revengeful affects. She was a 35-year-old

woman with dysthymic disorder and primitive character pathology. She was on multiple psychotropic medications which had partially but not completely helped to stabilize her mood. She had worked as a disc jockey for a local radio station until her psychiatric illness had forced her to take a leave of absence. There was a history of suicide attempts, self-mutilation, substance abuse, sexual promiscuity and frequent hospitalizations. The eldest of three children, she felt personally attacked and betrayed when at age 8, her mother abandoned the family for a female lover. Her father, to whom she had always been devoted, remarried one year later. Interestingly it was this act rather than her mother's desertion that she never forgave. From all accounts her father had been devoted and caring of his children.

The therapist was a man, a few years younger than the patient. The session was the fourth in a series of inpatient evaluations at the end of her first week of a psychiatric hospitalization. The patient entered, smiled, sat down, curled her feet under her and said, "Hi." She twisted her long straight hair around her finger.

Therapist: What are you thinking? (She smiled as if she had been expecting the question.)

Patient: Oh I was thinking about what I said to you last session, about giving people power over me by talking to them. I have balance when I'm alone. In relationships if they're weaker than me I feel okay, but if they're stronger, it upsets the balance—I'm not sure why.

Therapist: Anyone in particular have that power?

Patient: My doctor [referring to her outpatient psychiatrist].

Therapist: How does he have that power over you?

Patient: Just sitting there he can call my bluff on anything I do. Whatever I do can be broken down. I hate it. Makes me feel really awful.

Power and in particular the distortions of power in the transference and extratransference were the issues. The therapist addressed this directly,

Therapist: Do I have that power over you?

Patient: Yeah—I have to work really hard to stay in bal-
              ance. Makes me feel nervous. I wake up some-
              times and feel that anyone has that power over
              me and can hurt me. Other days I wake up and
              feel invincible. In the hospital I can't keep that
              up.

Therapist: If I have that power over you, does it mean I'm
              going to hurt you?

Patient: Yeah, it could. Even if you didn't mean it. Some-
              one always has that power; it's like a contest.

Therapist: What happens if you win?

Patient: I never feel settled in. It can always go away.

Therapist: If this is a power struggle, can you hurt me?

Patient: No.

Therapist: Is there anyone you want to hurt?

Patient: Yeah . . . my father, my doctor. I have a lot of ways
              to hurt them. I want my father not to exist. Other-
              wise he makes me feel like a nothing. Sometimes
              I think that if he were dead I'd feel better. I don't
              know. I just like it when he's sad.

She was describing the person in her world who meant
more to her than anyone. That she was furious with him for
remarrying was clear; that she hated him was also clear. But it
was a hatred that was deeply ambivalent, and it was this ambivalence rather than the hatred that was the issue, just beyond the
patient's consciousness, that needed to be brought into focus
and contained. The therapist, however, chose to stay on the
surface of what the patient was saying, and deal only with the
hatred. He asked her,

Therapist: So you can hurt your father, make him sad by—

Patient: I don't talk to him. Or I just tell him terrible
              things. That it's too late for me to change. That
              if I kill myself it's his fault.

She was describing sadomasochistic ways to inflict pain,
and not surprisingly she was staying with the manifest hatred,
leaving the latent ambivalence where it was, latent.

She justified her thinking by saying,

Patient: It's his fault my life is like this.
Therapist: Like what?
Patient: So confused.
Therapist: Do you believe that or say it to hurt him?

He was asking her to be reasonable, but she had already demonstrated that she had no intention of being reasonable, of willingly giving up her sadomasochistic pleasure. The ambivalence would have to be addressed first, but it hadn't been addressed, and thus her response was predictable. It would follow the unopposed affect of hatred and revenge:

Patient: I believe it. I like to hurt people I'm jealous of. Like my friend in the other hospital before I came here. I was feeling worse and worse. He was feeling better. He had the same doctor as me and they seemed to be friends. I wanted the doctor all to myself. I'd see them in the hall sometimes talking and laughing. I hated that so much. So I'd tell the doctor things about my friend and what he was doing—burning himself with a cigarette. The doctor took his privileges away . . . I made my friend hate the doctor so he couldn't even talk to him anymore. I ruined their relationship. That felt good. I liked doing that.
Therapist: Has anyone ever done that to you?
Patient: I don't think so. People who hurt me don't plan it out the way I do.
Therapist: What about with your father?
Patient: I expect too much of him, I expect him to give me something he can't.
Therapist: What?
Patient: I don't know. I expect him to understand me and talk to me like I'm a person. But it's never good enough. What I really want is for him to die. I don't know. I see how impossible relationships are. I can never be comfortable. There's no point.
Therapist: When did you want you father to stop existing?

The patient was not only recounting but creating with the doctor the chaotic and corrupt interpersonal world that she was describing. She was saying on the surface that the only comfort she had was in destroying the possibility of creativity and meaning that she saw in others, and especially in those that she needed. As the therapist continued to question along the surface of what the patient was saying (literally allowing the content of the session to be his sole point of reference), the interpersonal interaction moved further toward hopelessness and meaningless. A "safe" sadomasochistic place was being constructed by virtue of the fact that the ambivalence of her affects was being ignored.

The patient felt intense ambivalence toward people she needed. Her need for them became so intense that any disruption in her access to them became so painful that the only safe thing for her to do was to destroy what she needed from them in the first place, their love, their generosity, their empathy, indeed their very ability to help her. Because the patient was describing safety in this way, as a search and destroy mission aimed at those she most loved and needed, one would anticipate that she would need to actively sabotage the treatment.

For this patient at that time, the control and destruction of hope were felt to be safe. But safety derived from this depth of ambivalence will generate chaos. And because this was a construction based on chaos, it could not be understood directly and from within. The system would spin on itself. There would come a point then when the therapist began or should have begun to feel lost and confused. This feeling was the countertransference, where the therapist was able through self-reflection to recognize that the patient was forcing the affect of hopelessness into him (projective identification), and from that to realize that the more he questioned the patient in this way, the more confusion would result. If one reaches the point and recognizes that the hopelessness one is experiencing is the patient's active need to destroy meaning, then one has come to understand the patient's corrupt and ambivalent view of safety, where the possibility for love has been targeted.

But to continue to pursue meaning in the face of this kind of assault generates further chaos by empowering the patient's sadomasochistic design. And thus the therapist's last question, "When did you want your father to stop existing?" may have been wrong because it was addressing the surface of the narrative rather than the depth of the patient's pain and ambivalence. The question, by accepting the patient's construction that this was indeed her desire, let the patient know that the therapist shared this increasingly meaningless place that had fallen under the patient's control. If this route were pursued (which it was not), it would soon have terrified the patient with the thought that her destructive version of safety had been realized, and she would have been driven to act out.

What was the error? The therapist was following too closely to the description of hopelessness as if this were all that was being expressed. The patient was not describing one scenario. There was evidence that the patient was conflicted about her rage, and one very destructive way to resolve such conflict is to force someone you value to follow along with you on a hopeless path. Such an action resolves ambivalence and establishes safety but at a price. At a certain point, the countertransference alerts to the end point of meaninglessness, and the fact that it is the resistance that is leading the way.

Safety, like all other aspects of the evaluation, must be evaluated from multiple perspectives. What is safe, is not what a patient says is safe. What a patient says, the content, is a facet of the assessment. But like transference, the content is never accepted as valid without corroboration from other data, and this is especially true when the content indicates meaninglessness and despair. Thus if the patient is defining what she wants (content), and in listening one hears contradiction, then it is the contradiction that must be explored. Contradiction at this level and at this intensity, is usually based on intensely ambivalent affect.

So the therapist might have taken data from the content of the narrative, the observation of the dominant and contradictory affects, and from the countertransference, and said,

What you have been saying is confusing to me. But I wonder if that isn't just what you are really trying to tell me. That here in the hospital away from your regular doctor you've been feeling confused, frightened, and abandoned. And when you feel that way, whether it is about your father, or your doctor, I wonder if one reaction you have is to want to hurt them perhaps because you have felt hurt.

The comment addressed one aspect of the patient's ambivalent view of safety, that she wanted to be heard by those that she valued, needed, and envied. It also addressed her retaliatory rage, but in a more human context. She was angry and did want to hurt people, not because she hated them, but because she wanted more from them. Perhaps more than they could ever give. And despite the illogic of that wish, there was also a human basis to it, a basis from which hope could be addressed.

A patient's assumption that there is no love, humanity, or generosity is not an assumption that one should follow too far. Because if one were to follow the patient on this path, ambivalence would be lost, contradictory affects would disappear, tension would collapse, direction would be circular, resistance would rule. When dealing with a corrupt version of safety, the search for contradiction may be quite literally life saving.

Several months later, the patient, who was then in twice weekly psychotherapy, missed a nine o'clock appointment because she had overslept. She called the therapist and left an enraged message on the answering machine accusing the therapist of not caring enough about her. "If you cared about me," she screamed into his answering machine, "you'd have given me sleep medication so this wouldn't have happened," and then hung up. When the therapist called her back, the patient refused to take his call.

Obviously there were many complicated factors and numerous pieces of data in this material, but let us focus on the issues of safety. What the patient was betraying in this behavior was not just the attitude that the therapist had failed her. What had been revealed to the patient by her own reaction was how important the therapist had become to her. This then threatened her view of safety because as she saw it, the therapist now held the power. This contradiction, "Because you have power to help me, I hate you," must be brought slowly to awareness. It touches on primitive affect (see chapter 11).

But rather than deal with that issue, and those affects, the patient restructured the interaction around another affect, rage, in order to recreate a perversely safe place, one that was safe because she didn't have to attend to the affects of value, need, or envy. It was safe because it was bankrupt and thus corrupt. The multiple stories in the material would over time serve to help the doctor and patient see the multiple levels of ambivalence and contradiction.

Another example of perverse safety was a 30-year-old female patient who had been referred to me from an inpatient unit after having made a serious suicide attempt. She had a long history of self-mutilation and self-destructive behavior. Early on in the evaluation she indicated that in order to recover she would need me to supply her with "unconditional love." I asked her what that meant.

Patient: When I was growing up, my mother made it obvious that she loved my sister. I remember the day they brought Sandra home from the hospital. I was 5. My life effectively ended. I mean my mother clothed, fed, and bathed me but she never loved me—not the way she loved Sandra.

Therapist: So in order to get better you must— (She cut me off.)

Patient: No matter what, I need to know that someone will love me. No matter what. That's what's wrong with me. That's what I need.

Therapist: I see. So what you are saying is that you should be allowed to do whatever you want, and that I must respond with acceptance, generosity, trust. No matter what.

Patient: I never had that. Not since my sister was born.

Therapist: But that isn't love. That's dictatorship.

Patient: No, it's love, unconditional love.

Therapist: It's as if you are convinced that no one who has freedom would ever love you. Therefore you feel that you must find someone who will have to love you "no matter what." Maybe we need to look at your understanding of love and why it is you feel

you'd never be loved unless someone was forced
to love you.

Perverse safety always involves illogic. In order to move
from perverse safety to real safety, the illogic must be located
for it provides the opening to hope. When a patient's view of
safety is perverse, there may be the unconscious desire on the
part of the therapist to keep the treatment "safe" by being
supportive and by encouraging reasonable cooperation. This
rarely succeeds. It is far better to uncover in the formulation
the data of the irrational, the ambivalent, and the contradictory
rather than try to smooth these over in the hope that kindness
and generosity will somehow prevail. Kindness and generosity
are necessary but not sufficient.

Another example. The patient was a 35-year-old woman
who presented for treatment with a history of depression, separation anxiety, anorexia nervosa, and self-mutilation. There
was no history of physical or sexual child abuse, a very real
consideration given the constellation of this woman's symptoms. She entered the session, her fifth over a 3-week evaluation, actively reading a newspaper,

Patient:	While I was waiting I was doing the crossword puzzle. It was harder than I thought. The crossword puzzles in *The Times* get harder as the week goes on.
Therapist:	Last week you mentioned that you were looking for work.
Patient:	Yeah, I was. But nothing seems to be happening. I read the want ads. Nothing. So I went back to the crossword. Like I said they don't make it easy for you. (She has now mentioned the crossword puzzles twice. There was a long silence.)
Therapist:	What are you thinking? (The patient put her hand over her eyes, seemed to be crying gently, blew her nose, and then spoke with her eyes still closed.)
Patient:	Over the weekend I went into a drugstore. I just stood for a while in front of the section where

they sell razor blades. (She opened her eyes and stared at the therapist.) I really wanted to buy some. That's a signal to me. Later on I felt at first angry and then sad, but realized it was my own doing and for my own safety. (The patient stopped.)

Therapist: Did you buy the razor blades?

Patient: It was like a safety blanket. Having them and knowing I could use them if things got overwhelming.

Therapist: So you bought them?

Patient: Yes.

Therapist: How does that help, having razor blades?

Patient: I think the feeling that if I'm not safe I can scream loud enough. You're expecting—it's been said that things will be hard and I could fuck up. You said that. I don't know if I can yell loud enough so you'll hear what's going on. So I bought them on Friday.

Therapist: To yell loud enough?

Patient: Yeah. In part that's what it is.

Therapist: "It?"

Patient: The pain. The overwhelming pain and feelings. Feeling so scared. To see a cut, to see blood makes it better. (The patient again put her hand over her face and was silent.)

Therapist: What scared you over the weekend?

Patient: I just felt safer having the razor blades.

Therapist: Did you cut yourself?

Patient: No. I wanted to, but I didn't.

Safety for this patient included having in her possession the possibility of self-mutilation. Of being able to yell "loud enough." If cutting herself and seeing blood run from her wrist defined safety, then what was dangerous for this woman?

The answer is not easy and cannot be said with any certainty—indeed too little information was available to give an answer, and progression toward "the answer" would have to be made with many hypotheses including but not limited to:

affective disorder, impulse disorder, dissociative disorder, the need to control the therapist (sadomasochism), the need to make the therapist feel as helpless as the patient was feeling (projective identification working through the countertransference). But the example given held at least one other and more specific hypothesis.

The patient twice mentioned "crossword puzzles." Indeed while in the waiting room the patient was doing the crossword. Thus before the session began and again in her first words, the patient had referred to a search for the right words and even added that the puzzles got harder as the week went on. One can hypothesize that the patient was feeling that her own search for the right word grew harder as the evaluation progressed, that as she became more engaged in the therapeutic process, and as more regressive material emerged, she experienced greater difficulty finding the words to express herself, and therefore would have to search for other (nonverbal) ways to express her turmoil. She would act out what she could not say, become mute, put her hand over her face, cut her wrists, in an attempt to yell "loud enough." The therapist might have articulated this version of safety, if not to the patient, then to herself:

Therapist: It strikes me that you were having a hard time finding the right words to express what you were feeling over the weekend. Buying the razor blades was I think one way of ensuring that you would have the security and safety of being able to yell "loud enough." My hope is that as our work together continues, you will be able to express those issues in here with me.

The search for words was becoming harder and harder for this patient. Consequently, psychotherapy itself could become the very essence of danger, unless the therapist was conscious of where she was psychologically and neurobiologically inviting the patient: into a place and process where emotions would become more painful and where words would become more elusive. The therapist continued the session by asking the following question:

Therapist: What scared you about the weekend?
Patient: Well, it wasn't just a weekend. It was a holiday weekend. I was home for one day. There were lots of people around. My cousin was there—who's real interested in talking to me about how I'm doing. I mean what am I supposed to tell her? I'm fine. Right. Anyway her kids were there playing the piano and being master minds of that. My sister was there with her baby. Our mother coddling the baby. The whole holiday aspect of it. I don't know.
Therapist: The holiday aspect?
Patient: Yeah, being with all of these other people and not knowing how I was feeling. How to present myself. The number of people and who they were—
Therapist: Not being sure of—
Patient: Having to prove myself. Prove that I can handle that type of situation. Social, family. . . .

She stopped talking, and again covered her face with her hand. She wasn't crying. The patient stayed like that needing someone to define for her what was going on because she was in that unsafe place, experiencing a strong and painful emotion that she could not articulate.

Twice she had defined for the therapist what was safe, what was unsafe. If expressive psychotherapy were to be useful at all, then a hypothesis that would have to be tested was that this patient needed the therapist's help and active instruction in how to manage painful affect. Asking this patient, "What are you thinking?" or "What are you feeling?" might be asking her to go deeper into a labyrinthine crossword where words failed. So in one's formulation one might recommend a much more active, directive treatment that did not emphasize verbalization of feelings or thoughts until the patient had a better capacity for expression. And until such a state were reached, the therapist and not the patient would have to supply most of the replies to the question, "What are you thinking?" without ever having asked the question.

In Shakespeare's *The Tempest* Miranda says to the savage Caliban,

> I . . . took pains to make thee speak, taught thee each hour
> One thing or another. When thou didst not, savage,
> know thine own meaning, but wouldst gobble like
> A thing most brutish, I endowed thy purposes
> With words that made them known. (I,2, 350ff)

It is frequently the task of the therapist to endow the patient's purposes with words. And this is a task that may indeed take *many* hours.

If one can formulate a patient's logical or illogical view of safety, then part of the evaluation should include, or at least consider, the possibility of "pushing safety" as I have described it, in the transference. This is broached only if a reasonable human dialogue has been established. Going that distance with a patient is never comfortable and the assessment of the true danger must be made from an assessment of one's own anxiety (countertransference) as well as from what the patient says (content). But just because one is feeling anxious does not necessarily mean that one should turn back. With a sense of where the patient has been, where the patient is now, and where the patient's view of the world will lead, the therapist gathers courage to proceed with the patient into what is illogical and toward what is potentially dangerous. The confidence to go to the edge increases and indeed is possible only if one has the specific sense of where the "edge" is, and from this knowledge the confidence that one can get back.

To do this requires a map. With a map one has the confidence to move the treatment in appropriate steps away from the center toward the unknown edge where discovery and growth are possible. If one knows what transference paradigms are most safe for the patient, one can manipulate the transference with an expectation of what should happen. The results will indicate the validity of one's hypothesis. And by advancing to the borders of safety, one is not only testing one's hypotheses, one is also helping the patient to accept that such explorations can be made. In this way the patient learns that the illogical can be explored.

I was asked to see a 34-year-old man with chronic suicidal ideation. A biochemist working for a pharmaceutical firm, he was isolated, lonely, and had no social outlets other than playing ping-pong, a sport at which he excelled. Suicidal ideation was a constant issue in his life and in his treatment. He had never made a suicide attempt. Diagnostically, the patient met criteria for chronic dysthymia. Requests that he try medication were met with, "No! I won't take medicine. I'm not depressed. Either I'll work this out by myself or I'll kill myself." His suicidality was chronic. He did not meet criteria for involuntary hospitalization.

In the treatment, the referring therapist, a psychiatrist in his early thirties, had felt "trapped and frightened" by his patient. The therapist felt unable to say anything to the patient without worrying that he would attack him for saying the wrong thing and then torture him with his suicidality. As a biochemist, the patient frequently reminded the therapist of the lethality of the chemicals he routinely handled. The therapist feared that if he were to make an attempt, he would suicide.

A thin, finely boned, dark skinned, Hispanic man, the patient arrived for the first meeting dressed in a horizontally striped shirt, tight jeans, and heavy black boots. My first thought was that he looked like someone who had just left prison. He related how isolated he was and how hopeless he felt about ever finding happiness or love. He did not feel that he was capable of having a relationship with a woman because no woman, or man, could ever be genuinely sympathetic to his pain. After a first session devoted to the exploration of his depression and suicidality, he began the second session by stating, "Sometimes I wonder if there's a prognosis." I asked him what he meant.

Patient: How else could I feel about life? I was treated so badly—always. I was hit by both parents. When I tell people no one understands but me. No one

ever takes my side. If I could just get a divorce
from my parents. But people tell me I'm not supposed to do that. I just want to separate our lives.
I mean they fed and clothed me. They met my
physical needs. And there are no scars. No marks
on me. They paid for college. I just want to get to
the point that they're dead so I can put flowers
on their graves.

I was struck by the data of servitude: The therapist had felt
trapped and imprisoned (countertransference); the narrative
included the wish for an unattainable divorce; in appearance
the patient reminded me of a convict; he described the obligation of flowers after death. I hypothesized that obligation and
servitude lay on the edge of safety. I wanted to push him toward that,

Therapist: It was their obligation to feed and clothe you, so
             once they're dead it would be your obligation to
             put flowers on their graves?
Patient: Yeah. But only after they die.
Therapist: So it's a relationship of duties, obligations?
Patient: Yeah—they were always telling me what I had to
             do.

I wondered how imprisonment was related to the issue of
the transference and to the issue of safety. I asked him for
historical data as I listened for data about the transference,

Therapist: Do you still feel trapped by what they tell you?
Patient: Yeah. They still tell me what to do. I talked to my
             mother a year ago. Put your books in this room,
             wear these clothes, do this, do that. "Ma shut up,"
             I said. "You don't have to tell me what to do."
             I've unlisted my phone number. I won't give it to
             them. I'm gonna have a hard time getting any
             support for that attitude. My Ma got mad at me.
             A lot. I remember I was in my sister's bedroom.
             It's sunny outside. My Ma had me on her lap; my

pants are pulled down and she's hitting me with a hairbrush. She's counting to 10. "One, two. . . ." Her face and her voice are full of anger. Later it was with a spoon. Then I'm bigger and it's my father. He just yells—goes ballistic. Screams and slaps me across the face. Sends me flying. Or kicks me in the rear as I turn to run away. He doesn't count to 10. He just hits me once. He explodes. But they leave no physical scars. No one knows. No evidence except in my head and in hers [mother's]. I'm screwed. No way to fight back. No one will believe me. No way to fight back.

The sense in the transference and in the extratransference was that no one would believe him unless he forced them to believe him. I asked for validation of that idea,

Therapist: With no scars, without evidence no one will believe you?

Patient: Right. Like I need a polygraph—for me and for my Mom. I mean I told guys at work. No one takes my side. No one really accepts or understands what I'm saying. The prognosis for being hit like that by both parents—is it suicide? (He has been forced into something against his will. A prisoner.)

Therapist: Not necessarily. But it is a lot of pain.

Patient: I cry every day. It's in my head. Like a headache. [The association between low serotonin, migraine headaches, and depression would be explored.] This fight about what was. The anger. The effort to control the rage and not let it infect the rest of my life. My brain is always going. It's stuck in high gear.

Therapist: It's filled with thoughts about your mother, your parents, the beatings?

Patient: I want to sit my Mom down and with lots of people watching, get her to admit that she hit me. To get people to believe me.

This statement provided data about the history but also about the transference and about the therapist's countertransference of feeling "trapped and frightened" by his threats of suicide. The edge of safety had to do with this use of suicide to control others because underneath he felt too puny and weak to get anyone to listen to him. His predicament had forced him to that edge, to suicide. No one would listen to him freely. Therefore he felt justified in coercing others to his view. Coercion defined his strength and exposed his weakness. Because the transference contained all that, I wanted to go with him closer to that safe–unsafe edge that was defined by how isolated and powerless he felt. I asked,

Therapist: So your head fills with the thoughts that no one will ever believe you. Everyone will believe your parents?

Patient: I get that feeling with most women I meet. That they'll be on my Mom's side and that if I mentioned my Dad hitting me, they'll think that he hit her and that's why she hit me—that that explains it. It's like being the only black kid in a white neighborhood. Or the only kid hit by their Mom in a town where that just doesn't happen.

Therapist: No one sides with you?

Patient: Everyone's just gonna side with my Mom. They buy it. They all do.

He had defined what he meant by a prognosis. I said, "And so, the prognosis of anyone ever believing you is nil?" "Yeah there is none."

With this patient, pushing to the edge involved several factors. His referring therapist said the patient's suicidality left the therapist feeling trapped and unable to think or speak freely. Whatever he said was thrown back in his face as wrong, leaving the therapist feeling assaulted and the patient feeling misunderstood. As a result the patient felt more suicidal, and the therapist felt more paralyzed. Imprisonment was a powerful issue in the treatment, the patient by the therapist and the therapist by the patient.

Safety and danger seemed to revolve around obligation and freedom, around being the prisoner or being the jailer. The transference and countertransference reflected this paradigm. Pushing to the edge would involve moving cautiously with these issues knowing that suicidality was also part of the logic of his "safety." Suicidality in the transference became "safe" because it "freed" the prisoner and imprisoned the therapist. Suicide was the only way he knew to get someone to listen to him, especially a woman. Thus one would want to explore the issue of the safety and comfort provided by the thought of suicide because in the transference it also meant being heard. Pushing the issue of safety would expose issues of coercion, suicide, and communication in full knowledge of the risks. But not to approach the issue would be to accept the patient's insistence that it was too dangerous. And "it" for this patient was not so much the possibility of suicide as it was the possibility of communication. The freedom of movement, which in treatment translates to freedom of thought, had to be reestablished.

A dream the patient had several weeks later after treatment had resumed with his therapist, reflected movement along this path and further toward the edge of safety, communication and transference. The dream: "I am with a man with dark hair [the therapist had dark hair]. He came to watch me play ping-pong. He just watched. He didn't say anything." He looked at the therapist, then went on, "I went with him to Chicago. The train broke down. I turned to him and said, 'I'm sorry.' He said, 'It's okay. I'm with you.' " The patient stated right away, "It's about transference. It's about you. Isn't that what you call it, transference?" The therapist nodded agreement.

Patient: That's what I want you to be.
Therapist: Just silently watching and being there with you?
Patient: Yeah. The man in the dream was very nice. I knew him. But it wasn't you. You'd never behave that way with me. You'd never be nice to me the way he was. No one is. And if you say you are I

wouldn't believe you. I mean what does it mean
when I pay you to listen to me? Nothing.

In his dream the patient had moved toward the edge and
then come back. He had explored fleetingly what it felt like to
have someone, his therapist, willingly at his side. By exploring
the issues of coercion and communication, he had briefly been
able to entertain the notion of freedom.

By understanding his view of safety, the therapist would
anticipate a round of increased anxiety, suicidal ideation, rejection of him, his own anxiety and fears, followed by another
phase where he might again explore the patient's attachment
to him. Having the data of safety and transference enabled
the therapist to better anticipate the patient's reactions to his
interventions, and the resulting confidence to work on the
edge with this patient's dangerous affects and thoughts.

It was through approaching the issues of imprisonment,
communication, and suicide—by going to the edge not with
one but with all of these issues—that new data and new meaning were generated. Going to the edge of safety is about a
journey partly into the unknown, and one that must be taken
with as much data and with as many viable theories as possible.
To go blindly, without focus, would be reckless.

A 14-year-old Hasidic girl was brought to the emergency
room after taking an overdose of aspirin. Both parents were
extremely upset and ashamed that this could have happened.
They stated that they had no idea that their daughter had such
impulses. She was an excellent student, had no sleep or appetite problems, had not been sad or depressed, got along very
well with her friends and with her 5-year-old sister. There was
no prior history of suicidal behavior or depression. The parents
and younger sister were asked to leave the room and the girl
was seen alone by the emergency room physician, a woman.

The girl could not explain why she had taken the overdose.
She said that she had not been depressed. After an evaluation
that revealed little more, the girl told the doctor that she had
a secret but that she couldn't tell the doctor what the secret
was. She was too ashamed. The doctor wondered whether the

girl had had a sexual relation, had suffered child abuse, received bad grades, had failed in some way. After about an hour, the patient called the doctor closer and asked if she could write her secret on a piece of paper. The doctor got a pen and paper and handed it to the girl. The girl turned her back on the doctor and wrote something down. She crumpled the paper into a tiny ball, laid it on the table and then moved her chair into the corner of the room where she "hid" with her face in her hands.

The doctor first tried to comfort the girl, then picked up the tiny ball of paper. She opened it. The girl did not dare to glance at the doctor. The doctor read: "My sister nurses from my mother's breast."

The doctor looked at the girl with her face in her hands. Why was she hiding? Why would this confession about her sister cause the overdose? Why was it so unsafe for the girl to look at the doctor after confessing someone else's behavior? Safety. Transference. The girl was not confessing about her sister. She was making her own confession. She was jealous of her sister who was allowed to nurse from her mother. She wanted to do the same. And while there was no way to have anticipated that this was the girl's secret, once it was told, the issue of her emotional safety would have to be repaired without ever mentioning it, but also without ignoring that this had been a part of her shame, part of her safety, and part of the transference.

In the example just given, the girl's behavior, hiding in the corner, indicated that transference and affect were issues. Data from the mental status may or may not indicate what the transference issues are and where the edge lies. But very often the data of the mental status do help to locate where and how the patient feels safe which establishes a point from which to locate transference and affect.

Specific challenges to safety then occur through the transference. The therapist hypothesizes the patient's boundaries and then tests the formulation as well as looks for new data, by moving the transference to the edge or just beyond where he feels that boundary must be.

Another example is a session with the woman who worked for the pharmaceutical company that manufactured nicotine patches. The context of the material was that she had the weekend before called me, extremely unusual behavior for her, because she needed help to bolster her resolve not to smoke. I was, she had explained, the only person that she could turn to.

One hypothesis I held going into the session was that her call was exceedingly ambivalent. By identifying me as someone she needed, she also identified me as someone she feared. Just as she had feared that she might consume those she loved, I anticipated that she feared being consumed by those she valued. (Whenever you identify specific data in the transference or in the history, turn it around using affect as the axis, consider the data from the opposite perspective.)

The fact of her call, I hypothesized, had both increased and diminished her sense of safety. It increased safety in that she knew that she had been able to contact me. It reduced her safety by increasing her awareness of the bond that existed between us. It was the latter, her awareness of the power of the affect that was foremost in my mind as the session began. She stated:

> I don't know what to do. I want to stop smoking but when I stop all I seem to see on the street are families. I hate it. If I go back to smoking I'll feel like such a failure. But when I stop—I see families. Men and women with babies. When I'm not smoking—I know this is a little funny—but I start to see that men are more attractive to me. Then I start to think about sex. And then I see families. All over the place. Men, women, babies. I start to think about myself and what I could have had. And then I realize that I can't have a family. I'm too old to have a baby, a family. I never will. I know I never will. And that just feels like a total loss. (She looked at me directly.) What do you say to someone when they have lost something that they want and they can never have it?

I thought about her call over the weekend, that she was feeling closer to me, the material about families, babies, men, that she had been finding men attractive, that she had been having sexual thoughts, and mourning a family that she would never have. I thought about her version of safety. And finally I knew that if I addressed transference directly, she would reject the idea, so I said, "The issue of children is a sad one because the loss is real and there is little that I can say about that. But there is another issue. For the first time in a long time you have found men attractive to you. Can you tell me about that?'' Her rage explosively filled the room:

> You always fucking do that. You just go back to your men–sex thing. I just said I wanted to talk about family, about the loss of ever having a child and you go back to your thing. It's so predictable. There was one person in the whole world I was able to go to with this, with how much I felt I'd lost, and now there is no one. I can't talk to anyone. No one. Fuck!

She was mute with rage until at the end of the session, she stormed out of the office slamming the door behind her. Safety, transference, resistance.

8.

Resistance

*Freedom's just another word for
nothing left to lose.
("Me and Bobby McGee," Janis Joplin)*

*Extinction is just as important as
conditioning itself, since continuing to
respond to cues that no longer have
significance is nonadaptive.
(Kupfermann, 1981b, p. 572)*

One tests safety by increasing the level of stress either by dimin-
ishing structure or by approaching specific issues of the transference. An explosion of affect such as what was just described,
indicated that my comment had increased the level of danger
enormously, or there was a pool of underlying rage ready to
explode, and the slightest spark would ignite it.

It was as if the increased stress of sexuality, dependency,
and loss combined, and when ignited they changed her perception of herself, of me, of our relationship, and of the safety that
existed between the two of us. The reality of our antecedent
relationship had been replaced by another reality, operating
according to different rules, as if a whole new set of facts had
suddenly been revealed. But was the test of the safety successful? Were my hypotheses validated by her reaction? Was I right?
Was I wrong? What happened?

Hypotheses that I had had about her included: her overuse
of caffeinated beverages and nicotine; her possible need for

more medication; possible substance abuse; the effect of increased intimacy outside the transference; and the effect of intimacy inside the transference; the anticipation of primitive defenses; the anticipation of the affect of anger to defend against dependency. Behind all of that was the hypothesis that for this woman, safety was determined by her ability to control and maintain distance, and when that failed, intrapsychic and psychobiological forces were released in the transference and experienced as an acute threat to her safety.

As this session occurred after a weekend when she called me twice for assistance, I felt that her rage was provoked by the fear of having exposed her need and trust of me—exposed a level of dependency that terrified her. Her reaction added support to my hypothesis that she was someone for whom intimacy was overwhelming, and who protected herself on many levels from the conscious experience of dependence, affection, involvement, and gratitude because these feelings aroused such primitive terror. It also strengthened my conviction that she suffered from significant affective instability, and that her intense (almost fully paranoid) reaction to me might be in part biologically determined. The emotional lability then could either be due to underlying psychobiological imbalance (perhaps a mixed manic state), to substance abuse, to aspects of conditioned fear, or to some combination of the three. Another hypothesis was the possibility of child abuse or trauma that she had been unwilling or unable to discuss with me. This might account for perhaps some of the lability that had emerged with specific interpersonal triggers—her sense of being trapped in emotional ties, her terror of sexuality, her rage at me for suggesting such an idea in the context of the now denied, positive–affectionate transference.

Was the "test" a success? In that moment, no. A patient storming out of the office in rage and terror is not a therapeutic triumph. Had I pushed her too close to the edge of safety? Was my question wrong, that is to say was it unempathic? Perhaps I might have said, "I can understand your sadness that you will never have a child. Can you talk to me about that?" Or I might have asked, "Did seeing so many families leave you feeling lonely?" There were many other questions I might have asked or comments that I might have made. Perhaps an intervention anticipating her rage might have muted the storm. And thus I might have said:

In the past when you felt closer to people, you always reacted to that closeness with rage, as if to reestablish a "safe" distance. You've been talking about closeness—you've seen families, found yourself thinking about babies, about men, the two phone calls you made to me over the weekend. I hope you will be able to tolerate the anxiety that such feelings create and discuss those feelings further with me.

Perhaps she could have heard this. Perhaps at that moment when her denial was breaking down, nothing I might have said would have obviated her need to storm away from me, reestablish behaviorally a "safe" distance, and then return the next session to explore it anew. Perhaps. But I didn't in fact feel that my intervention was unempathic. Indeed I addressed the one ray of hope that I saw coming through in her story, and I felt that I was dealing most closely with transference, safety, and the increasing intimacy and trust that she had been exploring with me. Her reaction may have been a reaction to change itself.

In his play *Molly Sweeney*, Brian Friel (1994) described such a time of crisis when Molly's bandages were removed from her eyes. For my patient it was the breakdown of denial. And for both, safety was shaken by the challenge of a new vision. In the play the doctor, Dr. Rice, described his patient's predicament at the conclusion of a successful surgical procedure:

The dangerous period for Molly came—as it does for all patients—when the first delight and excitement at having vision have died away. The old world with its routines, all the consolations of work and the familiar, is gone forever. A sighted world, for that is the best it will ever be—is available. But to compose it, to put it together, demands effort and concentration and patience that are almost superhuman.

So the question she had to ask herself was: How much do I want this world? And am I prepared to make that enormous effort to get it? (p. 52)

No one accepts new vision easily. Almost invariably it is easier to stay with the known, even if it is painful, than to risk the unknown. Part of resistance is inertia, the comfort of the known, the fear of the novel. One resists new definitions, especially when they challenge self-definitions. What is resistance? What has been said about the constituents of transference can be said about the constituents of resistance. All those factors—psychological, neurobiologic, genetic, environmental, traumatic, operantly conditioned—are factors of the resistance. This chapter and the next will address predominantly the psychological factors of resistance.

Resistance may be conscious, as in the example of the Asian woman who feared I might think her crazy for believing in spirits. She turned the focus of each session away from her onto me. She did not want to risk my view of her, and more importantly she did not want to risk having to consider changing her view of herself. She therefore resisted revealing herself in any unstructured way because she knew there were issues that she very much wanted to avoid. She had to know where she was going before she headed out. She could answer specific questions, or talk about specific dreams, or talk about me in very specific ways. But she could not talk comfortably about herself without first knowing where the discussion would lead.

But what is being resisted or why it is being resisted is not always conscious. So what is safe or unsafe is not always known to the patient. Resistance by encouraging the failure of memory (repression) avoids unpleasure, shame, or embarrassment by keeping specific thoughts, affects, or desires unconscious. It is affect that is at the basis of such "decisions," what Freud called "unpleasure": "The basis for repression itself can only be a feeling of unpleasure, the incompatibility between the idea that is to be repressed and the dominant mass of ideas constituting the ego" (Breuer and Freud, 1893–1895, p. 116).

Freud further related resistance to transference. He felt that resistances arose particularly strongly against feelings or thoughts directed toward the therapist. "For it is evident that it becomes particularly hard to admit to any proscribed wishful impulse if it has to be revealed in front of the very person to whom the impulse relates" (1912, p. 104).

But to admit what one wants or feels toward someone else is to reveal something about oneself. When these impulses are resisted, it is again because one does not want to recognize something in oneself. Thus resistance can be dogged maintenance of a perspective. By insisting on one view of self and object (on one view of how one attaches to others), one resists the notion of another. That is to say, one transference paradigm, between patient and therapist, makes it difficult and sometimes impossible for the patient to meaningfully hear what is being said if that communication refers to meaning inherent in another transference paradigm. Thus resistance is not just the inability to remember a specific event; it is also the insistence on an object relationship or transference that precludes the possibility of another attitude, and this may be for psychological or biological reasons (see chapter 14).

The woman who worked for the company that manufactured nicotine patches, for example, could not safely listen to my interest in her newly found view of men because in the face of her increased dependency, that interest had also been directed at me (transference). Moving emotionally closer to me would only have increased the danger that I represented. Thus her paranoid reaction reestablished safety by creating a new affect and from that new affect distance that made it impossible for her to effectively remember the closeness she had been feeling toward me just the session before (resistance supported by the defense mechanisms of splitting and denial). So long as that affect and that transference paradigm were operative, any cooperative exploration remained impossible. This is also an example of the therapeutic alliance being overwhelmed and lost, momentarily or indefinitely, by affect.

Another example of resistance and the collapse of the therapeutic alliance is taken from a passage in Tony Kushner's play, *Angels in America*. It is a scene between the Roy Cohn character, the megalomaniacal lawyer of the McCarthy era, and his doctor, Henry, in which Henry is trying to tell Roy that he is probably HIV positive. What is demonstrated is how a patient, in this case a patient in a play, is unable to accept a new stressful reality and unable to accept the changed form of attachment that the new reality imposes.

The scene begins with the doctor,

Henry: Nobody knows what causes it. And nobody knows how
         to cure it. . . . The body's immune system ceases to
         function. At any rate it's left open to a whole horror
         house of infections from microbes which it usually
         defends against. Like Kaposi's sarcomas. These le-
         sions. Or your throat problem. Or the glands. We
         think it may also be able to slip past the blood–brain
         barrier into the brain. Which is of course very bad
         news. And it's fatal in we don't know what percent of
         people with suppressed immune responses.

Roy: This is very interesting, Mr. Wizard, but why the fuck
         are you telling me this?

Henry: Well, I have just removed one of these lesions which
         biopsy results will probably tell us is a Kaposi's sar-
         coma lesion. And you have a pronounced swelling of
         glands in your neck, groin, and armpits—lymphade-
         nopathy is another sign. And you have oral candidia-
         sis and maybe a little fungus under the fingernails of
         two digits on your right hand. So that's why. . . .

Roy: This disease. . . .

Henry: Syndrome.

Roy: Whatever. It afflicts homosexuals and drug addicts.

Henry: Mostly. Hemophiliacs are also at risk.

Roy: Hemophiliacs and drug addicts. So why are you im-
         plying that I. . . . What are you implying, Henry?

Henry: I don't. . . .

Roy: I'm not a drug addict.

Henry: Oh come on, Roy.

Roy: What, what, come on Roy, what? Do you think I'm a
         junkie, Henry, do you see tracks?

Henry: This is absurd.

Roy: Say it.

Henry: Say what?

Roy: Say, "Roy Cohn, you are a. . . ."

Henry: Roy.

Roy: "You are a. . . " Go on. Not "Roy Cohn you a drug
         fiend." "Roy Marcus Cohn, you are a. . . ." Go on,
         Henry, it starts with an "H."

Henry: Oh I'm not going to. . . .
Roy: With an "H," Henry, and it isn't "Hemophiliac."
         Come on. . . .
Henry: What are you doing, Roy?
Roy: No, say it. I mean it. Say: "Roy Cohn, you are a homo-
         sexual. . . ." And I will proceed, systematically to de-
         stroy your reputation and your practice and your
         career in New York State, Henry. Which you know I
         can do. (1992, pp. 42 ff.)

Resistance. What is being resisted? On one level one could
say that Roy was resisting the fact that he had contracted HIV.
On another level one could say he was resisting the fact that
he was homosexual. But that was only part and in fact it was a
minor part of the resistance. The essence of resistance is that
it refuses new information. "I Roy Cohn have had homosexual
relationships"—was not new data either for Roy or for Henry.
And while the information, "You are HIV positive," was terrifying, it too was known and heard by Roy.

The major issue of the resistance was neither of these facts.
The issue of the resistance had to do with attachment and with
affect. And in the example above, the resistance had to do with
a change in the attachment between Roy and Henry. For Roy
to admit that he had HIV meant that he had to admit that he
was very sick, and most difficult for a man who had survived
by his wits, arrogance, power, and sadism was to admit that he
was now suddenly dependent on someone else and by extension vulnerable to their wits, arrogance, power, and sadism. He
would have to trust Henry. This change in the transference,
though reasonable, was for Roy at the heart of what was unsafe,
and at the heart of what was being resisted.

Roy's need to dominate Henry as expressed in the transference, blocked the possibility of the full thought: "I am sick,
and need to have the advice of a doctor I can trust." The
former prevented the latter from entering consciousness and
experience. Because this attitude involved an object relation—Roy's attitude about himself, in relation to Henry his
doctor—the resistance was Roy's inability to allow the interpersonal interaction to change in accordance with a new reality.

Resistance maintained what was felt to be safe even if it meant having to deny what was real, logical, or truly safe.

Resistance is not so much about keeping a thought out of consciousness. Resistance is the refusal to allow certain attitudes, thoughts, affects into consciousness by virtue of the fact that other attitudes, thoughts, affects are maintained in their stead. Resistance is the insistence on an interpersonal perspective in the face of evidence that that perspective is incomplete—not wrong but incomplete.

Resistance is experienced by the therapist as obstinacy. A patient refuses to see or accept what seems reasonable, or persists in seeing something in the therapist that seems unreasonable. Stress often hardens the resistance, makes it bigger, exposes it, and because it becomes so glaring and garish, makes it that much more frustrating for the therapist (countertransference).

But by repeatedly showing what feels safe, the patient also exposes what is unsafe, and thus outlines in negative where the patient is prohibited from going. The danger of moving along the surface, of following the patient as if the patient knows where to go, is that one risks following the path of the resistance, a path that will fail to deepen, not lead to new data or meaning, and will sooner or later complete a circle. One does not follow the resistance. One must identify it, make hypotheses about what it is protecting, and then make hypotheses about how and when to challenge the false safety of the resistance.

Another example of resistance. The patient was the woman referred by her therapist and psychopharmacologist, who had avoided me, my gaze, my handshake; she had brought her own Kleenex and took them out with her. It was as if she were saying, "I will not be touched by you in any way." She was single, a successful fashion designer. She suffered from a long history of depression with suicidal ideation and behavior. She had abused alcohol and other substances. She had been treated with a combination of antidepressants and her baseline affect was improved. There were no vegetative symptoms; suicidal ideation had diminished. Her sense of herself and her basic underlying unhappiness, however, persisted.

Patient: Just so you won't be surprised, I'm not smoking.
               It'll last probably only a day or so. I almost called
               you on Thursday. I felt awful. The more I deal
               with people the worse I feel.
Therapist: The more people you're with the more threat-
               ening?
Patient: Yeah. That's how it is. Last night the phone rang.
               I hardly ever pick it up. I'm afraid to pick it up.
               It was Susan.
Therapist: Did you answer the phone?
Patient: No. I hardly ever do. It's safer alone.
Therapist: Safer?

The patient was describing a paradigm, a transference paradigm and a pattern of resistance. That it was safer for her to
be, or at least to perceive herself as being, alone. The obvious
flaw in her argument was that she was also in psychotherapy.
Acknowledgment of the very real intimacy that she sought with
me was being resisted. There were contradictions then between
the resistance ("I refuse to be close to anyone") and the transference ("I am confiding in you"), and in these contradictions
there were opportunities to examine her sense of safety. She
went on,

Patient: If I'm alone not talking to anyone, I don't have
               to worry about screwing up, about them liking
               me. I usually call people when I know they won't
               be home. Leave a message and fulfill my obliga-
               tions to talk. Anyway last week I saw James [a col-
               league at work] flirting with a very small, pretty
               blond. I was thinking why is this guy doing this to
               me? I had to just stand there and watch him. I
               wanted to die. Thursday was worse. They moved
               my office—to Siberia. It's obvious what they think
               of me, obvious what the message is. . . . Then
               James came to my office to complain. I was think-
               ing well this is nice; he's paying me a visit. He was
               talking very loud, complaining. I said keep your
               voice down, or the boss will hear you. He said, "I

want the boss to hear me.'' And that's when it hit
me. I mean that's why he came to see me. To get
a message to the boss. Used. . . . Whenever I start
to feel okay, something happens to remind me
where I should be. . . .

The patient was thus confiding to me that she should trust
no one—a contradiction. She also indicated that the consequence of violating that rule was shame (affect). To avoid that
consequence she had to stay emotionally isolated. She was establishing a situation where if she allowed herself to feel close
to me, she would by her own logic feel ashamed. The resistance
was foreordaining two possible outcomes: solitude or shame.

Patient: Saturday I went to Andy and Sally's for dinner.
              When I saw some of their friends on the train ride
              out, I hid. I just didn't want to be seen by anyone.
Therapist: That sounds hard, having to hide more than you
              can show.
Patient: It's always been like this. When I ran into James
              that morning—I felt so ugly and seeing him made
              it worse. More reasons to be alone.
Therapist: Is that when you were thinking about calling me
              last week (reintroducing aspects of the trans-
              ference)?
Patient: I get these bad feelings when I go to work—things
              that make me uncomfortable, sad, that embar-
              rassing things are going to happen. But I feel that
              no matter where I go I'll fail. And if I do ever feel
              good, these feelings will be dashed in a second.
              James—it was devastating. Every day I expect peo-
              ple to just smash me. I just thank God when I get
              through a day without being hurt.

Her association was to the fact that if she allowed others
to be aware of her attachment to them, she would be humiliated. She was then providing a context to the fact that she had
avoided what I had said. I decided to challenge the safety of
her resistance,

Therapist: You've defined your safety as being alone, not an-
               swering the phone, hiding from people on the
               train. You've defined your solitude as the safest
               place for you to be. But you wanted to call me, to
               bring me in to that place.

Patient: Last weekend was just luck. I can't always depend
               on a good weekend rescuing me. (She was still
               avoiding what I had said. I clarified)

Therapist: One thing for you to consider and I know this
               will make you somewhat uncomfortable. You've
               allowed me to be a part of your solitary existence.
               You've allowed me in. So it's not entirely solitary.

Patient: Yeah—I'm not sure what you mean by that.

Therapist: You've defined your safe place as solitary, but to
               a certain degree it's not. I'm part of it.

I was challenging her conviction that she was only safe
when alone. She chose to avoid what I had said consistent with
observations from the mental status exam: "Don't touch me."

Patient: I'm not fired yet. I did go to Andy and Sally's.
               I'm not completely cut off and alone. There are
               escape routes if I want them. (I decided to address
               the affect)

Therapist: Does it generate anxiety for you to contemplate
               that you've allowed me into your life in a powerful
               and intimate way?

Patient: I don't know. I guess. Relationship with you—it's
               one of two things. I'm really unhappy when I talk
               to you. Or if I get things straightened out, I'll
               never see you again. So no matter what, it's tem-
               porary. Makes me anxious that I can't talk to any-
               one except you. The disturbing things I only tell
               you.

She was moving from the pain of solitude to the pain of
shame. I decided to back off from that, to be more supportive
as I felt that she was as close to the edge of safety, of affect, as
she could go without pushing me away. I said, "Do you have

any idea why the idea of trusting me is so frightening?'' She looked at me then said in anger,

Patient: No. I just know it is, okay? It's just there, a fear, I can't grasp it. I can't say what it is. I can't—All I can say is that you're probably right. Okay? You get what you want? Damn, I don't get credit for anything. I'm trying to stop smoking. What happens? Do I get any credit?

The session had recreated what she had described with James, the feeling of trying to win a man's approval and ''What happens?'' Humiliation. The experience of shame was one that no matter how carefully I worded my interventions, kept recurring.

Patient: This morning, before I came here, I got very anxious. I dreaded coming to see you. I'd been alone this weekend. I didn't want to come out. I feel worse with people. When I talk to someone, it only gets worse.

Therapist: The dread you feel before coming to see me speaks to your conviction that the only emotion you will feel with me is shame. That what you show me will humiliate you.

Patient: The feeling I have, the shame, I can't get away from it, and if I do, it just comes right back. I don't want to go to work today. I'm really fighting with that.

Therapist: I wonder if what you're struggling with isn't also whether you feel safe enough with me. I wonder if that isn't where the fight is right now.

Patient: Yeah, that and that comfort is all that I'll ever get. I feel disdain for comfort. Coming here for comfort, it's cheap. I'm asking for something that isn't there, that no one can give so why ask?

Therapist: Perhaps because the issue isn't just about comfort. It's about trust.

Patient: I'm not trying to avoid that, but I have an early
             appointment and I have to go now.

Resistance is tenacious. The identification of the data of
resistance begins with the identification of the affects that recur
no matter what contradictions must be ignored, and with the
identification of what affects are being excluded. In this example the central issue was the affect of shame. She defended
herself against that by avoidance, isolation, projection. But
oddly what recurred unfailingly was her experience of shame,
and my feeling of frustration (countertransference). That
something else was happening in the transference that she was
beginning to trust me and to rely on me, not just as someone
who could and did offer her comfort but who also offered her
understanding, was fought fiercely and ambivalently. Attachment was fought off because of her conviction that with attachment came shame.

Thus there was a strange issue of control that was being
enacted in the transference. It was as if she would allow the
treatment to progress so long as she controlled the outcome—invariably solitude or shame. It was as if there were no
other alternatives. Safety, perversely, became the capacity to
get to that endpoint.

The identification of resistance has in part to do with the
identification of the affect that the patient needs to create and
recreate (psychodynamically and neurobiologically). By working toward the same affect, no new material was allowed to
emerge. Nothing new happens so long as resistance is in control. In working with this woman, the tenacity of her despair
made me mindful not only of the psychodynamics of resistance,
but also of the tenacity of affective illness especially in patients
with a significant comorbidity, in this case of substance abuse
and personality disorder (Thase, 1996).

In any evaluation then, it is crucial to know not only where
the patient wants to go, but where the patient does not want
to go, and where the patient may or may not be able to go.
This has to do with resistance, transference, and affect. These
will take a similar form; that is, the form of a structured interpersonal relation with the therapist. The elaboration of the

transference leads to the possibility of new data and new meaning, while the elaboration of the resistance leads to the repetition of the known by virtue of the repetition of the same patterns of affect.

Hypotheses about the transference and about the resistance then can be tested by observing what happens when the level of safety changes. These changes can be caused by issues outside of the transference—a frightening diagnosis is confirmed, a humiliating encounter with an ex-boyfriend occurs, razor blades are purchased. Or they can occur in the transference—the therapist unstructures the session, remains distant when the patient is needy, provides comfort, announces he or she is going to be away. When such changes occur, one observes what happens to the quality of the object relation, to the resistance, to the transference, and to affect—in particular to the quality and intensity of affect.

The greater the health, the greater the freedom. In the context of dynamic psychiatry, freedom of thought has to do with freedom of affect.

> Nothing. I mean nothing honey,
> if it ain't free.
> ("Me and Bobby McGee," Janis Joplin)

And when someone's thinking isn't free, there are at least four factors which must be evaluated, compared, formulated. They include: (1) the resistances within the mental status—particularly the patient's cognitive style; (2) the defense mechanisms which structure the transference and the resistance; (3) the history and how associative learning shapes transference and resistance through affect; and (4) the neurobiological control of affect.

9.

Defense Mechanisms

Diseases attack boundaries.
(Holtzman, 1996)

A very slender, elegantly dressed woman of 38 entered the office. She looked around the room disdainfully as she played with a strand of pearls hanging from her neck. "I don't know why I'm here," she smiled, and then corrected herself,

> No, I do know why I am here. I came to see you because I can't afford to see someone really good. I refuse to see a resident; they just experiment with people. So when Dr. Dean gave me your name—Dr. Dean is someone who I would see if I could afford him—I said, "Well all right." So, I guess you are going to say, "What brings you to see me?" aren't you?

Transference and resistance are structured distortions; and the components of the structure are defense mechanisms. As part of any evaluation it is crucial to identify the defense mechanisms, hypothesize their origin, their purpose, their function, and then test the validity of one's hypotheses. One is testing then not just "whole" transferences but specific pieces of the relationship as they emerge and are identified. These components have psychological and biological roots, and while it is not always possible to know what part of the structure is biological and what part psychological, both must be considered. This chapter will focus mainly on the psychological component.

119

The peculiar nature of safety and danger in the patient–therapist relationship causes more primitive aspects of
the patient's internal world to emerge. It is as if the more
normal socialized components of the individual's thinking and
behaving recede in favor of the more instinctive and the more
primitive. This shift in the nature and quality of the object
relations occurs along with a shift away from defense mechanisms that tend to dominate in the interpersonal sphere, toward those defense mechanisms that tend to dominate in the
more regressed, intrapsychic sphere.

Two factors in particular are responsible for this shift of
defense mechanisms. The first is the particular nature of the
safeties and dangers of the doctor–patient relationship. The
second is the relative lack of structure that can be introduced
into the evaluation process. Because of these factors, more
primitive affect, object relations, and defense mechanisms are
mobilized and the patient shows a side of himself that is not
usually shown except in the most safe and the most dangerous situations.

By manipulating the treatment in relation to transference
and resistance, more or less primitive affects can be fostered,
and with more primitive affect more primitive defense mechanisms follow. Through the transference and affect, the level of
the defense mechanism can, to a degree, be predicted. In the
example above of the slender woman with pearls, she was very
quickly giving a definition to the relationship and demonstrating defense mechanisms that had to have been operative as she
introduced herself to me. Because she had these views of me
on entering the office, before I had said much more than
"Hello," it was clear that her views were not about me, not
about the reality of an unfolding interpersonal relationship,
but about an internal intrapsychic distortion that she carried
with her as she entered an office and encountered me, her
doctor. This distortion was not about an interpersonal reality;
it was about an intrapsychic reality.

Intrapsychic reality is different from interpersonal reality.
The latter reveals how one interacts with people. The former
is an internal assessment of that interaction. The interpersonal
is the "real"; and the intrapsychic is the experience of the

"real." The transposition from the reality "out there" to the reality "in here" is complex biologically, psychologically, philosophically; suffice it to say that the transposition goes from the objective and the testable to the subjective and the personal. While the internal experience itself cannot be duplicated because it is subjective and internal, its components to a certain degree can be teased apart: affect, impulsivity, sense of self, sense of object, transference, resistance, defense mechanisms. These are not the equivalent of the internal experience but they are pieces of it. The internal experience has consequences in observable behavior and in communicable affect, and it is these consequences that can be assessed.

One proceeds from assessing the interpersonal, to identifying the distortions, clarifying how the patient views himself and yourself in that distorted interaction, and the affect that exists in that distortion. The therapist must make separate assessments: one of the patient's intrapsychic world and one of the interpersonal reality. The discrepancy between the two is largely determined by affect. The therapist must simultaneously hold and examine these multiple realities and affects if contradiction is to be appreciated.

From there one defines the defense mechanisms that must have been operative to sustain the distortion. Defense mechanisms are the prisms through which perception and affect pass. If one knows how they distort, one can make specific predictions as to how those distortions should influence subsequent behavior. From that prediction, one may have a better sense of whether one's view of the person's internal world is accurate. By the accuracy of one's predictions, one lets someone else know that they are not wholly alone with their internal experience.

To return to the data, a very slender, elegantly dressed woman of 38 entered the office. She looked around the room disdainfully, playing with a strand of pearls hanging from her neck. Then she said, "I don't know why I'm here." She smiled at me, and then corrected herself,

No, I do know why I am here. I came to see you because I can't afford to see someone really good. I refuse to see a resident; they just experiment with people. So when Dr. Dean gave me your name—Dr. Dean is someone who I would see if I could afford him—I said, "Well all right." So, I guess you are going to say, "What brings you to see me?" aren't you?

"No," I thought, "that wasn't what I was thinking." I was a bit stunned actually and was silent for a minute. I must have smiled because she threw out at me, "Why are you smiling?" "I didn't mean to," I answered, "but if I did, I guess it was because I hear you anticipating the outcome before we have begun."

Whatever she may have said next, I was thinking about defense mechanisms because of the intensity of the affect and because of the distortions that had already occurred. I needed to understand those distortions in order to understand the intrapsychic representations that she had presented of herself, of me, of us that I had already witnessed.

Defense mechanisms distort perception. They are not the cause of the distortion any more than prisms are the cause of rainbows. They are the vehicle of the distortion, and as such she saw me as an incompetent who couldn't help her: devaluation, projection, denial. Others could help her: Dr. Dean who could be seen as a wonderful doctor partly because he was out of reach: primitive idealization, externalization, displacement.

I was thinking of "part object dyads," a useful concept when facing primitive affect and defenses. Part objects pertain to a specific form of object relation based on the defense mechanism of splitting. Thus she saw me as incompetent, stupid, beneath contempt. She saw Dr. Dean as worshipful, brilliant, beyond reach. There was one implied view of herself (superior, brilliant, and pleasantly amused) that existed in relation to me, and another view of herself (rejected, unworthy, forever in mourning) in relation to Dr. Dean. These paired part self part object representations were mirror images maintained separately by the defense mechanism of splitting. After a while I did ask, as she had predicted, "What brings you to see me?"

She smiled contemptuously. I felt a little annoyed. She stated, "I've had an eating disorder, anorexia nervosa, since I was 14." She smiled again as if there were a victory in that. I soon realized there was. She continued, "I've seen the best. None of them have been able to help me. So now I've come to see you."

It wasn't so much that she expected me to fail. It was that she was growing increasingly desperate—anorexia nervosa of 24 years duration offers a very poor prognosis. So she wasn't really expecting me to fail, rather, she had given up hope, she was expecting to fail. She wanted to let me know that she was planning to make her failure mine (projection).

There were two "realities" operating simultaneously. The first was the interpersonal reality: A newly established doctor in his new office was greeting an elegantly dressed, slender woman who had come to him for help with what in her particular case might be an incurable illness. This interpersonal reality would have to be compared and contrasted with the second, or intrapsychic reality: a pathetic, incompetent, newly established doctor would make a fool of himself as he tried to rescue a brilliant, elegantly dressed, but tragically doomed woman.

The distance between the two was the distance between the interpersonal and the intrapsychic. Both "realities" were valid representations of an interaction, but from different perspectives. By comparing these two perspectives one could better understand what must have occurred in order to have created the differences (how the light must have been bent and by what kinds of prisms in order to get the two patterns of color that were playing on my office walls). The greater the distance from the one to the other, the more primitive were the defenses.

Certain defense mechanisms had to have been operating in order to have established the distortions of affect and perception. Devaluation, denial, projection, primitive idealization had thus been identified. One examines subsequent interactions with the expectation of specific distortions according to these defense mechanisms.

The patient returned for the next appointment, on time, wearing another elegant suit. She mentioned that her grandmother had recently died leaving her a lot of money as well as a wardrobe of Chanel suits. She asked whether I had ever heard of Coco Chanel. I indicated that I had heard of the designer and then asked a question about her weight, to which she smiled as if she had once again identified my narrow, pedestrian mind. She brushed a fleck of something off of her Chanel suit, "What about my weight?" She didn't want an answer. She continued, "Women look at me on the street. I can tell what they are thinking when they stare at me." My thought: "What a poor, wretched creature." Hers: "Envy. They just see how thin I am and they fill with envy." She looked away as if the question were not worth examining, then added as an aside, "What about my weight, doctor?"

Consistent. Structured defense mechanisms established a pattern of transference and object relation that was buttressed by a resistance against the very affect, envy, that she seemed to be seeing in others, projection, wherever she looked. She had not only in the transference defined me as contemptible, but she had also identified women on the street as enviously turning and staring at her. Both the interaction that she was creating with me (transference) as well as the one that she was describing on the street (extratransference), reflected her sense of herself as someone surrounded by inferiors. Because of the structured way in which she perceived herself and those around her, anyone turning to stare at her *must* have been staring because she had something they wanted. Defense mechanisms: devaluation of others, primitive idealization of self.

The next week she returned again on time, and paid the bill that I had given her the week before. She complained how dirty the neighborhood was where I worked. And then almost casually added how little she was getting for what she had been paying me. She thus had introduced an inconsistency in her intrapsychic perception. In every evaluation, indeed in any session, one is particularly mindful of internal illogic, because it offers the opportunity of showing the patient some of the consequences of primitive defense mechanisms. Sooner or later there must be internal contradiction because primitive defenses maintain a separation between the interpersonal and the intrapsychic, between data and affects that are not compatible. This separation is usually at the expense of humanity, at the expense of the patient's awareness of his or her own humanity and the humanity of others, and therefore the price is very, very high.

Any evaluation should include the search for and possible confrontation of internal illogic and of defense mechanisms to see how the patient deals with the possibility of a new perspective. This is not the same as a confrontation of what is inconsistent according to generally held beliefs: such as "Two and two is five"; "New York is west of Chicago"; or "The doctors in Presbyterian Hospital are agents of the KGB." Rather it means looking for inconsistency within the patient's own system of affect and logic. And to identify inconsistency at this level, one must enter the system of the other.

An example will serve. A lawyer presented to the emergency room convinced that former Soviet agents had planted electrodes in his ears to control him by telling him what to do and what to think. He was understandably very upset with the ENT (otolaryngology) service when the doctors there failed to discover any devices in his ears. When he was referred to psychiatry, he continued to be upset with my inadequate understanding of the situation and with the fact that I had failed to do anything about the KGB agents who were operating "freely in this hospital." Soon he began to suspect me of being one of them.

Paranoid schizophrenia is a neurobiological illness which leads to cognitive and behavioral decisions based on psychotic beliefs. This man's internal belief was that Soviet spies were trying to control him by talking to him. The internal inconsistency was not the electrodes, the Soviet conspiracy, the fact that the ENT resident could not find the devices in his ears, or that I might be an agent of the KGB All of these were consistent with the belief: "Soviet spies are trying to control me." What was inconsistent, however, was the fact that he had chosen to come to a hospital. "What strikes me as odd," I said to him, "is that you, a lawyer, someone who is very well acquainted with the workings of the Justice Department, the FBI, and the police, would come here, to a hospital, to see me, a doctor, when you believe that your problem is that KGB agents have illegally planted electrodes in your ears. Is it possible that the reason you freely chose to come here is that part of you wonders whether the voices you are hearing may be the work of an illness and not of spies? And therefore the reason you chose to come to a hospital is that part of you believes, as do I, that you are ill and need medical not political help?'' The patient did not accept my argument, but he did accept medication and hospitalization. Confrontations to be effective must find the inconsistency within the patient's system of logic.

And so to return to the example of the woman with pearls. She had just paid her bill, and then commented offhandedly about my incompetence. She went on about some problem at work. After a few minutes, I said to her, ''It's curious that you come here on time session after session, pay me good money, all the while trumpeting what an idiot I am and how I can't help you. I don't get why a woman as smart as yourself would continue doing something that you are convinced is pointless.'' She smirked, looked around the room and pointed to Dr. Dean's ''light blue Bible'' that was on my shelf, ''That's a comment right out of his book.'' She smiled triumphantly, ''Can't you do any better than that?'' One should not, however, expect that patients will instantly grasp the ''wisdom'' of one's confrontations.

Thus, rather than recognize the illogic of her behavior, maintained by splitting, devaluation of me, primitive idealization of Dr. Dean, her defense mechanisms grew more rigid and the prevailing part object dyad of grandiosity (herself) having to ''suffer'' the indignity of a contemptuous object (me), continued, and continued, for several weeks. Resistance is tenacious. It is fueled by neurobiological factors which are structured by defense mechanisms. ''I had so hoped you would come up with something more original than that,'' she told me. ''I am so disappointed in you. I am sure Dr. Dean would be as well.''

My ''amusement'' with the patient was beginning to wear thin. This went on for another week. Then there was a change—not in her, but in me. I began to dread the thought of seeing her, and then I found myself worrying that she would call Dr. Dean, a mentor and respected teacher of mine, and complain to him about what a poor doctor I was. I began to fear that he would take her criticism of me seriously and that my image would be sullied. As I thought this through I realized that I was feeling somewhat frightened of what this woman could do to me and my reputation amongst my colleagues with just one well-placed call to Dr. Dean. I also realized that I was beginning to see things in a refracted light, that my vision was beginning to match not the interpersonal realm between myself and Dr. Dean or between myself and my patient. Rather it was beginning to match the intrapsychic representations of my patient. I reread some of Dr. Dean's "light blue Bible" as she had called it. I also reread some of Lewis Carroll's *Alice's Adventures in Wonderland* (1865/1947). In particular the first chapter, "Down the Rabbit Hole," where Alice had just been watching the elegantly dressed White Rabbit dash across the lawn:

> Alice started to her feet, for it flashed across her mind that she had never before seen a rabbit with either a waistcoat-pocket, or a watch to take out of it, and burning with curiosity, she ran across the field after it, and was just in time to see it pop down a large rabbit-hole under the hedge. In another moment down went Alice after it, never once considering how in the world she was to get out again. (p. 12)

I realized that I too had gone down after "it," and that the fear and paranoid distortions I was experiencing were my patient's, and that she, like the rabbit, had taken me in, or placed in me her intrapsychic world. Obviously this was an example of countertransference, but it is important to recognize that one does not just objectively and comfortably observe the way someone else feels, but one also begins to distort and misrepresent the interpersonal world with the defense mechanisms that had once seemed the sole possession of the other. Defense mechanisms are, like white rabbits, quite real. I realized that I was experiencing directly what it was like to have to cope with her level of fear, her sense of vulnerability. I was experiencing what it was like to be her (projection and projective identification).

In the following session there was a change which led to further confirmation of my hypothesis of the defense mechanisms and of how and why they were operating in her and in me. She entered looking, for the first time, sad and more than just a little frightened. She confided that she had had some trouble at work—she was a corporate executive at an ad agency. Her boss had yelled at her for having failed to attend an important meeting. She felt humiliated and threatened by him. She spent most of the session explaining what an unpredictable man he could be especially when he was angry. As the end of the hour neared, she turned to me and asked, quite sincerely, "Would it be all right if I stayed in your office for the rest of the day?" I asked, "What do you mean?" She answered without hesitation and in all seriousness:

> I'm afraid to go out. So what I want to do is stay with you. I want you to protect me. I could stay under your desk or behind the curtains. Your other patients wouldn't mind; they wouldn't even notice I was here. I want to stay here. Please. I'm frightened.

I thought for a moment she was joking; she wasn't. She was serious. I watched her now curled up in the chair looking like a poor, wretched creature. I was wondering whether she might need antipsychotic medication; I was wondering whether she would need to be hospitalized; I was wondering who my next patient was and would that patient mind finding a seriously underweight woman in a Chanel suit hiding in the corner behind the curtains. I was also aware that I knew more or less exactly what she was talking about, and that what she was saying was not altogether unexpected. I had been experiencing the same paranoid reaction. I was now certain that what I had been experiencing had been hers and that her experience had been placed in me through the defense mechanism of projective identification. I had been viewing the world through her prism.

I empathized with how frightening it was not just to feel so vulnerable but also to have things seem to change so rapidly and completely. I discussed issues of her physical safety. Suicidal ideation was not in evidence. "I'm fine. Never mind. Really this was silly of me. I'll be fine." I said to her, "I think we should talk about what's going on." She shook her head, "I'm fine. That's all you need to know. That's all anyone needs to know. I just want to stay here. Please, may I stay here?"

She remained in the chair, still shaken. I went out to inform the next patient that I would be late for his session. I came back. I discussed her fears, her isolation. I discussed issues of safety. I offered her medication. After another half hour, perhaps it was longer, she seemed calmer. I arranged to see her the following day. She returned the next day on time: composed, intact, and contemptuous. What was going on? Something very significant had changed in her perception of me. But I hadn't changed. I was the same human being. Then what had changed? There was an intrapsychic change in her. It reflected an external stressor, a resistance interpretation, a change in the part self part object dyads, perhaps a change in her psychobiological processing of affect, and a change in the configuration of the defense mechanisms. There had been a shift and it was a shift that had been predicted, that when stressed her defense mechanisms would not be able to support her intrapsychic distortions. The stress had come from both inside and outside of the transference. Extratransferentially there had been her boss's anger. Within the transference there had been the interpretation of her internally illogical attachment to me. The structure of the object relations then shifted.

When first seen, she had felt herself to be powerful, dangerous, and out of any human's reach. She was connected to me by her contempt. She viewed me as a fool for believing that I had anything to offer her. Hope and love—humanity—were dumped into me so she could mock them unambivalently.

But when her safety was shaken, things changed both psychologically and biologically. First denial failed her, and she found herself confronted with a changed intrapsychic reality. It wasn't me or the world that had changed. What had changed was her sense of safety, bringing about a change in affect, the neurobiological integration of affect, and a consequent change in her defensive structure and in her intrapsychic world. No longer protected by contempt, she was overwhelmed by fear. Once afraid, she could no longer deny her need for me. So suddenly I, the object, took on value and from that she was forced to accept a different version of herself. No longer powerful and full of contempt, she was now a poor, wretched creature who needed another's protection. The mirror images had flipped. The locus of power and need shifted around the fulcrum of affect. Because of the power of affect, the object relations that had been operating collapsed and were replaced by others. Splitting shuffled the defense mechanisms, now in the service of a different intrapsychic configuration and a different affect. The primitive fear that had been dormant arose, and when it did, it returned with all of its power (see chapter 11 and LeDoux, Romanski, and Xagoraris, [1989]).

As the session drew to a close and she "heard" my offer of help and availability, the original danger, of needing me, returned and she began to revert to an old intrapsychic pattern buttressed by original defense mechanisms. By the next session she was her old self again; she had moved in the course of one day from one internal view of the world and of safety, to another. She was quite certain about each view while in the grip of one affect (contempt) or the other (primitive fear). There was no ambivalence. This absolute certainty in the moment is not about cognitive certainty, it is about the power of primitive affect.

Another experience introduced by primitive affect and the consequent response of primitive defense mechanisms and especially splitting, is fragmentation. It is a terrifying experience. The interpersonal world between this patient and myself had remained relatively unchanged. I was there to help her as her doctor. She was coming to me for help as a patient. There were few if any major threats to the safety, consistency, or trust of our relationship. The major change had been intrapsychic brought on largely because of a shift in affect. When the patient faced a totally new and disorganizing experience of the world, little outside had happened to indicate why she should be going through such internal chaos. This forced her to believe that either the external or the internal was in crisis. Neither belief is particularly comfortable, easy to accept, easy to articulate, or easy to live with. In *The Cocktail Party* T. S. Eliot expressed one side of the dilemma,

> I should really like to think that there's something
>   wrong with me—
> Because, if there isn't, then there's something wrong,
> Or at least, very different from what it seemed to be,
> With the world itself—
> and that's much more frightening!

That would be terrible. So I'd rather believe
There is something wrong with me, that could be put right.
(quoted in Gray, 1992, p. 26)

Many don't share this view and tend to insist that given this set of circumstances, it would be less frightening to believe that it is the world that is fragmented and not one's mind.

The identification of the defense mechanisms helps the therapist predict the chaos, and by virtue of anticipation is not overwhelmed, frightened, or defensive. By virtue of hypotheses, one is better able to help the patient be safe and make sense of what is at bottom a very terrifying and disorganizing experience. The anticipation of chaos at this level becomes not just a validation of data and hypothesis, but also an empathic treatment of another human being's fragmented intrapsychic world.

Evidence of defense mechanisms should be sought in the history, in the mental status, in the transference, in the resistance, in the countertransference and in the comparison of each piece the one with the other. The more primitive the defense mechanisms the more rigid a hold do they have on someone's thinking and behavior. The data of defense mechanisms therefore are hugely important in making hypotheses about the kinds of thoughts and behaviors, the consequences, that one should anticipate in one's patient (transference) and in oneself (countertransference). Because they are structured, their prevalence is widespread.

A 42-year-old man had been referred to psychiatry from the rehabilitation clinic. The referral noted that he had had a right cardiovascular accident 6 months ago, and that whatever recovery of function he had made was now at its limit. He was referred for evaluation of "depression." The patient entered wearing a Yankee's baseball cap and shirt. He was muscular, handsome. His left arm was in a sling; he walked with a cane. His left leg was in a brace. He sat down and smiled at his therapist, a 25-year-old woman. He pulled at his cap with his right hand and said as if in greeting, "We had a stroke." He looked down at his left arm. He looked up at the therapist,

Patient: I wanted it to be quicker than it was possible, to
                get better. It takes so long."
Therapist: Tell me how you've been feeling.
Patient: I really don't know. Sometimes good, sometimes
                not so good.
Therapist: Not so good?
Patient: I don't know how to say it. I have problems with
                my arm, my leg, my whole left side really. I mean
                I can walk. But not real well. I know it'll take a
                while to get better.
Therapist: The doctors in rehab medicine—
Patient: They've been very helpful. They have. It just takes
                so long.
Therapist: Were you working when this happened?
Patient: I worked as a stage manager. In the theater. I
                always took care of myself. That's the hardest
                part. . . . (He began to get tearful, took a tissue.)
Therapist: It must be hard, not being able to work.
Patient: No—I took care of myself, you know. I took care
                of myself. (He began to cry. The therapist
                watched him.)
Therapist: Have you had any previous health problems? Dia-
                betes? alcohol? cigarettes?—anything like that?
Patient: (The man pulled himself back together, wiped
                away a last tear.) "No."
Therapist: What are your plans now?
Patient: I plan to go back into show business. I plan to go
                back to being a stage manager in the theater.
Therapist: Do you think you'll be able to?
Patient: Yeah. I want to. I think I'll be able to. Sure.

Thus an athletic, previously vigorous and healthy man who
had suffered a right cardiovascular accident (CVA), with moderate left-sided hemiparesis was convinced that he was going to
return to work as a stage manager, a job requiring full physical
mobility. He was indeed impatient with the slowness of his recovery but seemed convinced that he would recover.

One operative defense mechanism was denial. He seemed
unwilling or unable to face the medical probability that he had

recovered much of the function that he was going to recover, and that he would have to begin to face the prospect of limited independence, and a compromise with his former capacity and desire to take care of himself. Was that the only evidence of a defense mechanism? No. The therapist was also using denial, consciously, or unconsciously. At the point where the patient was saying, "I took care of myself, you know, I took care of myself," she chose to change the topic of discussion from his depression and sense of helplessness (the reason for his referral) to risk factors for hypertension and vascular disease. It was at this point that she chose to ask, "Have you had any previous health problems? Diabetes? alcohol? cigarettes?—anything like that?" She was feeling, perhaps, the injustice of a young, healthy, attractive man who had suffered a cardiovascular accident, and chose at that moment to deny that injustice and that fact.

When she elected to use denial, his denial returned. The doctor then was using a defense mechanism that had "belonged" to the patient. Was her decision wrong? Not necessarily. Was it conscious on her part? I don't think so.

Defense mechanisms are not mindful of boundaries. When one discovers a defense mechanism operating in one's patient, not infrequently one discovers the same defense mechanism operating in oneself. Just as I had found myself becoming more fearful and paranoid when dealing with the "Chanel lady," so too the therapist in this example was using the defense mechanism of denial that had first been her patient's. Defense mechanisms are communicable—"Diseases attack boundaries." What one sees or hears in one's patient is often what one may hear or find in oneself if one is willing to listen for it. The validation of defense mechanisms is often made through the honest investigation of one's own attitudes and behaviors.

The validation of defense mechanisms occurs at multiple psychological loci—in the patient's attitude toward the doctor (transference), in the patient's attitude toward others in his life (history), and in one's own attitude toward the patient (countertransference). Whenever they are identified in one source, they should be anticipated and sought in others. To find the patient's defense mechanisms operating in oneself is

not a failure of therapeutic technique. It is a natural consequence of interpersonal interaction and reflects a healthy re-
sponsiveness and openness to one's patient. And so long as one
is aware or becomes aware of the process, it is valuable. The
danger is not that one is open to the communication of primitive defense mechanisms; the danger is in refusing their
meaning.

Communication occurs at many levels and through many
channels. The direct expression of an experience can occur at
the level of defense mechanisms—I became afraid that my patient was going to ruin my reputation by calling Dr. Dean. I
had become paranoid—projection, projective identification.
By then stepping back and observing my own reactions, I was
better able to understand my patient. This came not by directly
listening to her words, but by the nonlinear communication of
defense mechanisms.

Allowing and recognizing such shifts can be extremely important sources of understanding. They can also be quite destabilizing in that one becomes, in the moment, as unstable and
unsafe as one's patient. One must be able to hold onto other
sources of data, other awareness, one's colleagues, one's teachers, a hobby, a good book, in order to work at this level with
primitive defense mechanisms operating in the patient and
in oneself.

Two examples have been given of the data of defense
mechanisms in both the transference and the countertransference. The following is another example of data from multiple
sources. The evaluation session was of the hospitalized female
patient, a disc jockey, whose view of safety included being able
to destroy those she cared about. She was seen on a Monday
morning.

Therapist: How was your weekend?
Patient: I saw my father and my stepmother. I'm trying to
             keep that out of my mind. Made me feel sick. I
             got so upset with them. I started yelling at my
             stepmother. They left.
Therapist: What made you so angry?

Patient: I don't know. Well, I do. I wanted to break them
                up, but I know that's not gonna happen. I want
                to say they hurt me, but really I've hurt them. I
                feel guilty about that. I feel I've hurt my step-
                mother so much. I'm so jealous of her having my
                father. But I've always hated her. I was desperate
                after she left. I called my sister and told her how
                I wanted to kill myself.

The patient was describing powerful and primitive affects
including jealousy, envy, despair, guilt. In dealing with those
affects there was evidence of projection, externalization, and
acting out. Rather than deal with the affects as they arose, the
patient tried to rid herself of them as best she could. Thus
calling her sister with a suicidal message may have been an
example of trying to cope with the affect of guilt, or it may
have been acting out behavior aimed at forcing despair into
another person ("Because I hurt, I am entitled to make you
hurt"—projective identification). But the patient's sister
would have none of it, "My sister just got mad and hung up
on me." The doctor, however, couldn't hang up, and asked,

Therapist: Did you want to kill yourself?
Patient: Yeah. I feel hopeless about everything. I've given
                up. I'm disgusted with myself. Other people say
                things that make sense. I listen to what they say;
                I think "yeah." But it makes sense only when they
                are there.
Therapist: And after the person walks out of the room?
Patient: It's gone. Meaning just goes.

Two issues had been introduced involving defense mechanisms. First she had described how she used projection: "I try
to fill my sister with my despair in order to torture her." She
thus identified how comfortable she was with sadism. But second, she also revealed how she needed those very same people
she wanted to hurt: "When they leave me, meaning just goes."
She was describing an internally illogical system: I try to harm
those I value.

At this point, the therapist, having witnessed in the extra-transference the patient's attempts to effect a sadomasochistic enactment, should have anticipated that the patient would do the same to him, use projection to fill him with despair, try to control him with suicidal ideation, and then construct a hopeless scenario with which to torture him. The patient would feel powerful by virtue of the sadistic projection, and then enraged when denial failed and she was forced to realize that she could not prevent the therapist from leaving at the end of the session, taking all meaning with him. When one identifies defense mechanisms operating in one aspect of the clinical presentation, such as in the history, anticipate that they will be used in another aspect, and especially in the transference.

Patient: It's not enough for me to live for myself. When it comes to that I'd rather die.
Therapist: You want to live for someone else?
Patient: Yeah for Dr. Schwartz.
Therapist: The doctor you saw when you were in Los Angeles?
Patient: Yeah. I never got over him. I want to kill myself because I want him to know I killed myself.

There was then more and more data supporting the notion that when the patient felt pain, she wanted others to experience her pain as well. Projection and projective identification were evident in both the extratransference and in the transference. The patient had called her sister to tell her she was suicidal but the sister had hung up. She had turned to her doctor, a captive audience, and was doing with him what she had done with her father, her stepmother, and with her doctor in Los Angeles, making him experience the pain of her hopelessness, and trying to punish him for being someone whom she valued but could not control absolutely. (Phenomenologically she was exhibiting chronic dysthymia, borderline and histrionic behavior. Structurally she was exhibiting defense mechanisms of projection and acting out. Neurobiologically she was exhibiting primitive affect with probable subcortical dominance of conditioned responses.)

The therapist addressing only the content of the session asked, "How would Dr. Schwartz feel if you killed yourself?" "He'd be very upset and sad. He's very sensitive and caring. He'd be affected," she said.

At this point in the evaluation, one should confront the patient and her defense mechanisms because one had a hypothesis supported by data from the history and from the transference that she was trying to reconstruct hopelessness in another to momentarily feel power. One should confront the patient with the internal illogic, and help her return to a capacity to think in a way that did not depend on denial. Where was there evidence of denial?

The patient refused to accept the fact that the control that she had over others was limited. Specifically she was denying that people she attacked would refuse to listen to her, that the resident would ever leave the room, that the session would ever end, that her sadomasochism would have consequences. One would not want to confront this level of defense directly. It would only collapse the patient into a more primitive and therefore more desperate state of fear and psychobiological organization. Rather one would want to both confront and support the patient's defensively structured denial in order to try to make it safe enough for her to examine (in this or in some subsequent session) the power of the underlying fear and the illogic that this was imposing on her thought. The therapist might have said,

> You describe these people that you want to hurt; your father, your sister, your doctor in Los Angeles, and now me. What we all seem to have in common is how much you value us. That contradiction must have occurred to you as well. I think we need to look at it.

Thus, he would be encouraging the patient to join with him, and thereby letting her know that he was aware of her hatred toward him, and still welcomed a joint exploration of that ambivalently held feeling.

The identification of the defense mechanisms helped to identify these structures, and once recognized, there was a need for a response. Or at least the recognition of the very real

dangers of allowing the patient to continue to direct the session
when it had become clear that resistance and defense mechanisms were doing the bidding of a sadomasochistic navigator.
To not act at this point, to continue to follow the patient, would
be to risk allowing her to lead the treatment deeper into hopelessness. If this went on too long, there would come a time
when not only the patient but the therapist as well would be
confronted with a deep sense of futility and despair. At that
point, the therapist would risk returning hopelessness in an
unmodified form (countertransference).

To avoid this, one must hypothesize, frame, and move from
within. The illogic and contradictions of defense mechanisms
are discovered from within the individual patient's specific
state. It is from within that specific and subjective state that one
must advance. But one cannot ever fully effect a sick perspective, that is via identification. Rather one must move from that
place to a perspective of reason and then all the way back,
allowing the defense mechanisms to help guide the passage to
and from illogic and reason. It is by this use of defense mechanisms that one avoids getting paralyzed with the patient by
identification; but it is also how one avoids maintaining so firm
a defensive grip on reason that one fails to effectively include
the patient.

> It's very sad, really: all my life, I've been praised
> for my intelligence, my powers of language, of insight,
> In the end, they're wasted—

writes the poet Louise Glück,

> I never see myself,
> standing on the front steps, holding my sister's hand.
> That's why I can't account
> for the bruises on her arm, where the sleeve ends. . . .
>
> If you want the truth, you have to close yourself
> to the older daughter, block her out:
> when a living thing is hurt like that,

in its deepest workings,
all function is altered.

That's why I'm not to be trusted.
Because a wound to the heart
is also a wound to the mind.
("The Untrustworthy Speaker," 1990).

Defense mechanisms help reveal the data of the chaos, how to get to it, how to get away from it, and how to return once again.

PART III

The Centrality of Affect

As long as the patient is in the treatment he cannot escape from this compulsion to repeat; and in the end we understand that this is his way of remembering.
(Freud, 1914b, p. 150)

There is no doubt that we are dealing with a removal of inhibition. Any hypothesis of an irreparable destruction of the conditioned reflex cannot stand for a moment, since in every case of extinction the reflex invariably becomes restored in a longer or shorter time.
(Pavlov, 1927, pp. 66-67)

Emotional memories established in the absence of the sensory cortex probably by way of the thalamo-amygdala projection are relatively indelible.
(LeDoux, Romanski, & Xagoraris, 1989, p. 241)

10.

History and Affect

> *The play is memory. Being a memory play, it is dimly lighted, it is sentimental, it is not realistic. In memory everything seems to happen to music. That explains the fiddle in the wings. I am the narrator of the play, and also a character in it.*
> (Tennessee Williams, 1945)

Where is now and where is then? Where does the present end and the past begin?

Daisy: I was thinking about the first time I ever went to Mobile. It was Walter's wedding. 1888.

Hoke: 1888! You weren't nothin' but a little child.

Daisy: I was twelve. We went on a train. And I was so excited. I'd never been on a train, I'd never been in a wedding party and I'd never seen the ocean. Papa said it was the Gulf of Mexico and not the ocean but it was all the same to me. I remember we were at a picnic somewhere—somebody must have taken us all bathing—and I asked Papa if it was all right to dip my hand in the water. He laughed because I was so timid. And then I tasted the water on my fingers. Isn't it silly to remember that?

Hoke: No sillier than most of what folks remember. You talkin' 'bout first time. I tell you 'bout the first time I ever leave the state of Georgia?

143

Daisy: When was that?
Hoke: 'Bout twenty-five minutes back.

(Uhry, 1986, pp. 29–30)

The history obviously provides a great deal of information. From the history one begins to look for patterns and from those patterns to make diagnoses and predictions—about the course of treatment and about prognosis, about the future. One studies history, be it medical, political, natural, or individual, in order to better understand where one is now, how one got there, and where the trajectory of the past will intersect with the future.

The history in the doctor–patient relationship differs, however, in one significant respect from the history of a nation or a river. As a patient tells the therapist his history, the therapist becomes by virtue of the telling, part of that history. The part that the therapist plays in the patient's past, present, and future is revealed as one listens to the many layers of history. The very telling of history creates a tension between past and present by creating a tension between the therapist and the patient. The therapist enters the patient's history through that tension, through the psychology and psychobiology of attachment.

Because of the nature of such factors as safety, danger, stress, transference, there is fluidity in time and memory that is to a certain degree created by and is unique to the doctor–patient relationship. The therapist becomes a character in the history of someone just met. There is expectation, fear, shame, fantasy, hope. Past and present are pulled together in the tension of the relationship, in the tension between the person who listens and the person who speaks.

An example of this in the extreme is provided by Langer (1991). He describes this experience in the context of an Auschwitz survivor, Edith P:

> When Edith P. confesses that in Auschwitz you didn't feel and you didn't think, she is recording not a mental and emotional numbness endemic to the place but a totally foreign atmosphere inhospitable to the responses that normally define a human being. The resultant disunity, which alienates one from one's own nature,

remains in memory if not in daily fact a perpetual source of despair, even though it may not dominate one's present life. (p. 104)

The telling of a tale changes the teller in ways that are different from writing or thinking about what happened. "Memory sacrifices purity of vision in the process of recounting, resulting in what I call tainted memory, a narrative stained by the disapproval of the witness's own present moral sensibility . . ." (Langer, 1991, p. 122). Telling history changes history. But telling an interviewer what one had to do to stay alive at Auschwitz is hardly analogous to relating one's illness to a doctor. That is true and not true. Telling an intimate tale opens one up to affect which opens one to the telling of affectively encoded memory.

The woman who had been referred to me by her ailing therapist and psychopharmacologist described her work history,

> If I feel good at my job, I know these feelings will be dashed in a second. What happened to me at work was devastating. And it's happened before. I go to a new job, open and honest. And what happens? They just take my ideas and then trash me. I've come to expect it. Nobody wants me. Nobody cares about me. I'm treated like a leper—and when I talk to you about it, when I tell you what happens it just makes it worse [affect, transference]. It's pathetic that you're the only person I can talk to. It's pathetic that you've become so important to me. It's pathetic—(she was now angry). Pathetic. I mean you're not a friend. This isn't a real relationship. I pay you to sit there and to watch me. What good is it gonna do me?

Telling someone one's history creates affect, that affect generates tension, and from that tension, comes new data. There are expectations and apprehensions: The telling changes what is being told and adds material that goes beyond the story itself. In this instance the patient was telling me, in the history, about difficulties she had had with employment and was establishing with me what it was like to be watched, as she saw it, with indifference. She had created not only a story but affect in the context of attachment that was itself both a part of and separate from the story.

With this data I would listen to the rest of the history for evidence of her experience of indifferent providers anticipating that I would hear in the history evidence of those affects and object relations that I was witnessing in the transference. Through this tension, I would expect to find the conduit between the past and the present, and a route to new memory and new affect, and to how the one was influencing the other. There were two streams of memory, one worded, one sensed, coming from different parts of her brain, that were coming together in a river that was not entirely one.

If this idea seems a bit radical, perhaps absurd, it is. But it is a crucial assumption if the history is going to fulfill the promise of delivering the data that are capable of being delivered. The patient makes you a part of his history through affect and attachment, through the transference, through the countertransference, through the telling of the tale. The affect may pertain to the story; it may pertain to some aspect of the therapist in that moment as the one who listens to the story; it may pertain to both. Listen to affect both in the context of the extratransference narrative and in the context of the transference, in reaction to the verbal communication by the patient, and in the context of the experience with the patient. The telling of history is the telling of a story, but in the telling multiple stories may be being told simultaneously. These are separate stories from separate areas of the brain. "The brain clearly has multiple memory systems, each devoted to different kinds of learning and memory function" (LeDoux, 1996, p. 198). It is crucial therefore that one listen to the story on as many levels of story as are being told, and further to recognize that as the story is being told the relative contributions to the story from different parts of the brain may be changing. This change may be the result of the influence of affect as generated by the story itself and also by transference. Just as Edith P in relating about Auschwitz was sinking deeper into shame as she told her story to her listener, the affect of shame that she was experiencing may have been modifying not just how she felt about what she was saying, but also about herself and about what she was remembering. Transference acts on affect; affect influences transference. And these together influence where memory is coming from, from what parts of the brain.

As a patient describes his relationship with each and every character in his story, the therapist makes the assumption that the patient includes him, as one of the characters of the story, as he sees you now, as he will come to see you in the future, as an evaluator of his story, as an accuser, as a savior, as a voyeur, as someone with whom the patient is in tension through affect. And one must observe in what ways this is influencing what is being told and how it is being told. One enters the data, reacts to them, and allows that reaction to be a guide as one listens. One makes the assumption that the affect that is being discovered in the patient through the transference, but also in oneself through the countertransference, is affect that is having an impact on how and what is being remembered. One is listening then not just to symbolic, verbally encoded history, registered by the hippocampus and neocortex, but also to emotionally encoded history registered in subneocortical structures of the brain. The relative freedom that the patient has from his own story depends in part on what parts of the brain are contributing to the story. There are stories which offer very little safety because they offer very little access. When these stories are told the patient's conviction that he or she is alone is not the fault of the listener, nor is it the fault of the teller. It has more to do with where the story is coming from biologically.

"I'm gonna tell you something," Magda F relates about her surviving the Holocaust. "I'm gonna tell you something now. If somebody would tell me this story, I'd would say 'She's lying, or he's lying.' Because this can't be true. And maybe you're gonna feel the same way. . . . Because nobody, but nobody fully understands us. You can't . . . you're trying to understand me, I know, but I don't think you could. I don't think so." (quoted in Langer, 1991, p. xiv)

The patient referred to me by her therapist and psychopharmacologist related the following,

> I remember when I was 9, I had this pain in my belly. It wouldn't go away. I told my teacher. The school nurse thought it was indigestion. I told my mother; she said go to bed. My father thought it

was for attention. I was in pain and vomiting. I saw a doctor. He
thought it was indigestion. My father yelled at me, "Knock it off."
It went on for 3 weeks. Finally another doctor saw me and decided
to operate. My appendix had ruptured. Only then did my father
believe me.

The data of the history indicated a pattern: employers,
doctors, teachers, parents ignored her. In her mind, as I listened to her tell me the story of problems at work, I had become one of those people who sat and listened as she suffered.
I was one of those people who would offer her nothing. "It's
pathetic," had a context. I belonged both to her past and to
the present through the common denominator experience of
"indifference" to her suffering (projection). "It's pathetic,"
because she "knew" that her hope for an engaged, human
interaction with me was something that she had learned was
impossible—"pathetic" to even hope. As she was telling the
story she was experiencing humiliation as a cognitive reaction
but also at a visceral level as something that she had come to
expect as part of attachment. There was the indication of this
other level of story that was relating how dangerous it was for
this woman to want or to expect someone else to believe her.
It was as if there were a primitive story behind the story that
she was telling that seemed to say, "My very survival demands
that I not turn to you or to anyone because those that I need
and love will ignore me causing me even greater pain."

She continued her own declarative story: "When I'm
alone I feel comfortable. That nothing can happen to me. And
as long as nothing can happen, I'm okay. But as soon as there
is the possibility of things going on, there's danger. And more
than likely the results will be painful."

The primitive story provided a context for the more conscious story. To avoid pain meant avoiding the stimulus and
hope that lead to primitive affect. There was internal conditioned learning built on the avoidance of attachment behavior.

Further, she seemed to have no allies against her pain, or
did she? The transference, history, and mental status indicated
one: the affect of rage (sadomasochistic rage). Her statement,
"You're not a friend. It's pathetic," was a step on the way

toward creating in the transference that affect, and thus a hypothesis would be that there would be tremendous resistance against her relinquishing this view of herself and of others and the affect that maintained that view and that protected her from the humiliation of desire, "I am someone that no one cares about. I am someone who will always be alone." Rage, by driving people away and by defending her like a cruel knight against the loneliness it brought, was established as the predominant resistance. Resistance was generating an environment for her objects, in this instance me, and also an environment for her perceptions. A set was established, on both psychological and biological ground. The affect of rage was in fact establishing the very context it sought to defend.

Resistance and history were operating together to recreate the past in her memories but also in the present as a guarantor that the history *would* be repeated. In one sense she was coming to me for help. In another she was coming to me to prove to herself that she could not be helped and would inevitably be humiliated. Psychologically, the former can be seen as the working alliance; the latter as the resistance. Neurobiologically the former can be seen as an aspect of symbolically encoded memory in the neocortex; the latter as an aspect of emotionally encoded memory below the level of the neocortex. Both are accessed as the history and transference interact in the telling.

The nature of spoken history is intimate. The semistructured, semisafe atmosphere of the therapist–patient (dyadic) relationship opens the potential for a psychologically fluid and vulnerable space. One enters that space and the story created by the patient by listening with empathic identification, and thereby opens oneself and makes oneself vulnerable to the cognitive and physiologic experience of the patient's affects. Because of the therapist's identification both with the patient and with the therapeutic process, one listens with un-self-conscious curiosity. This does not mean that one retraumatizes a patient by forcing him to repeat something that he experiences as shameful. What it means is that by allowing oneself to empathize as closely as possible with the patient, one's questions are not asked from a distance, but are close, and while they may be painful, they also convey your psychological presence. The patient is not alone, and the therapist's intimate presence begins to weave into the patient's life story.

Thus in taking a history one is not just an independent and objective observer, one is a participatory witness. In listening to the patient recount the details of his life, one moves into the story, identifies with the teller, and then moves back and reflects on what one has heard. The model is not that of a mechanic listening as a motorist laments the symptoms of a beloved old car. Rather one listens like a child who enters with emotional abandon as a storyteller weaves a marvelous and horrifying tale. At the same time, one listens like an observer standing emotionally apart observing and listening to both the child's reactions (your own) and the storyteller's yarn (the patient's) from an emotionally safe place.

There should always be this back and forth movement. The therapist enters into the story with the patient and then moves away to think about the story, experience his or her own reactions to it, to the patient, observes the patient's reactions to what he is saying, and to you as the witness-participant in the process. This back and forth must be part of the history-taking process lest the history be reduced to just a list of symptoms and complaints. This emotional interaction allows not just the data of cognitively encoded, declarative memory, but also the data of emotionally encoded, sense memory. One must be open to these multiple histories, multiple sets of memory, if one is to find their truths. Empathic identification is a psychological and also a neurobiological aspect of history and memory.

A 27-year-old copy editor presented for treatment with the chief complaint that she kept going from relationship to relationship. She felt that she was unable to sustain a loving bond. In discussing her history she related that her parents had divorced when she was 12 years old. She said in disbelief, "It totally blindsided me. My brother wasn't as surprised as me. Not seeing it coming in was almost as bad as when it hit."

One would want to know more details particularly because the patient has identified it as an affectively overwhelming experience and because of its possible connection to her inability to sustain attachment. The therapist asked her,

Therapist: It felt like a bomb exploding?
Patient: Exactly.
Therapist: Where were you when it "hit"?
Patient: The kitchen. My mother called us in. We all sat around the dinner table. And then my father told us.

One might then want to ask: What did he say? What did your mother say? Your brother? Did you say anything? What did you do next? Did you go to someone for comfort? Did you isolate yourself? Did you blame yourself? Did you cry? Did you talk to your brother? Did you run away? Did you hide? Did you draw? Do you still have any of the drawings? What did you do that night? What did you do the next morning? Ask questions from the table.

In working with this woman, one would want to include as part of the formulation, that she associated loss with surprise attack, "blindsided." This association may have been more than a figure of speech; it may have been a deeply felt experience pertaining to the nature of intimate relationships. She may not only have stored it as a vivid memory, but have recorded it as an affective experience that she may need to reenact in intimate relationships and in the transference (the lack of intimate relationships was, after all, her chief complaint). One would anticipate that this woman might create through masochistic and sadistic object ties situations where she would suddenly be left by others or leave them. If one began to find these patterns in the history, transference, countertransference, then one would need to work to make this pattern conscious to the patient lest this history be enacted on the treatment. The force of history depends on several factors, but perhaps one of the most important is where and how it is remembered (quite literally in what parts of the brain).

A 30-year-old man with a history of depression, multiple suicide attempts, ego syntonic homosexuality, social isolation, and a family history of suicide was telling his female doctor one of his early memories.

Patient: I used to get these asthma attacks. My father would sit with me and then if it was bad, he'd

	carry me to the bathroom. He'd turn the shower on, and just let the shower run. I haven't thought of this for a long time.
Therapist:	You were how old?
Patient:	Four. I was no more than 4.
Therapist:	You were with your father?
Patient:	Yes. We were in the bathroom. The shower was on. There was steam. I felt the steam. That was soothing. I remember the room. The whiteness of the walls covered with drops of water—how soft everything felt. And how it was hard to breathe. But I don't have asthma anymore. That's a relief. (The doctor brought him back by noting)
Therapist:	Your father was holding you in his arms?
Patient:	Yes. That was soothing too.

By empathically identifying with the patient, the doctor stayed very close to the patient and was able to understand that it was not just the steam that was soothing but his father's presence; it was not the tile walls that were "soft" but the touch of skin; it was not just the asthma that was making it hard for him to breathe. Thus as the patient started to move away from the intimacy of the scene, it was the doctor who brought him back: "You were in your father's arms?" for she had felt the story's incompleteness, and the patient's ambivalent desire to leave it incomplete. Partly as a result of her presence and the unspoken and probably unconscious comfort and safety that she had provided, the patient was able to return to it and confide something. That it was in this setting that his father first began to sexually abuse him, which further helped to make sense of the patient's focus on texture, and added another dimension to his difficulty breathing, and to a deeper understanding of his father's subsequent suicide and the patient's guilty reaction to it, and thus his genetic, psychological, and conditioned attachment to self-destruction. The doctor was already a part of the history through transference. Her secure comfort, both like and unlike his father's, was there in the present and through the opening of affect was there with him in the past as well.

The history, like therapy itself, is done in the intimate space of empathic identification. One must be inside the story deeply enough to sense whether it is complete or incomplete, whether it is logical or illogical, whether it is emotionally rich or shallow, whether it is declarative memory or emotional memory. If as the listener one does not have an emotional response, one makes the assumption that the story is incomplete and asks for more data or for clarification. Only when one has a clear emotional response can one ask, "What were you feeling?" because only then does the therapist have his own reactions to compare with the patient's.

In this case, when asked, the patient replied, "It's so long ago. I can't remember," indicating the need to distance himself from his father, from the emotion, from the memory, and from the therapist; that he had gone far enough in their third session—data about the history and also data about the transference.

The doctor, having felt the power of the intimacy, moved back, and as the objective observer wondered about the patient's need for distance. One would not ask this patient, "Why can't you remember?" Instead the doctor looked actively in the history for anyone with whom the patient had experienced closeness. She did not do this by asking, "Who were you close to?" because it would have given the patient the opportunity to answer, "No one." Rather the doctor returned to the detailed unfolding of the history listening for the answer to the unspoken question ("Whom was this man close to and what context had made intimacy possible?") as she inquired about his parents, siblings, his friends.

Patient: I had a dog.
Therapist: What was your dog's name?
Patient: Ginger.
Therapist: Tell me about Ginger.

She knew that the patient's relationship to his dog was not incidental and indeed one would surmise that the dog may have played a huge role in the man's life. Any other intimate relationship might have been too threatening. Then she compared this historical data with the unfolding transference data and the limits that he imposed on closeness.

A patient who shared a powerful story, and then withdrew emotionally from that experience, is different from someone who related in such a way as to make initial empathic identification difficult if not impossible.

> I always felt my mother was, you asked me about my mother so as I was growing up she seemed to be responding to how the hell do I know? I mean last night she called. I held the phone really far from my ear, like this, she just talked. Whose anxiety is it? She won't stop. Talked and who is she talking about or to? Do you think it was me? Not on your life. Talking. Talking. Talking not to me or mine I can assure you of that. She won't stop.

In listening to this patient, it was hard to stay close, to remain identified with what he was saying. At times I was not sure what he was saying. I felt a little assaulted (mental status, transference), so I asked, "Did you feel assaulted by your mother?" He looked at me and asked, "How did you know that?"

I knew from the transference, from the countertransference, from combining that data with the history and from using the data of the one to help clarify and elucidate the data of the other. I also knew, again from the mental status and the transference, that he didn't really want an answer. "I always felt that she was responding to her own anxieties and never to mine. I didn't think she knew what mine were. I remember the first day of school." And then he described his first day of school and his mother's way of dealing with his anxieties, by accusing him of being "selfish," and then focusing on her own.

In order to obtain a meaningful history from this man, one needed to deal with his style of speech (mental status), and a way of interacting (transference), that made meaningful communication difficult, leaving the listener cut off (countertransference). But of course that is a communication: "It is dangerous for me to allow you or anyone else, especially my mother (history), to get emotionally close to me because if you do, you will fill me with your anxiety. So in order to keep you away from me and in order to communicate to you what her assault felt like, I will attack you with words the way she attacked me" (affect and projective identification). The here-and-now thus added data to what the patient's experience had been like: The lack of meaningful communication that the patient was forcing on me *was* the communication.

How the patient makes the therapist a part of the history is not always obvious because the issue addresses memory and how the past sometimes opens to allow a seeming stranger in. For example, the 45-year-old nicotine patch company employee mentioned earlier, related her memories of having been at camp when she was 4. Her mother was a counselor at the same camp.

> I was sitting at breakfast at one of those long camp tables. I was the youngest camper the camp ever had. I'd been sick. My first day out of the infirmary, I saw my mother come into the dining hall, and sit down at her table—with the "squirrels." I was a "tadpole." I picked up my bowl of oatmeal and walked over to my mother. Another counselor saw me coming and intercepted me. She led me back to my table, and said, "She's with her girls. You can't go there. You're not one of her girls." I could see her talking to her "girls." I remember wanting my mother so much. . . . I remember the smell of that oatmeal. I can still smell it.

We discussed this memory and other aspects of her relationship to her mother. She had also discussed her smoking and her disgust with the habit. The next session she came in and stared at me. She waited as if she were expecting something from me. Then she asked,

Patient: Well?
Therapist: Well what?
Patient: Don't you want to ask me anything? (The previous session was very much on my mind.)
Therapist: In fact I was wondering what your thoughts were about your mother, and about the experiences at camp that you related to me last session. (She shook with disgust.)

Patient: You knew how important it was for me to stop
                smoking. I had told you. You just ignore what's
                important to me.

The history absorbed me into her past as a figure deeply
needed and longed for, and at the same time, a figure who
remained unempathic and unresponsive. It was as if she were
there with her bowl of oatmeal unable to cross the room to me
as I remained involved with my concerns while I ignored hers.
The past and the present merged like two streams of memory.

In addition to placing oneself in the history in the context
of the object relation, one listens to the affect the patient is
experiencing in the transference and that you are experiencing
in the countertransference, and then look for the place of those
affects in the history. The affects in the present can and should
be used to guide one's searches in the past. In her case the
barrier was there again in the present as it had been in the
past, but it was she who had created that barrier and then
placed it between us by the use of projection. ("You just ignore
what's important to me.") It was as if she were reliving the
painful affect she had, or may have, once experienced when
she attempted to approach her mother.

The history provided data supported in the transference.
There was a line between her and me just like the one between
her and her mother, one she had learned not to cross—data
were coming from multiple sources. But her behavior in the
present while adding data about intrapsychic function did not
confirm what had happened 40 years ago. If anything it loos-
ened the past and opened it to questions, and in a sense those
questions brought the past closer to the present. Because it was
now suspect. And because it was now clear that her vision of
human interaction in the here-and-now was unreliable, it was
possible that either her memory of the past was skewed, or that
the past was significantly interfering with her view of the present. In either case, because of this unreliability, the past had
been brought closer. It might be brought close enough to be
examined if and only if the present were also made safe enough
to be questioned. If the present could be made safe enough,
the past could be changed.

History reveals patterns. Patterns of the past must be compared to patterns in the transference and countertransference. These patterns provide clues to the predominant affect, sense of self, sense of object, defense mechanisms, distortions. But another pattern in the historical data needs to be considered as well, "I remember the smell of that oatmeal." A powerful sense memory. Why was it so powerful? Empathically one could say that a small child's perceived rejection by her mother is a powerful moment and therefore was remembered. Why was it remembered as a smell? The question of memory recalled as sense memory was one that Freud had investigated with his patient Miss Lucy R., "When I asked her what the smell was by which she was most constantly troubled she answered: 'a smell of burnt pudding.' Thus I only needed to assume that a smell of burnt pudding had actually occurred in the experience which had operated as a trauma" (Breuer & Freud, 1893–1895, p. 107).

Freud had argued that such memories are retained as vividly as they are because they occur in the context of trauma and therefore that the brain registered memory differently depending on the state that it was in at the time of the registration. This argument has since been validated. The brain registers and recalls emotional experience and emotion itself differently, in a different place, under the influence of different neurochemistry, than it does nonemotional experience. Powerful affect has loci and neurochemistry of its own, and because of this, there are two forms of memory, predominantly neocortical, and one predominantly subneocortical (LeDoux, 1996). While these two memories do communicate, there are times when one form of memory may exercise more authority than the other. It may or may not always be obvious which is dominant at any given time.

In general, perception is assigned its affective tone by the amygdala, part of the evolutionary primitive subneocortical brain that via its afferent and efferent projections is "charged with maintaining the balance between the internal world and external reality" (van der Kolk, 1996b, p. 214). These perceptions are then coordinated with more general experience and especially the experience of memory by integration with the hippocampus and the neocortex. The hippocampus is crucial for the encoding and organization of memory while the association areas of the neocortex integrate and eventually store long-term memory. The amygdala thus receives perceptual input from at least two general sources: from the thalamus—a direct waystation from the sense organs via thalamo-amygdala projections, and from the cerebral cortex itself via thalamo-cortical-amygdala projections. "The former provide course representations, but reach the amygdala quickly while the latter provide detailed stimulus information, but reach the amygdala more slowly because of the additional processing stations involved at the cortical level" (LeDoux, 1995, p. 223). Because of these afferent projections to the amygdala and because of its primitive and basic position in the mammalian brain, some perceptions reach the amygdala neuroanatomically and neurophysiologically before perception can be said to have reached thought. Thus in certain circumstances one would be reacting to perception before one had registered just what it was one was reacting to. LeDoux continues, "The thalamic inputs thus may be useful for producing rapid responses on the basis of limited stimulus information, whereas cortical inputs are required to distinguish between stimuli" (1995, p. 223).

> [In certain circumstances.] The emotional evaluation of sensory input precedes conscious emotional experience: People may become autonomically and hormonally activated before they are able to make a conscious appraisal of what they are reacting to. Thus a high degree of activation of the amygdala and related structures can generate emotional responses and sensory impressions that are based on fragments of information, rather than on full-blown perceptions of objects and events. (van der Kolk, 1996c, p. 294)

This response, which applies to perception, may also apply to memory. This would mean that under certain specific circumstances one might react to perception (processed through subneocortical structures) without awareness, and that under other certain specific circumstances one might react to primitive memory (stored in the amygdala) without knowing why. And thus,

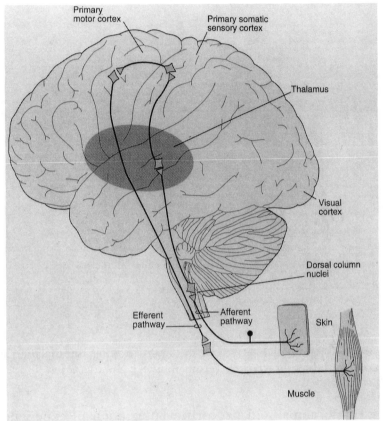

Figure 10.1   Sensory input travels from the skin, eyes, ears, and other
organs of perception to the spinal column and brain stem, and then to
the thalamus—a central cluster of neurons in the diencephalon ("the
between brain"). From the thalamus there are reciprocal connections
to many other areas of the brain including the sensory cortex, the hippocampus, and the amygdala. (From: Kandel, Schwartz, & Jessell, 1995,
p. 85)

It is also conceivable, if not likely, that the amygdala system can
store information that is not processed by the hippocampal system.
These "implicit" (unconscious) emotional memories, when activated, would lead to the same kind of arousal condition as when
explicit memories are activated, but in the absence of explicit (conscious) knowledge of why the arousal occurs. (LeDoux, 1993a,
p. 71)

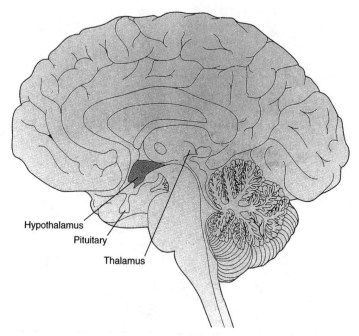

Figure 10.2 A medial section of the brain showing the thalamus in relation to the cerebral cortex. (From: Kandel, Schwartz, & Jessell, 1995, p. 600)

Hippocampal and neocortical integration of experience does not fully occur in such circumstances. For this reason, these perceptions, memories, responses are not fully verbal nor conscious; they are registered neuroanatomically below consciousness (in systems analogous perhaps to the Freudian id).

Traumatic history (see chapter 12) is recorded very much in this way with subneocortical and amygdaloid dominance; it is often recalled with powerful immediacy and presence. A woman who had suffered from years of child abuse related,

Patient: I had this terrible dream about something my father did or didn't do to me. Sticking his fingers inside of me. When I woke up I was on the floor of my closet covered with clothes.
Therapist: In the dream or in fact?
Patient: In fact.

She had no idea of how she got from her bed to her closet. During the course of the session, it became clear that she had had a dissociative reaction after having awoken from the dream. She then added, "The dream was real. I mean I had the dream; I was asleep. But what happened in the dream really did happen. I'm sure of it."

A more subtle example is taken from the following. It is an example where the normal integrative function of the hippocampus is compomised but not so damaged as where ongoing abuse has occurred. The history is from a 48-year-old married screen actress, and mother of two. As a child she had been a "superstar." Her career began to fade after her marriage to an international financier. She had a 20-year history of psychiatric illness and was on medications for atypical depression. Significant to both her genetic illness as well as to this piece of history, the woman's mother had "abandoned" her at birth, and then again at age 3, and finally by suicide when she was 15. The following is her description of saying goodbye to her mother who was being sent to a mental institution:

> They were sending her away and it was as if I knew, as a 3-year-old, I knew that she would die. I just knew it; I don't know how. I don't remember knowing, I just knew. My life seems clearer to me in metaphor. I didn't want to leave; I was so scared. They made me go [she was being sent to live with relatives]. I was afraid to leave my mother. There was nothing I could do about it. There were no explanations. My mother was in bed, having to say goodbye to me. I couldn't feel. I couldn't think. It wasn't happening to me. My aunt pulling me away. I hate my aunt. I still do. I can still see that moment come in to me. It just entered me but it never sat down.

The threat of the loss of mother is overwhelming to a 3-year-old, and arouses primitive affect because survival is threatened. Lower order circuits are favored in such circumstances because of the age of the child and because of the intensity of the affect.

It was too much to take in. It goes on but it wanders around in there, never finds a place. The way all these things keep resurfacing, keep wandering, it's like being possessed. [Hippocampal integration is necessary for linear, temporal, and spatial encoding of memory and under intense affect without hippocampal processing, memory loses its context.] I didn't know what was happening. Being sent away got more and more frightening. It never settled down [memories established below the level of the neocortex]. As soon as there was stress, when my father got sick, when my dog died, it would rear up again [state dependent memory]. "Don't make me go. Don't throw me away," that's how I experienced it. I felt like an abused dog and like an abused dog I was connected with my anger and her rejection [the failure to delineate specific affect]. It was so vivid. Like colors [intense, nonverbal, symbolic memory]. I just saw it as colors. That's what it was like. . . . My life seems clearer to me in metaphor.

In a situation of intense affect, the amygdala's responses to sensory input (rate of firing) are heightened. Because of the amygdala's neuroanatomical position in the mammalian brain, and also because of neurophysiological and neurohormonal changes that occur when that firing rate is increased, sensation is preferentially received and preferentially stored as emotional memory. Perceptions under these conditions are less likely to be ordered in a linear narrative by the hippocampus. Nor do they preferentially reach areas of the neocortex, particularly Broca's area of the left cerebral hemisphere where symbolic representation and verbal encoding of personal experience are thought to take place (van der Kolk, 1996c). For all these reasons highly emotional events, while retained in the history, are not retained in the same way as are more evenly received, significant experiences. Highly emotional and stressful history tends to be less well organized in time and space, and recall tends not to be always in words so much as in sensory fragments. "One can hypothesize that when this occurs, sensory imprints of experience are stored in memory; however, because the hippocampus is prevented from fulfilling its integrative function, these various imprints are not organized into a unified whole" (van der Kolk, 1996c, p. 295). And thus the patient's psychologically and perhaps neurobiologically valid conclusion, "My life seems clearer to me in metaphor."

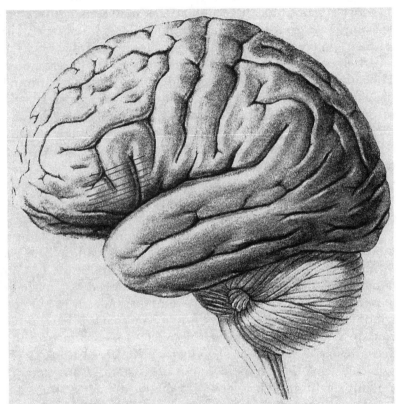

Figure 10.3.   This diagram shows the surface of the brain and outlines Broca's area of the neocortex where symbolic representation and verbal encoding of experience take place. (From: Martin, 1989, p. 398)

There are then at least these two basic ways in which perception is registered as memory: emotional memory and declarative memory, the former is located in lower order structures, especially the amygdala, and is primed for immediate response; the latter is more fully integrated in the hippocampus and the neocortex where stimuli can be evaluated and compared with prior experience before a response is initiated. The retrieval of emotional memory is state dependent, that is, emotional, affectively charged memories tend to be recalled when the subject is experiencing a similar emotional state as the one in which the memories were laid down. Emotional memory is crucial for survival in a Darwinian sense and for this reason is basic to the mammalian brain. Thus when faced with an emotionally arousing, potentially life-threatening situation, one does not have to think through each step of one's response. The subneocortical system responding to prompting through the amygdala and emotional memory provides a fixed rapid response pattern of neurohormonal, neurophysiological, and neuromuscular actions not on the basis of a careful evaluation of the situation but based on affective arousal. The emotion, memory, and responses of this system may be recalled when similar situations are encountered, and significantly, through the transference when a similar interpersonal context is being experienced.

The retrieval of declarative memory on the other hand is more under the control of conscious will. Sometimes these two forms of memory come together in the telling of the history; "emotional and declarative memories are stored and retrieved in parallel, and their activities are joined seamlessly in our conscious experience. That does not mean that we have direct conscious access to emotional memory; it means instead that we have access to the consequences—" (LeDoux, 1994, p. 57). Clinically what this means is that in many situations remembering and relating will be a complex mix of memory, affect, and experience coming from different areas of the brain.

So remembering the smell of oatmeal when threatened by the loss of one's mother is not so much a memory retained because of the quality of the oatmeal, nor was it likely recalled because of the desire for a pleasant, soothing smell, but because in an emotionally heightened moment, the affective tone leads the amygdala to preferentially receive sensations at the expense of hippocampal and neocortical integration. It was a memory that was recalled when the subject was in that similar state of emotional hunger. Thus the memory contained both the declarative memory of the hippocampus, the memories of what had happened some 40 years ago, as well as the emotional memory that had been powerfully encoded because the amygdala had been aroused by fear of not being able to get to her mother at the same time that the smell of oatmeal had been

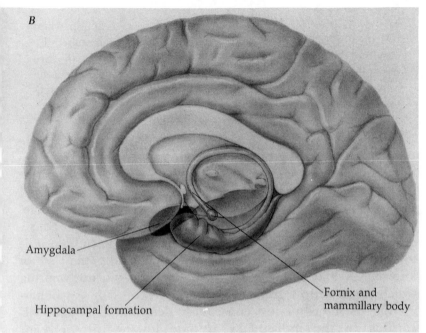

B

Amygdala

Hippocampal formation

Fornix and
mammillary body

Figure 10.4. The amygdala and hippocampus are structures deep inside the brain on the inner aspect of the temporal lobe and can be seen in this medial view. Once thought to be part of what was known as the limbic lobe, an evolutionary primitive core of the mammalian brain, the amygdala and hippocampus are now more correctly understood as structures of the brain's complex memory and arousal system. (From: Martin, 1989, p. 18.)

perceived. Thus the longing for her mother and the smell of oatmeal may both come back as a memory because they were laid down at the same time and under the same conditions. Indeed the smell of oatmeal may recall the feeling of loneliness that she had once experienced. These memories were separately encoded but associated and thus one facilitated the other (see Kandel et al. [1995] for a further discussion of long-term potentiation and Hebb's rule). And thus again according to LeDoux,

Emotional memory may be stored within declarative memory, but it is kept there as a cold declarative fact. For example, if a person is injured in an automobile accident in which the horn gets stuck in the on position, he or she may later have a reaction when hearing the blare of car horns. The person may remember the details of the accident. . . . These are declarative memories that are dependent on the hippocampus. The individual may also become tense, anxious, and depressed, as the emotional memory is reactivated through the amygdalic system. (1994, p. 57)

We find ourselves experiencing or reacting to things without fully appreciating or understanding why because the emotional memory is not always recalled with the full significance of the associated event. Because emotional memory is encoded more in lower order than in neocortical structures, these memories can affect behavior, perception, memory—consequences—without full conscious awareness. (Recall Freud's understanding of a related idea, "The hysterical patient's 'not knowing' was in fact a 'not wanting to know'—a not wanting which might be to a greater or less extent conscious.") Behavior may be more or less consciously determined not just according to the individual's attitude toward the behavior ("wanting or not wanting to know" is a cognitive neocortical assessment), but also according to what level in the brain had access to the perception, and thus according to what level of the brain has access to ensuing memory. When memory is encoded more as an affectively laden emotional memory than as a linear narrative in time and space, then affect operating subneocortically is beginning to make behavioral choices with less than full conscious input or awareness (more or less "unconsciously"). "If, for genetic or experiential reasons, the lower-order pathways are more efficient at triggering the amygdala than are the higher-order pathways in some individuals, we would expect those individuals to have rather limited insight into the nature of their emotional reactions" (LeDoux, 1995, p. 229).

These neurobiological choices may be reflected clinically in the following account given by the 48-year-old screen actress who had been taken from her mother as a child, "When I get upset I get like that abused dog, and I go to hurt someone, I go for the jugular. I don't want to. I don't mean to. It just happens and I can't help myself." The association of pain and rage was for this woman almost total and both were established in object relations—the pain and terror of losing her mother, the rage at her aunt as the instrument of that loss. And thus when threatened with loss, she reacted with rage according to associations that were laid down in her brain probably below the level of the neocortex and probably according to synaptic connections that are not easily undone. When coming to an appointment with me she described the following,

> I got a taxi cab to come here. I was late I know that, but then this idiot of a cab driver was driving so slow. I thought I would never get here [the threat of loss, but in this case not the loss of her mother (historical), but of me (transference)]. And then I started screaming at him, screaming. I was screaming at this poor cab driver. I don't even know if he speaks English. When I got out of the cab, I was just shaking. Look, look at my hands; I'm still shaking and I don't even know why.

The fact that she knew that her behavior was irrational did not help her to control it. It did not help her because the knowledge was in one area of her brain and the behavior was from another. The threat of losing me was associated with the subneocortically registered terror of loss, her mother, and associated further with primitive rage at the person who was threatening her survival, her aunt, but now the hapless cab driver. The two emotions, fear and rage in response to loss were associated in areas of the brain outside of the control of logic (the neocortex). Just as the smell of oatmeal and loneliness had been associated in the previous example, both reactions had been fixed according to long-term potentiation and Hebb's rule (two events that are encoded at the same time are linked because of synchronicity).

This association of events, emotions, and perceptions is further complicated by the influence that the amygdala may have on perception itself. "Projections from the amygdala to sensory processing areas may allow the amygdala's appraisals of danger to influence ongoing perceptions of the environment . . ." (LeDoux, 1995, p. 226). Perception may not only reach these lower order pathways before the neocortex because

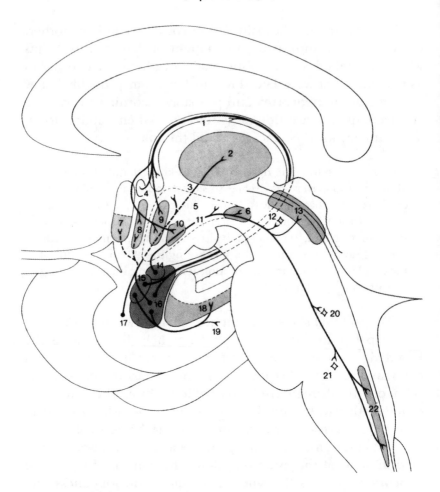

Figure 10.5. A view of the brain stem, diencephalon, and subneocortical structures showing projections from the amygdala. Projections from the amygdala to the thalamus and to the neocortex may influence how perceptions are received and remembered. The amygdala is represented by numbers 14, 15, and 16; and the thalamus by number 2 in this diagram (From: Nieuwenhuys, Voogd, & van Huijzen, 1981, p. 210.)

of the neuroanatomical hardwiring, but these areas of the brain, and in particular the amygdala, may influence how perception is received and what memories are brought to bear on perception once it does get there. These lower order pathways

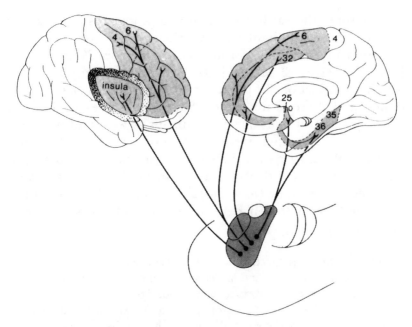

Figure 10.6. Projections from the amygdala to the cerebral cortex. (From: Nieuwenhuys, Voogd, & van Huijzen, 1981 p. 211)

have a huge influence on how the neocortex interprets perception, "Pathetic. I mean you're not a friend. This isn't a relationship, I pay you to sit there and to watch me. Pathetic...."

Patterns in the individual's history may take on a life of their own, and must be investigated not just as a streak of good or bad fortune, willful obstinacy, or the result of good or bad parenting (although this may be the case and sometimes the cause). The behavior must also be evaluated as possible neurobiological, conditioned stimulus–response paradigms organized around painful or pleasurable affect, where the unconditioned stimuli are affects below the neurophysiological level of consciousness, and where choices are being made below the level of consciousness at the level of subneocortical structures.

Thus a rat learns to react behaviorally (response) to an otherwise neutral light stimulus (conditioned stimulus) if the light is paired with a painful shock (unconditioned stimulus).

After a time, the rat will respond with a fear response to the illumination of the light because it has learned that a painful sensation will follow (classical conditioning, see Kupfermann, [1981b]; Vertes & Miller [1976]). The rat cannot choose whether to react or not to react to the light; it has been conditioned and there is no choice. Such associative–conditioned learning can and does occur in humans as well, and obviously can operate at a much more subtle level, where the stimulus, for example, may be the behavior of an important object in one's life and where the reward or punishment is not an externally mediated event (foot shock) but internally experienced emotion (affect) that had been assigned to the stimulus by the amygdala.

> Thus the developing child learns—internalizes—emotional conflict, and just as Vertes and Miller's rats came to react behaviorally and neurophysiologically to an innocuous light paired with a painful stimulus, so does a person grow to reexperience anxiety, shame, disgust, or their signal affect each time he detects within himself a feeling that, when vented earlier in life, provoked a distressing parental response. (Schwartz, 1987, p. 484)

And as with the rat, once these behavioral response patterns are established, they become fixed. That is to say, so long as the conditioned and unconditioned stimuli are presented the response will persist. Indeed even if the unconditioned stimulus (the foot shock) is discontinued and the animal's associated response to the light stops, the entire conditioned learning can be reestablished very quickly indicating that conditioned fear responses can be inactivated but are never lost, an observation that Pavlov made in his original experiments (Pavlov, 1927). These responses are indelible memories encoded not so much at the level of the neocortex and hippocampus but at the level of the amygdala through lower order pathways over which the organism has no direct control (see LeDoux et al., 1989). The rat cannot make a decision about its reactions to the light any more than Pavlov's dogs were able to make decisions about their response to the bell. The rat freezes, the dog salivates, the fashion designer declares herself pathetic, the actress screams at the cab driver, behaviors once associatively learned are outside of conscious control. There is, then, this unconscious memory to which we do not have direct access except through the experience of its consequences, examples of what Freud called "the compulsion to repeat" but a compulsion understood not on the basis of neocortical resistance but as a consequence of subneocortical neurophysiology, a distinction that is clinically crucial.

To return to the example of the copy editor mentioned earlier who had felt "blindsided" by her parents' divorce. She had been in treatment with her male therapist for 6 months. She had come 20 minutes late to the first appointment and lateness was an issue throughout. ("Above all, the patient will begin his treatment with a repetition. . ." [Freud, 1914b, p. 150]). During the previous session she had been discussing problems at work, especially with her boss Harry, toward whom she had felt some sexual interest but who was oblivious to anything but work. Lately he had been swamping her with work. She arrived late, "I've been doing nothing but work. Harry keeps misunderstanding all the issues. He never tells anyone what's going on. It's almost paralyzing me."

Her therapist asked, "Harry misunderstands all the issues? Do you feel supported at all?"

Patient: Not really. Harry's very narrow. In all the decisions at work, he just covers his ass. I ask him a question and he just gives vague general answers. There's so much work; I do most of it. I'm exhausted all the time.

Therapist: With all this work, I wonder what it feels like to be coming up here to see me? (encouraging the transference)

Patient: I felt awkward about coming up here. Hard to come all the way up here and then I have to go back to work. I ask myself, "Is it worth it?" I don't know. I ask myself what am I getting out of this? I keep coming hoping that things would fall into place. They haven't.

Therapist: You seem angry with me because you feel that therapy isn't doing what it's supposed to be doing (encouraging the negative transference).

Patient: It would be easy if I could get angry at you but on the other hand I like you. But I don't like the process. I just feel that sometimes we stare at each other and I'm not sure what it's leading toward. I think it's helped me in the past but I'm not sure where it's going. I don't get a response from you. I mean I could stay at home and write in a notebook. What's the point of this?

The therapist, who continued to take notes, then asked,

Therapist: I know my line of questioning was making you angry. But that's what's happening right now? You're angry at work, angry with me. Surely you're angry when someone reflects what's going on in general with your life and how you see the world.

Patient: I feel there's nothing I can do about work and I don't even feel safe enough here to talk about it. I really have to go back to work now.

One could question this interaction at several points. The purpose of introducing it, however, was to demonstrate that the patient and therapist were moving toward a conclusion that should have been recognized and dealt with more actively. The patient's subneocortical memory operated with the conviction that in intimate relationships ("I'm not angry with you, I like you") one person or the other will be "blindsided." As a 12-year-old it had been her; in most subsequent relationships, she had done her best to make sure it was someone else. In this therapy, it was becoming increasingly clear that unless the issue of intimacy in the transference and the patient's sadomasochistic patterns of dealing with intimacy were dealt with, the therapy would be blindsided by a lower order memory and its destructive way of reestablishing safety. "You, like Harry, have never made it safe enough for me to deal with those issues openly," was an underlying issue reflecting a failure to actively engage the positive transference, deal with the countertransference, and subneocortically patterned memory. The fact that the therapist was having trouble overcoming his own passivity with this woman (he tended to mirror the patient rather than to engage the issues) indicated that there was a lack of freedom in the treatment in general. When one discovers a lack of freedom in the way that one thinks about or approaches a patient, one should suspect the possibility that subneocortical issues are being stirred both in the transference and in the countertransference.

Thus patterns in the history may be important for at least two similar but different reasons. Historical patterns may represent a series of interpersonal perceptions that were processed through the hippocampus, neocortex, and Broca's area, organized into a narrative in time and space, and thus were symbolically and cognitively understood aspects of the behavior between self and object. Patterns processed by the cortex in this way could be said to function as symbolically encoded, linear memory.

Or patterns may have begun as events (the isolated "foot shocks" of good or bad parenting or experience) that brought on immediate affective responses that were learned more as an affective response at the subneocortical level of the thalamus and amygdala than as a cognitive response processed at the level of the hippocampus and the neocortex. This form of learning would have been a result of neurobiologic changes similar to those that occur with the conditioned reflex such as the rat reacting to the light. This is learning more at the level of reflex than at the level of reason.

But in the case of human beings as opposed to rats, those situations include not just a classically conditioned fear response to a "harmless" light bulb, but complex interpersonal and behavior responses involving thought, memory, and affect. These more subtle responses toward significant others may be kept out of consciousness at the level of something like an operantly conditioned reflex. Patterns of behavior, thought, memory, affect that are avoided ("repressed") or repeated ("the compulsion to repeat") at the level of a conditioned response, may be operating neurobiologically more under the influence of affectively conditioned "reflexes" stored in lower order pathways than as neocortical "wants." These more primitive psychical systems are not as amenable to logic and thought. These are issues which are generated mainly through the transference and which may be responsive only to actions through the transference. With this in mind, the therapist in the above example should anticipate that unless he began to deal more actively with the conflicted nature of the transference, including the positive transference and how the patient had a history of fleeing intimate relationships, she would blindside him and the treatment as well.

There are then two patterns of history which lead to two patterns in the unconscious, unconsciously stored in separate areas of the brain. First, ideas may be unconscious because when the information was presented to the neocortex, the neocortex found the ideas incompatible, and initiated a defense in response to the anticipation of anxiety, and thus as Freud described it, "This effortless and regular avoidance by the psychical process of the memory of anything that had once been distressing affords us the prototype and first example of *psychical repression* (1900, p. 600). Repression for Freudian-based psychoanalysis has meant that there was a cognitive assessment of the situation followed very rapidly by the initiation of a defense. The defense was initiated in order to avoid a thought, fantasy, or behavior if allowed into consciousness would bring on pain. Thus an assessment, based on an anticipated conflict and affect, led to a defense, all of this taking place, speculatively, within the neocortex.

The second reason why an idea may be unconscious has to do with a reflex that operates through the subneocortical areas of the brain and therefore without full cognitive assessment and at a level where affect is its own motive. Here it is not conflict that drives an experience out of consciousness. Rather, perception and encoding of the experience occurred along lower order pathways reinforced by projections to the neocortex. There may then be gaps in the history (amnesia) and unwilled consequences in behavior for two very different reasons: one because something was felt to "stink" and was repressed; or two because smells were associated with an event and thus "whenever I eat oatmeal I feel lonely." There are at least two distinct forms of memory to explain why one can't remember something, or to explain why one finds oneself always remembering something at a particular point in time, or always reacting to certain stimuli in specific ways, screaming at cab drivers, "blindsiding" intimate relationships, recalling the smell of oatmeal.

These explanations are not always revealed in the declarative history because the explanation may be in another history. The one history reflects symbolic, declarative memory largely encoded in the hippocampus and the neocortex and accessible verbally; the other, the more primitive emotional memory largely encoded in the amygdala and accessible more in the transference. These two histories reflect the workings of two systems of memory. "Studies of brain mechanisms of emotion have pointed to the amygdala as an important part of the aversive emotional memory system, and to the hippocampus as part of the system involved in cognitive or declarative form of memory. This does not prove that the systems operate by different information processing rules, but it certainly leaves open the possibility" (LeDoux, 1995, p. 226).

One of the first researchers into this area of investigation, interestingly, was Freud. In 1895 he wrote "The Project for a Scientific Psychology," in which he attempted to demonstrate the neurophysiological basis of thought, wish, and affect. What Freud was attempting to define in theoretical terms, was how behavior was "facilitated" (reinforced) or "inhibited" (extinguished) according to the "pleasure-unpleasure principle" (according to the reward or punishment that a stimulus generated). His construct accounted for how memory could be explained according to the "experience of satisfaction," that is, according to affect. Freud had connected stimulus and affect to response at the level of the cell. He speculated correctly that certain stimuli, by arousing certain affects, lead to preferred paths of flow across the synapse where transmission was independent of cognitive assessment. He was developing a pure neurophysiology of psychology; it was an undertaking that he more or less totally and reluctantly abandoned after 1895

("I have not always been a psychotherapist," Freud needed to remind his reader as he was embarking on that new path [Breuer & Freud, 1893–1895, p. 160]).

But the basic structure that Freud had sought to establish was correct: Learning does occur at the cellular level; it is mediated at the level of the synapse; it does involve change in synaptic transmission; and it is very much affected by emotion. Some of these changes seem to be mediated by the excitatory amino acid transmitter glutamate and the process of long-term potentiation (see Hebb, 1949; Kandel & Spencer, 1968; LeDoux, 1996). While the reasons for the change vary, the nature of the change is rather stable: "This process . . . involves a change in the efficiency of synaptic transmission along a neural pathway—in other words, signals travel more readily along this pathway once long-term potentiation has taken place" (LeDoux, 1994, p. 54). Although listening to a patient's history from the perspective of the single synapse is, as Freud conceded in 1895, still impossible, it is now possible to listen from the perspective of the system of synapses as well as from the perspective of the totality of the individual (Kandel, 1979). And one should attempt to do both.

In listening to the history, one should listen not just for patterns of object relations qua object relations. One should also listen for evidence of neurobiological learning, facilitated pathways, in the form of affect and object relation at the level of reflex (the amygdala and the subneocortical system), and at the level of reason (the neocortex). Because both patterns are organized around affect, it is affect that remains the guide to their understanding and to perspective. It is affect that will help one understand whether someone is responding at the level of cognition and choice, or at the level of instinct and response. It is affect, its quality and freedom, that helps to indicate what system in the brain is potentially dominant.

In the clinical situation, there are two levels of questioning that follow. First: What affects are avoided? What affects are sought? What self-object representations are being repeated? What self-object representations are being repressed? How much freedom is there in the response? The second line of

questioning: What are the stimulus–response patterns sur-
rounding the affect? What self-object representations are being
reinforced? What self-object representations are being extinguished? Is there evidence of subneocortical dominance? How
much freedom is there in the response?

Because the data are integrated through affect, the data
must be addressed both as data of psychology and as data of
neurophysiology, both as histories of events expressed through
declarative memory in the narrative, and as records of affect
revealed in the emotional memory expressed in the transference. One should anticipate that the more primitive forms of
memory will be revealed in the transference through attachment behavior where affect is more likely to be most directly
and intensely expressed. Freud knew this, "This struggle between the doctor and the patient, between intellect and instinc-
tual life, between understanding and seeking to act, is played
out almost exclusively in the phenomena of transference"
(1912, p. 108). But while Freud felt that transference was revealing the repressed conflictual wish, it is important to recognize
that the transference may also be revealing the memory of a
series of perceptions processed through the synapses of the
thalamo-amydgala projection and encoded as nonsymbolic
(nonhippocampal, nonneocortical) memory in the amygdala.

The evaluation and understanding of primitive affect and
part self, part object representation should be addressed in this
manner. A hypothesis of listening to the history is that the
quality of the affect and the wholeness of the internal representations are a function of the relative inputs to perception and
memory from the amygdala, the subneocortex, the hippocampus, and the neocortex. The more there is evidence of reflexive
responses to affect (all or nothing "thinking"), the more is it
likely that the affective response is being mediated at the level
of the amygdala. So too the more there is evidence of part
self, part object representations, the more likely is it that the
behavior is operating at the level of reflex. The more likely is
it, too, that the affect that is driving the behavior is primitive
and conditioned. What one sees clinically are not the neurobiological encodings themselves but the consequences of these
encodings as revealed in the object relations and affects in the

history, the transference, the countertransference, the mental status. The corollary is that the more there is evidence of whole object representations and a greater range of affective expression, the more likely is it that the assessments are being made at the level of the neocortex. The more that the patient can think about an affect before responding to it, the greater is there freedom and the more is it likely that the affect is being processed through the neocortex where delay and thought are more possible.

One is listening then for completeness of object relation, range of affect, and response to affect. One is listening for more or less reflex, more or less freedom in the patient's thought, feelings, and actions. While this conceptualization is hypothetical, it is based on research with animal models and with people who have suffered intense and overwhelming affect. This does not prove its clinical validity. However, it does provide a compelling basis for such beliefs.

The following example is taken from the treatment of the lawyer mentioned earlier who had tremendous difficulty allowing me to collaboratively participate in his psychotherapeutic monologue, as if it were dangerous for him to listen or to respond to anything that I might say. The example demonstrates, I believe, the importance of conceptualizing the data from the history and the transference at different neurobiological levels of integration.

The patient's father was a salesman in the diamond trade who was "either on forty-seventh street, in Switzerland, yelling at me, or asleep." His mother, a Holocaust survivor, had throughout his early childhood been extremely vigilant lest anything untoward happen to her son, her first born. She doted on him. But as difficulties surfaced, she demanded perfection, and when these expectations were not met, she withdrew in anxiety and frustration. Her involvement, as he told it, was a mix of intrusive demands and aggrieved disappointments.

Diagnostically he evidenced affective disorder, depressed type. There were no data to support a diagnosis of mania, mixed mania, or hypomania. There was a possible diagnosis of obsessive–compulsive disorder in childhood. On axis II there was a personality disorder, with narcissistic, obsessional, and schizotypal features. Medications had improved his overall functioning, especially his mood and obsessional thinking. However, he remained socially isolated and tended to block intimacy on any level.

The following are from two consecutive sessions. I select these rather long passages because they demonstrate not only the complex data of object relations but also the interaction of affect, object relations, and neurobiology at the level of both reason and reflex. The material followed a session in which for the first time ever, he had addressed questions to me. Was I married? Did I have children? This was extremely unusual behavior for this man—not only were they direct questions to me, but he seemed genuinely curious about the answers.

After some exploration with the patient, I decided to answer his questions, not because I advocate self-disclosure as a therapeutic method, but because I felt that for this man the risk of showing me his curiosity was enormous, and I wanted to reinforce this behavior. The next session occurred 3 days later. He began:

Patient: I had two dreams. In the first I was in a room looking for someone. I was yelling out, "Hello, hello!" There was no answer. In the second, I'm watching two nomads fighting in the desert. The one takes his sword and sticks it in the back of the other's head. Like pithing a turtle. When he pulls the sword out, the guy falls to the ground. Then he cuts off the guy's head and his hand. (He went on without a pause.) As a child I was always afraid of being alone in the house. Afraid of the basement and of the attic. I was a mess when I was a kid. I must have been brainwashed into thinking I was a normal kid.

Brainwashed? Was that a reference to the second dream, thoughts being forced into him. By others? By his mother? With a sword, by his father? Had he felt threatened by my answering his questions the previous session?

Patient: I called out to my mother a lot [first dream?]. It was my mother who I viewed as protecting me

from my father. Like if I wet the bed, she'd tell
my father that I had to be reprimanded, and he'd
yell at me. He'd yell and yell and yell. When she
got too scared at his yelling, she'd step in. But the
funny thing—(He looked at me) the me now is
the same person that I dimly recall lying in bed
and wetting night after night [enuresis to age 12].
Screaming. Banging my head. I used to call out
for them to come. I was inconsolable. She'd come
in. Offer me platitudes, warm milk, cookies. Nothing soothed. I just had this feeling of being brainwashed. Everything felt so contrived and false. On
the rare occasions when I get close enough to
people, I don't feel the reality of their feelings.
And now I'm so confused about my own feelings.

Therapist: You've been talking about brainwashing. Like in
the dream someone's head gets stuffed. By whom?

Patient: My parents live in a comic strip. They couldn't
deal with me. Who could? My symptoms reflected
on them. It's as if they were saying, "Our kid reflects on us. It's too frightening. They [the symp-
toms] have an origin that's too familiar. We can't
get too close." We have to say, "It's him. Not us.
That's *his* problem. We will help *him*. But 'Us?'
Problems? No. His problems don't come from us.
We can't allow that thought. It's not us. It's him."

So when they tried to help me, their help
was shallow. Nothing. Hurt without healing. They
were breaking some law. Got to be some law about
this. No power to turn things around. Just turn
things over. Problems. My unhappiness reflected
on theirs and reminded them of their misery with
themselves. I was threatening to them. So they
threatened me. Talion. That was the law. I was
forbidden to be unhappy. Peeing in bed? yelling
at night? head banging? "What do we do?" Hide.
They were simple people from a simple land.
Hide. They had no other resources. Their anxiety
about themselves, about their marriage, it was all

stuffed into me. They couldn't go, where could they go, to a rabbi, a psychiatrist? Where could they hide it all? In me. The only place. If they got discouraged or afraid, they'd say it was him. "It was him," they'd say. It was me. And then she'd say, "Here have a cookie. Stop being unhappy." I felt like occupied France. What about the Nazis Ma? Did she forget? My unhappiness reflected on her.

Therapist: The two dreams may also be about—

Patient: In the first I don't know, I think in the first dream—

Therapist: Lemme just say—

Patient: I'm sorry. I don't mean to cut you off.

He paused. I thought that in the material, the mental status, and in the transference I was encountering his persistent need to maintain safety by maintaining emotional distance from me and emotional control over me. I said to him, "I wonder if there wasn't a time when your life seemed to depend on your being able to cut off from others. I wonder if a way to stay safe was to find a way that no one could get to you."

He interjected, "The guy lost his head in the dream." I agreed,

Therapist: Yes. No small price. The two dreams—perhaps they were two aspects of the one issue that you've been describing. Intensely alone in the one wanting to find someone who might understand you, and in the other brainwashed when you got close—by other people's anxieties? It must be very lonely having to stand so far back from people and cut them off for fear of what will happen if you get too close.

I wasn't sure if he was listening to me. When I finished the sentence, he immediately began,

Patient: I was always a disappointment. When you let someone get close to you, there is the potential

	to disappoint them terribly. I'm their bad seed. I feel I've failed them by not responding to what they've tried to do. If anything I'm afraid of that feeling being stuffed into me.
Therapist:	The feeling of?
Patient:	Of being so unreachable and inconsolable that whoever wants to be near me or is drawn to me—I feel I can't give people the response that they want. They'll get discouraged and give up on me.

There were numerous references to the transference. But there were also references in the material, the transference, the mental status, and at times in my own frustration with understanding (countertransference) just what it was that he was talking about, to the need not to communicate, not to make himself heard, not to let himself be understood by others. It was as if he had learned that there was a price to be paid for establishing clear communication with others or with himself, and that this learning had been conditioned.

The next session was 3 days later. He entered, sat, and stared. Then offered, "Hi." I offered, "Hi," partly because it seemed polite, but mostly because in the dream before the previous session, he had called out and no one had answered. He was silent for several minutes. I asked, "Did you have any thoughts about our last session?" He said, "I didn't think too much of it, not in plain thought no." I wasn't exactly sure what he meant by that; I said nothing. He said,

Patient:	I was in a restaurant this morning reading. Then I just started crying. I couldn't really cry because I didn't want to cry. There used to be this waiter there. I didn't ever like him very much, so I'd never cry in front of him. But he wasn't there. I hadn't seen him in weeks, and there was a new waiter, and so I ordered eggs, coffee, and—

I was having trouble following his tangential movement away from affect, so I interrupted him: "What were you crying about?" "I guess . . . Well . . . Last session one thing you said put me in touch with the tremendous loneliness and anxiety at the same time.''

He had thought about last session. I had predicted the opposite: That he would deny involvement and the intimacy of "taking me with him" between sessions. He went on,

Patient: I was reading these poems. I project these passion-
            ate poems I was reading onto women and
            sex—these complex relationships I have in my
            head. These poems can transform. I'm experienc-
            ing these poems—I can't think of the right word,
            elegant, or I'm not sure what.

Obviously I was having trouble understanding what he was talking about. I felt this confusing form of communication (mental state) was part of the resistance, and part of his condi-tioned fear of communication, so I said to him, "Maybe you're having trouble finding the right word because the feelings you're struggling with are not about the poems so much as about what you and I were talking about last session." He nod-ded, or seemed to.

Patient: The poems, well Keats. All right. Yeah. I mean I
            think the poems triggered it. The poems were
            talking about loneliness and anxiety. The poems
            just happened to be, the beauty of the poem. That
            was the trigger.
Therapist: To here?
Patient: These beautiful women I saw and the
            poems—written two hundred years ago. It was
            beautiful. Yesterday.
Therapist: You felt sad reading the poems, seeing these
            women, after the session?
Patient: I'm not used to trusting emotional truths. I under-
            stand I generated this explanation, I don't trust
            it. I don't have it on videotape. Maybe underneath
            if I stop looking at women, stop that distraction,
            everything is a mystery to me.

One of his obsessional symptoms included thinking for hours about women that he had seen on the street. He continued.

Patient: Part of that will really make me feel like crying a lot, and I did have this thought about this. Now that I've stopped obsessing, these women were on my mind as I was having breakfast—I didn't let them come along. When I was in there having breakfast, I was free. I just wanted to be at peace after being there. I did think that this reaction, this crying, this sadness is underneath, lying there in wait. I came to some intuitive feeling, that it's important for me to get there. That these strategies and habits I've developed to protect myself from getting there, and that they'll dissolve only if I recognize that there is something important lying behind this.

While what he was saying was not easy to follow, he had nonetheless communicated a meaningful idea, that some of the obsessional symptoms might be a way of avoiding what lay underneath. I said nothing. He seemed sad, almost at the point of tears. He continued,

Patient: I can't help not thinking about women. I think I fear having them in my mind—thoughts—but I'm more afraid of not having them to hold onto because when I clear all that away, I'm not happy. There's a true unhappiness beneath and behind all that.

I made a point of clarification, "It's almost as if you've 'chosen' the pain of obsessing about these women, over some other pain."

I was thinking that his obsessive thoughts about women were an operantly conditioned response to avoid some other more troubling thought and its associated affect. In the transference he had demonstrated over and over how much he feared emotional and empathic connection to me; my hypothesis was that this paradigm provided a map. He avoided connection except at an obsessionally hollow level because of his terror that if he allowed himself to connect to others, they would fill him with their anxieties and defeats. This pattern of conditioned avoidance and controlled contact was one that he carried from his childhood encoded predominantly in the emotional memory of the amygdala and subneocortex reflecting childhood attachments that were being repeated now with me in the transference. This idea on one level is an extension of the work of Konrad Lorenz (1965) and Bowlby (1969), and thus, "Social mammals are intrinsically motivated to seek out recognizable attachment figures, and the nature of what is recognizable is likely to be heavily influenced by what is present at the time of formation of the original attachment bond" (Amini et al., 1996, p. 231). The system that encodes these earliest bonds in all mammals is the subneocortical emotional memory and is largely unconscious. It was the experience of these bonds that I felt my patient was avoiding in the transference through his obsessional symptomatology. He went on,

Patient: When I was a kid, I'd think about girls but it wasn't a torture then. I'd think about Marcy Rothman. And then Donna Glickman. It wasn't about sex; I didn't know what sex was. I obsessed about other things too. When I was 8, 9, I'd wake up in the middle of the night thinking "I'm really on edge now because I can't think about what's bothering me." I had to have something to occupy my mind.

Therapist: Such as?

Patient: Well like I forgot my books at school. I used to bring home a ton of books, like this—[demonstrates a ton of books]—But I'd always forget one. My parents'd have to drive me back to school to get the book. I mean this wasn't once or twice. It was two, three times a month. I'd have to go back and get it. Find the janitor, "Glenn," I was on a first name basis with the janitor. I had all kinds of obsessions. Things I had to do. Arrange my papers. Move my boxes. My sneakers had to be lined up with their laces in a certain way before I went to bed every night, or else I couldn't sleep. My father used to come in and kick them just because he knew it drove me bananas. I'd have to get up and arrange them all over again. He'd laugh. I had to. My socks had to be just a certain way. I had this recurrent dream, "My parents take me back to school to get a book. I look in my school desk and I find the front of my finger in the desk." [He looked at me and shrugged.] I know. I know. How obvious. You don't have to say it. Finger-penis. I know. I'm pretty sure it was my finger. There probably was a choice somewhere, to chose a path of least resistance. I felt no one could help me with it so I figured so long as I can keep my mind on something and adopt perfectionistic type goals, good grades, model behavior, everything was fine.

Therapist: Until?

Patient: Until I started jerking off. That was a bad thing I couldn't resist. At first it was no big deal. Something I did to relax, help me go to sleep. Then I put it together with girls. I don't know how that happened. First it was without girls and it was okay, but then I made the connection.

He started to cry. I hadn't anticipated this demonstration of emotion. I had never seen him cry before. At the beginning of the session, he had mentioned how he never cried at the restaurant because of the waiter. But there was a new waiter. Had he experienced a change in our relationship, I wondered. What had made it safe enough to expose this much emotional memory to me, to cry in front of me? Because I wasn't sure what the answer might be, I said nothing. He went on,

Patient: While I was in there [the restaurant], an older woman came in wheeling a baby carriage. A grandmother—grandchild, had to be. She came in and I felt terrible and selfish. That I had failed my mother in some terrible way. . . . My parents are simple. They must've been so happy to have a boy child. Passing on the name. She must've been so happy. But I ended her happiness. I let her down just by being alive. My mother is older than that woman in the restaurant. I never gave her the happiness that she deserved.

There were many thoughts going through my head. The obsessions about women on the street and their connection to his thoughts about his mother. The dream and its blatant oedipal implications, losing his finger-penis. The transference and his increased trust of me. Every situation described in one way or another one affect: fear. He was afraid of everyone, including himself. I wanted to try to make it safe enough for him to explore affect further. Therefore I chose to stay with the affect in the context of attachment,

Therapist: Maybe the tears and sadness you are feeling have to do with the distance that you've had to create between you and your mother as you've been telling it. But also between you and others in general. You and me in particular. As if that were the only way for you to stay safe.

Patient: I can't help it. I find it so awful being close to my mother. The idea of closeness is loathsome. Intellectually, I can understand how it'd be nice to—I wouldn't have all these psychiatric maladies for one if I weren't. These tears are about that and more. I don't take it all on myself. But whenever I'm near her. Whenever I feel her, I feel her saying, "You're a failure." That it's me. Everything that was wrong in her childhood, her marriage, everything that was wrong between her and her father [there had been child abuse], with her life. "It's him," I felt her saying. It's him. . . . It's me.

The data from this material came from many sources. In the mental status there was tangentiality, circumstantiality, and at times illogicality. His style was obsessive, overly inclusive, sometimes difficult to interrupt or to follow. He limited my involvement, kept us both at a safe distance from one another by attempting to limit how much I could understand. In the transference, as with women on the street, he maintained contact in a controlled and distant fashion. He wanted me as an object to talk to, just as he wanted women as objects for masturbation. Emotional involvement was restricted. There were limits that he could not cross with me or with women, without tremendous anxiety. In the content of the session, he described how his interactions with his mother filled him with her anxiety and with her sense of personal inadequacy as a mother, woman, wife, daughter. It was as if her sense of herself as a failed woman were being stuffed into him. The affect he experienced was intense anxiety whenever he experienced emotional connection, a reaction seen in the mental status, the transference, the content of the session, the history.

From the perspective of object relations alone, I hypothesized that there was a part self representation that wanted to be known and that suffered tremendous loneliness and that therefore wanted to attach to the object. This part self-object representation came to sessions faithfully, desperate to attach to me and to be understood by me. It was also the part of him that dreaded the end of each session, and that would speed up his speech to prevent me from announcing that the session was over. Another part self was terrified of attachment, and thus saw me as a dangerous part object (projection of his own competitiveness and aggression). I was someone who would stuff him, leaving his skull filled with my anxieties. Defense mechanisms of splitting, denial, devaluation of self, and projection of rage supported these part self-object representations.

But by combining the data of object relations with the data of operant conditioning and lower order memory, there was another perspective that needed to be considered. This man sensed from an early age the dangers of intense involvement with his mother. Her level of anxiety (or importantly his experience of it) was enormous, generating an ongoing atmosphere of tension and danger. This hypothetically led to heightened subneocortical arousal. In a state of general heightened affect, boundaries are blurred—indeed heightened arousal by making one more focused on the environment is designed to generate a state that incorporates one's surroundings, prepares internal state for external action, and by its focus brings the external close. Affects do connect the external to the internal, and if external arousal is forced and ongoing, then the boundary between self and other becomes vulnerable by virtue of this shared internal intensity and external threat.

This sense that others were forcing their way into his mind was his ongoing experience, reflecting heightened anxiety and arousal. It was a state beginning, I would argue, with his earliest attachment bond. His experience of maternal intrusiveness was enormous. The demands for perfect harmony between mother and child reflected perhaps her own fears of loss as a Holocaust survivor, sense of inadequacy, and desire to repair her own very damaged childhood. The danger and anxiety she tried to tamp down were instead communicated to her son. The presence of the object (stimulus) and the experience of the object's disappointment and fear (the unconditioned response) were associated such that avoidance of affective contact and meaningful communication became the safe response (conditioned avoidance).

In order to avoid the intrusive experience of his mother's anxiety, she had to be avoided, but she couldn't be. Attachment was conflicted. In order to avoid pain, he had to keep his needed and longed for mother both near by and at bay. He responded to the approach of the object with complex and contradictory signals every night when he would scream, wet his bed, or head bang. He both felt the terror of his mother's approach as well as the need for her empathic understanding and comfort. Obsessional symptoms became an operantly conditioned response to this need–fear dilemma. He could call for her secure in the fact that his symptoms would not allow intimacy, that his obsessional thinking and character were in strict control.

This behavior began with "neutral" acts, arranging papers, books, shoes, socks as a way of overcoming the internal sense of danger. In early latency masturbation was added to these obsessional behaviors. "At first it had nothing to do with sex. I didn't know what sex was." With the "discovery" of sex and its connection to masturbation, masturbation became a multiply determined solution: it was a way to alleviate anxiety, a way to deny meaningful contact through the sexualization of all human contact, and given his moralistic, Hasidic household a way to feel intense guilt. Masturbation thus intensified as the other behaviors faded.

These data would have to be combined and evaluated clinically. I would have to decide when he was operating more at the level of operant conditioning, and therefore when his freedom was diminished and the reestablishment of safety would be the first priority. At other times when he seemed to be "making sense," and was able to communicate with me, it would be more likely that he was thinking and seeing me more clearly and less as a dangerous part object whose (projected) rage had to be avoided. At such times, affect and safety might not have to be the primary focus, but the better understanding of pathological defense mechanisms (splitting, devaluation, projection) might then be the focus of my interventions because his affect presumptively would be operating more freely and be integrated at the level of thought, not conditioned reflex. The levels of intervention are based on the determination of the level of the affect, an evaluation which is made in part by a comparison of the patterns of affect in the history and the transference.

Treatment with this man continued and progressed well. The primary mental status index I used to evaluate his progress was centered on how well I could understand him as opposed to how much obsessional detail he would introduce as a way of destroying communication and interest. However, a time came when there was a disruption in his life; his mother took ill and he was having to make frequent visits to see her, at first in the hospital and then as she recovered, at home, his childhood home.

After one such visit, I asked him how she was faring. He began a long and confusing description of the train ride to the suburbs, about how he had to wait to get a cab, how they picked up two other passengers. He went on about this for some time. I pointed out that he had avoided the question. He nodded in recognition, and then after a perfunctory answer as to her health, went on about how he hated Connecticut. I wasn't sure what he was getting at, except that I was aware that I felt excluded and irrelevant to his monologue. I attempted to communicate this idea to him. After I had said something about this to him, I realized that what I had said was confusing and must have been hard to follow. This seemed to cause him no bother. He agreed with what I had said as a matter of course. I interrupted him again and said, "It's striking to me that sometimes when I talk to you, what I say comes out all confused and hard to follow. As I think back on it, what I said a little while ago was very unclear. It's hard for me to understand what I meant." He nodded and said, "Jamming frequency. I think that sometimes, maybe most of the time, I operate on a jamming frequency."

I knew what he meant, I nodded and said, "Yes, I think I know what you mean." We both sat for a moment realizing that we both understood very clearly something that had been going on between the two of us. He seemed calmer and said, "I'm afraid you'll give me something that will eat up my mind."

I thought of the pithing dream. I knew that what he was describing was not some paranoid psychotic reaction but rather was a valuable communication that he had made because he had been feeling safe enough with me to experience the truth of it in himself. He continued, "I get afraid that something will get sucked into my mind and not be able to get out. You'll make me frightened. If I have any emotion, I get frightened of it. Any emotion frightens me."

I did not ask him for further clarification. I felt that this was as far as he could go with it, that for now this was as much language as he could place on a primitive emotion and perhaps memory, and therefore to ask him "Why?" would have led away from the truth of what we had discovered and led him into obsessional resistances, and back into a "jamming frequency." Indeed I felt that we had gone a long way toward establishing a context where it was safe enough for him to think about what was dangerous, that he had gotten to the point where he was able to communicate his fear of connection and affect.

Another example: A 39-year-old woman, with a history of multiple psychiatric hospitalizations and many failed treatments, had been referred for consultation because yet another treatment was failing. On our first meeting, she entered my office and in greeting said, "Hola!" I smiled and said "Hello." Then this attractive, and from the history very troubled, young Jewish woman from New Jersey, who spoke this one word of Spanish, said "Hello." Her mood stayed artificially upbeat until she began to describe a particular incident in her past. And then everything changed, in the past, 30 years ago, and in the room where we sat.

The summer of her ninth year was the first time in her life she had ever been separated from her parents for any significant duration.

> I didn't want to go to camp. I hated it. I spent 10 days in the infirmary. I don't think anyone knew what was wrong. Something was wrong. Finally at the end of the month my parents came up to see me. I didn't want to stay there anymore. I couldn't. I was crying and pleading for them to take me home. I just couldn't bear the thought of being away from them.

At this point, she pulled her legs up to her chest, and curled in the chair with her hands covering her face. After some hesitation she said, "I was afraid they were going to leave me there."

As I looked at her, curled in the chair and afraid, I felt that the fear she expressed was not just about the past, but was there in the room as she told me the story. Partly the affect was shame for being such a "crybaby." But it was also fear, terror, really, of abandonment, perhaps as she had experienced it 30 years ago.

I would then listen for terror over interpersonal issues as a powerful presence and organizer in her history. The experience of terror over abandonment is different from the experience of sadness over separation. The affect in the story, but more significantly in the room with me as she told the story, was terror. I would then go back to the history mindful of the mental status, searching for other data corroborating or refuting this hypothesis. If the hypothesis were valid, I antici-pated the patient would reexperience terror with me over any felt separation. This would be revealed, and thus tested, as anxi-ety between sessions. But the intensity was such that I wondered whether she would experience fear if there were any separation not just from one evaluation session to the next, but if I had a view that differed from hers (if I were not perfectly identified with her). This hypothesis could also be tested by observing her reaction when internal illogic was confronted, when defense mechanisms were identified, or whenever I for whatever rea-son, failed to understand or be in agreement with her.

Affect then should be used as a guide as one gathers the data of the history. In obtaining the history one must follow the progression of the story as it is told. But one must also observe the affect that the patient is experiencing both as the affect applies to the history, and as it applies to transference, and as it applies to reason. Affect as it is experienced is very different from affect as it is told, psychologically and neurobio-logically, and these differences must be observed and ac-counted for.

The back and forth of history manifests on multiple levels. First at the level of content, second at the level of affect, third at the level of reflex, fourth at the level of reason, fifth at the level of freedom. All aspects must be examined separately from the history and then reapplied as guides to the history. But the data of the affect did not make sense. Why had the telling of this tale from summer camp delivered her into a state of terror now? Why had her affect changed so quickly and so profoundly?

11.

Affect and Primitive Affect

> *The fact that words denoting feeling*
> *are predictive of behavior means that*
> *they can be used in a rigorously*
> *scientific way....*
> (Bowlby, 1969, p. 121)

Affects can change, sometimes quickly, sometimes subtlely producing changes that are reflected internally through perception and externally through behavior. Brian Friel described an aspect of this action of affect in his play "Molly Sweeney":

> All of us live on a swing, she said. And the swing normally moves smoothly and evenly across a narrow range of the usual emotions. Then we have a crisis in our life; so that instead of moving evenly from say, feeling sort of happy to feeling sort of miserable, we now swing from elation to despair, from unimaginable delight to utter wretchedness. The word she used was "delivered" to show how passive we are in this terrifying game: We are delivered into one emotional state—snatched away from it—delivered into the opposite emotional state. And we can't help ourselves. We can't escape. Until eventually we can endure no more abuse—become incapable of experiencing anything, feeling anything at all. (Friel, 1994, p. 50)

In any formulation, it is crucial that specific understandings of affects be reached. Affects are the links that afford an understanding between biological function and psychological

195

function; between the amygdala's demands and neocortical thought; between internal and external; between action and reflection. Affects provide a connection from the individual to his environment and back.

Darwin (1872) was among the first to propose and undertake research into the complex biosociological importance of affects and their expression.

> We have now, I think sufficiently shown that when any sensation, desire, dislike, etc., has led during a long series of generations to some voluntary movement, then a tendency to the performance of a similar movement will almost certainly be excited, whenever the same, or any analogous or associated sensation . . . is experienced. (p. 48)

Darwin demonstrated the important communicative value that affect afforded a species, and thus argued that behavior and expressions that were most "efficient" would be biologically favored—that is to say inherited. Freud was very much aware of Darwin's work, and took that insight a step further:

> And what is affect in the dynamic sense? It is in any case something highly composite. An affect includes in the first place particular motor innervations or discharges and secondly certain feelings; the latter are of two kinds—perceptions of the motor actions that have occurred and the direct feelings of pleasure and unpleasure which, as we say, give the affect its keynote. But I do not think that with this enumeration we have arrived at the essence of an affect. We seem to see deeper in the case of some affects and to recognize that this experience could only be a very early impression of a very general nature, placed in the prehistory not of the individual but of the species. (1916–1917, pp. 395–396)

Contemporary understandings of affect include this complex mix of biology, heredity, neuromuscular expression, object relations, and approach–avoidance behavior. And thus: "Affects are behavior patterns that include a specific cognitive appraisal (basically, of perceived reality as 'desirable' or 'undesirable'), a specific expressive facial pattern, a subjective experience of pleasurable (rewarding), or painful (aversive) quality, and both muscular and neurovegetative components" (Kernberg, 1991, p. 210).

Affect is probably the first communication, and as such is the first word of attachment behavior: "Affect is the innate, universal language we are born with; our nervous systems come prewired with knowledge of and readiness for this language, and it is a language independent of abstract symbolization or verbal capacity" (Amini et al., 1996, p. 229). Affect is the connection to our first object.

Affect is not simple. It is a complex state that is the vector sum of various environmental, behavioral, biological, and hereditary inputs. Because of this complexity, it is not always possible to know which specific inputs are operative at any given time. But also because of the complexity, it is reasonable to consider affect from multiple perspectives. By so doing one has a greater chance of gathering enough data to locate the subjective and objective meaning of affect.

In the previous chapter, the patterns of history were described as they related to the neurobiological data of affect. In this chapter the volatility of affect will be explored, how people can be "delivered" in noncrisis situations from one emotional state to another. The following is a description from a patient, a 30-year-old medical technician with mixed character disorder and affective instability who was being treated pharmacologically for affective instability. There was no history of physical or sexual abuse. The interview was by a therapist of about the same age as the patient. The setting was a long-term hospital unit. The therapist began by asking, "How long have you been here?" The patient looked at him, tucked a strand of her long brown hair behind her ear, and smiled.

Patient: Five months, oh my God, it's been a long time.
Therapist: How has it been?
Patient: One of the most difficult things I've ever done. But it's been really helpful. It's hot in here isn't it? (She crossed and uncrossed her legs. Undid a button. He nodded; it was hot. She leaned forward.)
Patient: To make a separation from my parents. I can't be alone. Or let's say I wasn't very good at it, but

I'm getting better. I've been learning to use my strengths. Be more self-reliant. So that not everything is a crisis. (The therapist leaned back as he began to take notes.)

Therapist: What do you mean? (She leaned back.)

Patient: My moods can change just like that, within the same hour, the same day; they can go from hopeful to "forget about it." (Her moods were indeed changing. The therapist continued to take notes. She watched him.)

Patient: I can hold on better now and not act on it [affect and impulse control]. But when people I depended on—my doctor, my parents, my usual support systems—are away, I just panic. I lose a part of myself because the people weren't there [intense separation anxiety, lack of internalization]. The feeling didn't last that long this time; I mean I survived it. I'm better able to say the person's coming back, that the feeling will go away so I don't act on the self-destructive thoughts. But when I'm scared or panicked or alone, I think about killing myself, as if that's the only way for the feeling to stop [acting out, resistance, affective instability]. In the past, the level of anxiety and despair'd get so great—in my mind and physically too in my body [somatization]. Just panic. I feel I can't stand it. Now I have more confidence to go through to the next thing and the next thing before I'd take the opportunity to cut myself.

Therapist: You cut yourself a lot? (She looked at the therapist, studied him like a specimen.)

Patient: It's like a tranquilizer. I'd focus on that and everything else would be shut out [dissociation]. A tranquilizer you know, you've heard of it—it's not like I thought this up by myself. You've heard of razor blades and self-mutilation, haven't you doctor?

The tone had changed. A new defense mechanism, devaluation, was evident perhaps as a resistance for having confided so much to a "mere" therapist who wasn't responding. It was as if signals were being received from a different area of her brain, unconsciously warning her that she was going to experience "unpleasure," and in response to that affectively driven signal, her interpersonal behaviors, the part self part object representations, were changing. She was no longer "enjoying" the interview. She was no longer flirting with the therapist. Fear was encroaching. Defense mechanisms were changing, and he, the therapist, was moving into the storm of her developing affect ready, willing, and unprepared,

Therapist: What do you mean? (She looked at him, shrugged, took out a cigarette. Lit it, exhaled.)
Patient: Well underneath I can feel really angry at being so disconnected. This may sound stupid to a healthier person [devaluation]. But at times I feel there's nothing I can do or say to make a difference. Of course it's a way to get attention but I don't think I want attention. I want . . . I don't know what I want. (The therapist continued to evaluate this information at face value.)
Therapist: What did you get angry at?
Patient: Usually I feel angry if I feel that people aren't understanding me. If they're leaving me at a time when I need them, or using me in some way. Just not being there. They can be physically there but not emotionally there. (She was addressing the transference point blank, and the issues of attachment, intense separation anxiety, and unstable affect.) I begin feeling really alone and overwhelmed and feel I need help. But then I turn down help [narcissistic defenses against disorganizing affect in the transference, against reexperiencing abandonment issues]. I sometimes can't see that the help is really there. I feel no one's helping me, that there's no one there but that's

not really true. (She was perhaps unconsciously
giving him one last chance.)

Therapist: Can you give me an example? (Indicating that he
still hadn't recognized that she was staring right
at the very example he was asking for.)

Patient: Well last night. I was having this severe back pain.
The nurse didn't want to give me a prn for pain.
She was giving me this lecture about addiction.
Fuck her, I thought. I felt I'd love to scare the shit
out of her. There was a water pitcher. I wanted
her to feel the pain that I was feeling. So I threw
the water pitcher at the wall.

The intensity of the affect was so great that she was convinced that communication was impossible through language.
The intensity was such that action, "I will make you as afraid
as I am afraid," was the only communication possible. She had
done it the previous night after all. She smiled, "I guess that
was pretty borderline hunh?" "It didn't show great impulse
control, no." She nodded, cocked her head to the side, the
cigarette near her face,

Patient: You want to know what I'm feeling now, right
now? I feel you're using me. Taking advantage of
me. I mean I crave someone to listen to me, to
be supportive, but then when it happens, I can't
deal with it. I'll downplay it. Change it. I have this
fantasy that you can't wait for this to end [primi-
tive affect in the transference fueling issues of low
self-esteem, projection of contempt, loss of reality
testing]. I bet you just can't wait to go to lunch
so you can tell the other therapists, "I saw this
real borderline, named Grace." I don't feel like
your patient. I feel like your object. That if I can't
have the person's full attention, I have to shut
down completely from receiving anything. I feel
like saying, "Daddy, read me a bedtime story."
So what does that mean? That after all that I've

told you, I want you to read me a story? What do
you think that means, "doctor"?

The therapist said nothing. Grace smiled triumphantly, snuffed
out her cigarette, "It doesn't mean shit." It meant chaos. The
chaos of primitive affect, and the need for greater safety.

In order to begin to know what was going on, one would
need to contain the chaos, and thus contain the patient's swell-
ing emotions during the course of the evaluation so that one
could have the time to begin to formulate and understand
this material which was coming at the therapist from many
directions at once. The first inkling of meaning might then
have come from the countertransference.

The therapist acted as if he had been overwhelmed and
rendered passive by the patient's forwardness and aggression.
One might hypothesize that the patient was also feeling overwhelmed by the emotional chaos that was her daily bread and
that his experience was hers and therefore that she was using
the defense mechanism of projective identification. One might
have tested that possibility by suggesting to her that perhaps
she had been feeling overwhelmed, but that in the evaluation
you and she were going to better define and treat her pain, a
generic, supportive statement about safety. From a technical
point of view, then one might have hypothesized that the patient's increasingly confrontational behavior toward the therapist was caused by the relative lack of structure that he was
offering her, and that with structure, affirmation, and support
the patient's function and integration would have improved.

While it may have been that the patient's cohesiveness
could have been temporarily strengthened by a more active,
affirmative interview, there was in the material ample evidence
that this woman's overall level of functioning was chaotic both
within and without the treatment setting. She had, after all,
informed the therapist that the night before she had thrown a
pitcher of water when a nurse wasn't quick enough to respond
with medication for her pain (i.e., data indicating that she dis-
tances those she needs, and thus a warning that she would do
the same in the transference).

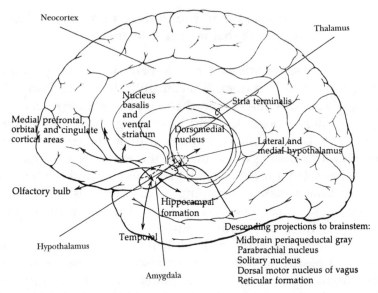

Figure 11.1. A schematic diagram of the brain showing the interconnections between the amygdala, the thalamus, and the hypothalamus, and other structures. (From: Martin, 1989, p. 383)

She had said that she disorganized when separated from important care providers, her doctor, her parents, her nurse. This was a statement of history, her past medical history as well as history from her childhood. And the statement was supported by her behavior in the transference. As the therapist remained silent and distant, she became more impulsive and disorganized. In a sense his unwitting reserve created an opportunity to test the hypothesis. The transference had recreated what was the pathologically (dis-)organizing experience of her life, "People I need are hardly ever there for me, and when this happens, I feel enormous pain. This pain is intolerable. I can't think anymore. I have to act out self-destructively to override the pain, or I have to get to someone else to comfort me. What is clear to me is that alone I cannot cope with the affect. It is too painful, and I am too weak." But once having tested a hypothesis, it is then necessary to reestablish safety.

Why had her affect became primitive? Why had her moods changed, "in the same hour . . . from hopeful to forget about it"? Affect is organized in the central nervous system at different levels both of which pass to the amygdala where emotional tone is registered. There is a lower order pathway that deals automatically and reflexively when perception indicates danger. In the lower order pathway, stimuli travel from the organs of perceptions through the brain stem to the thalamus and then directly to the amygdala. From the amygdala an immediate response is organized. This makes sense if there is danger or even the possibility of danger. It is a system whereby speed is gained; accuracy is lost: "Emotional processing is initiated very early in the sensory processing sequence, long before the system has had the opportunity to construct real-world objects and events out of the available sensory cues" (LeDoux, 1992, p. 275).

The higher order pathway involves a more complete evaluation of sensory input before being passed on to the amygdala. This processing involves projections from the sense organs to the thalamus and then to the neocortex before being sent to the amygdala for its emotional tone. In this thalamo-cortico-amygdala projection sensory input travels across a greater number of synapses as the route goes to the neocortex where more complex patterns of memory and learning are added to the perception; the perception is given a context. This route takes more time to complete but it gives a fuller appraisal of what is going on before a response is generated. In both systems it is the amygdala where emotional tone is finally generated.

One might ask what happens if the quicker thalamo-amygdaloid path initially registers danger, and then a few milliseconds later information from the thalamo-cortical-amygdaloid system adds information indicating that the perception is harmless? For example the gunshot you thought you heard you realized was the sound of a car back firing. Under most conditions the amygdala would make adjustments and the overall affective response would reflect the slower but more complete appraisal of the neocortex: the noise is not dangerous; evasive measures are not indicated. Normally this is how the systems work—normally but not always.

"In real-time processing, the amygdala receives input from both the thalamus and cortex, and either or both of these systems can be the basis of emotional learning. However, because

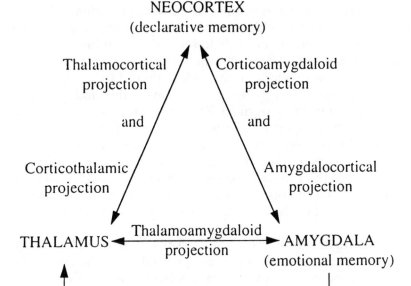

Figure 11.2. Declarative memory registered in the neocortex and the hippocampus is more complete but takes more time to access. Emotional memory registered largely in the amygdala is less inclusive but can be accessed very quickly. To a degree amygdaloid memory can interfere with cortical responses to input because of amygdalo-cortical projections.

sensory information reaches the amygdala from the thalamus before it does by way of the cortex, thalamic inputs have the opportunity to directly influence the amygdala's response to cortical inputs" (LeDoux, 1992, p. 276). In other words, the initial, more direct input from the lower-level system may so influence the amygdala that it "refuses" to listen to neocortical reason. And thus LeDoux continues,

It is easy to imagine that individuals may differ as a result of constitutional (genetic) differences in the extent to which the thalamic or cortical pathways predominate in the initiation of emotional processing through the amygdala. If so, this could influence the extent to which an individual has control and feels in control of his or her emotional life. (1992, p. 277)

This has tremendous clinical implications. Because of the fact that in the transference more primitive affect tends to be generated, the emotions of the transference are potentially the emotions as routed through the more primitive thalamo-amygdaloid system.

In the interview described above, one can hypothetically argue that different biological levels of affect regulation were contributing as the quality of Grace's experience changed, that different neuronal integrations were taking place as her perception of the external variable (the therapist's involvement or lack thereof) was changed from her expectation of a relatively involved, attractive young man to the reality of a relatively uninvolved, attractive young man. This perceptual change of an external variable created a change in the patient's sense of safety which may have then facilitated the more primitive thalamo-amygdal projection and have triggered more primitive areas of the central nervous system in response to increasing levels of perceived danger in the transference, and thereby creating a more neurobiologically primitive mix and more primitive affect. When this happened, it was as if she were "in crisis," and as Brian Friel wrote, as if she had been "delivered into one emotional state—snatched away from it—delivered into the opposite emotional state." It was not an act of will, not a decision. "And we can't help ourselves." It happened on its own.

This shift that was observed clinically may have reflected a relative shift away from neocortical and hippocampal influence over perception to a more direct reaction to perception that was less under willful control. Higher-level circuits involving neocortical and hippocampal input are necessary for the more even evaluation and appraisal of a conditioned response:

Whenever a conditioned stimulus is paired with an unconditioned stimulus, some conditioning accrues to the background or to contextual stimuli that are also present in the environment. . . . The hippocampus . . . may be a kind of higher-order sensory structure in fear conditioning. That is, the hippocampus may relay environmental inputs pertaining to the conditioning context to the amygdala where emotional meaning is added. . . . Once learned, this kind of contextual fear conditioning might allow the organism to distinguish between those situations in which it is appropriate to defend oneself against a stimulus vs. situations in which it is not necessary (e.g., a bear in the woods vs. a bear in the zoo). (Le Doux, 1995, p. 214)

As relative neurophysiologic influence shifts from the hippocampus and neocortex to thalamo-amygdala projections, there is a shift from contextual appraisal of perception to conditioned response to perception. As this happens there is less and less biological freedom for the individual to recall memory, evaluate criteria, decide on a course of action. The external becomes internal, boundaries collapse, and there is the call for immediate action—a bear!

In the clinical example, there was possibly, and I must stress *possibly*, a neurophysiological shift away from hippocampal and neocortical dominance to a simple conditioned fear response mediated more and more directly through the amygdala. As this shift occurred, Grace was increasingly unable to make a contextual analysis of what was going on, unable to effectively use hippocampal and neocortical input as to what her perceptions really meant. "The hippocampus, with its abundance of multi-modal and demonstrated involvement in processing of spatial and relational information is well situated to provide the additional processing involved in dealing with such a highly complex stimulus as environmental context" (Rogan & Le Doux, 1996, p. 471). But increasingly all that Grace was able to experience was isolated affect, in this instance fear. The context of the fear became less and less identifiable and grew as neocortical and hippocampal influence were neurobiologically compromised.

In order to distance herself from this neurophysiologically mediated crisis, Grace mobilized new affects, particularly rage. This "new" affect then allowed her to reconstruct reality, and

to distance herself from the stimulus, the unresponsive therapist, by changing her relation to him through the use of defense mechanisms. He was devalued, and as this now devalued
part object was no longer needed or longed for, and most importantly like a bear in the zoo, in that caged and devalued
context, he was no longer feared. Defense mechanisms and the
shift of part objects changed the balance of power and thereby
changed the affect. By hating him, she no longer needed him.
She was able to feel triumphant as he was made to feel insecure.
But once gone, she would feel abandoned after having driven
him away.

What is common to both the psychological as well as the
neurobiological understanding is affect. This is not a new idea.
Freud as well as other theorists saw affect as central. But Freud
understood affect as a unitary concept "like an electric charge
spread over the surface of a body" (1894, p. 60). This contributed to the notion that there were unitary measures of affect:
there was a measure of "aggression" and a measure of "love."
More "measure" indicated more "affect." Someone who was
inappropriately emotional was being unreasonable because of
the "quantity" of affect.

What has become clear is that the subjective quality of an
affect is not just a quantity and is not defined solely by an
amount. But rather the influence of affect on thought and
behavior is determined by the balance of where it comes from,
by quite literally what cells in the central nervous system are
firing and at what rates and thus what contributions are being
made by which specific systems of the brain. Inputs from certain
cells imbue affect with verbal meaning, others are more inclined to lead to immediate action, increased heat rate, others
to paralyzing fear, others to avoidance, others to approach.
Depending not so much on the "quantity" of affect but on
what areas of the brain are contributing to the experience of
affect, determines how the affect will be read and what thought,
behavior, or action is most likely to follow. "Affects are emotions of course—but more . . . affects are the perceptible, felt
accompaniments of the neurophysiologic activation of parts of
the brain. . . . Available evidence suggests increasingly that, as
do sensory data processing and motor activity, so do affects

themselves seem to originate in anatomically identifiable neural circuits . . . " (Schwartz, 1987, p. 472). The perception and
experience of affect changes when the input changes from one
area of the brain to another. The origin of the affect may be
of greater significance than the amount.

Affect then is not just an internal, subjective experience.
It is a complex psychobiological experience that orients the
individual to the environment, and prepares the individual for
specific behavior. "What is crucial to an emotion is the orientation it provides," commented Jonathan Lear (1990, p. 89) in
his analysis of Freud's theoretical understanding of affect. But
it is also crucial to recognize that affect is not just a psychological but also a biological orientation. As with Grace, the patient
described at the end of the last chapter who was relating being
left at summer camp by her parents was also experiencing the
full force of emotion. It was not as if the abandonment were
happening thirty years ago; the affect was there in the moment,
and had been made more and more acute by the neurobiological shift from neocortical memory and orientation to the state
dependent memory and orientation of the amygdala. The
more the cells of the amygdaloid system are contributing to
one's interpretation of reality, the less will that interpretation
be open to discussion or delay.

A 28-year-old woman with a history of dysthymic disorder,
generalized anxiety disorder, and avoidant personality disorder
entered a session. She sat down, looked away, and in a quiet
voice proceeded to explain why she felt that she could not
accomplish any of her life goals, that no one would ever take
her seriously (transference and extratransference), and that
she could never learn how to interact with others comfortably
(issues of axis I diagnoses, medication, safety). She cried
quietly,

> I can't accomplish things the way other people do. I don't have
> the skills. I walk into a room and people know how backward I
> am (an attitude toward the environment). I went to the school
> registration and they'd ask me a question and I wouldn't have a
> response. I didn't know what they wanted. I could tell after I left
> that they were all thinking, "God who is that poor girl? I hope we
> haven't terrified her" (projection). Ever since I was 12 I'm always
> watching other people, how they interact, trying to get a clue

how it's done (conditioned behavior or genetic). I feel I've been programed to believe that no one will give me what I want. The attitude, the tone in my voice. People know that I don't know what to do. I look at them and know what they're whispering about me, "Poor JoAnne."

The patient's long history of avoidant behavior, dysthmia, and the affect of fear (anxiety) had established an orientation that was not only influencing her response to people, but also influencing her perceptions of people on a biological basis. In this context the issue of projection needs to be understood not only as a psychological defense mechanism operating on objects in the environment, but also as a biological projection influencing how perceptions are received. This woman's long history of fear and anxiety had hypothetically influenced how her perceptions were organized by favoring, genetically or through conditioned response or both, certain perceptions registered in the amygdala according to the dominant affective tone. This core affective might influence not only how perceptions were registered, but which perceptions were received. "Projections from the amygdala to sensory processing areas may allow the amygdala's appraisal of danger to influence ongoing perceptions of the environment" (LeDoux, 1995, p. 225).

The patient covered her eyes with her hands and turned away. I said,

Therapist: You seem almost afraid, as I were one of those people who were quietly whispering, "Poor JoAnne."
Patient: Well aren't you?
Therapist: No. I'm thinking how hard it must be to think clearly when there is all this internal "noise" confusing you with what other people may or may not be feeling.

Because affect orients the individual for behavior, one can witness someone else's affect, and perhaps, have some idea what part of the brain the affect is coming from. The central nervous system goes public, so to speak, through affect. The data supporting this theory (see Kandel, 1983; Kupfermann,

1981b; LeDoux, 1995; Schwartz, 1987; van der Kolk, 1996b)
cannot be proven in a clinical evaluation. But clinical data can
be observed, and from this one can hypothesize central nervous
system input, or more importantly in the clinical setting, have
a better sense of the quality and neurophysiological level of
the affect and thus those situations where words and symbolic
communication are likely to be heard and those situations
where actions are more likely to be needed. Having a clinical
hypothesis as to what level of the central nervous system one
is "talking to," gives one a better chance of communicating in
a way that will be effective. By observing affect and having a
sense of the level of its psychological and neurophysiological
integration, one can make hypotheses as to what is likely to
happen under specific conditions and in response to specific
interventions. One can hypothesize how best to communicate.
One can in this way anticipate whether one needs to address
issues of meaning and logic, support and safety, or boundaries
and limit setting; and then one can observe the results of these
interventions.

Thus with the patient, Grace, one could hypothesize that
she had entered the session feeling needy and vulnerable—the
difficulty of separation from her parents, from her doctor, the
incident with the nurse all contributed data to support this
hypothesis. One could empathize with her feeling humbled by
being interviewed by a therapist who was about her age when
she herself had once studied to be a medical technician. She
quickly tried to establish a bond with the therapist. He was
courteous and available, but undemonstrative. The patient began to react to his distance as though it were aversive and unsafe, one of several hypotheses that the therapist should have
formulated early on in the session given the patient's history
of volatility and demonstrated need for immediate assurance
and availability. This map had been available to him, but he
had not made use of it.

Defense mechanisms became evident, and were designed
to avoid the affects associated with separation. She flirted, and
when this failed, she used denial to deal with the student's
remoteness. The breakdown of these defense mechanisms and
the shift to more primitive defense mechanisms indicated a

shift to more primitive psychological and neurobiological processing. References to unresponsive caregivers began, but were ignored. As this continued, the direct experience of aversive affect (the foot shocks) increased as safety in the transference was unwittingly diminished. The conditioned learning came back quickly. More and more primitive affect began to organize the patient's behavior and defensive structure (affects orient one's attitudes toward the environment as well as record one's responses to it).

The patient's internal, unconscious conclusion was that humiliation was inevitable. By associative learning, the patient knew on an unconscious level that given the history of her dependent needs (unconditioned stimulus), and given the therapist's detached responses (conditioned stimulus), this affective response was inevitable. Her conviction that humiliation was inevitable led to a further deterioration of reality testing and to a deterioration of the treatment alliance. A cycle had been set off beginning with a painful perception ("the therapist is not responsive to me") that led associatively to painful memories (via interconnections between the amygdala, the hippocampus, and the neocortex), leading to increased vigilance (via projections from the amygdala to sensory processing areas). This in turn led to increased lower-order pathway dominance as the affect of fear and the anticipation of pain began to influence external reality (and perception). A cycle had thus begun where input to the amygdala via thalamo-amygdala projections had primed communication between the neocortex, hippocampus, and the lower-order pathways such that all higher level processing was performed in the context of extreme fear and arousal. Reality testing was failing because all systems had been biologically prepared for a danger that was more internal and past than external and present. "It is highly likely that the amygdaloid complex has a tonic influence on behavior. One possibility is that the amygdala is influential in setting the emotional set point, or mood, of the organism" (Amaral et al., 1992, p. 56). If the set point was fear, then responses would be quick with little time for cognition or reflection as to the context of the interaction.

The patient was unable to integrate, for example, that this was a first meeting with a therapist who was clinically inexperienced. This was not information unavailable to her, rather it was information that she was unable to use. She could not think her way through to any conclusions other than those that had been made for her by her affect. She could not get to the thought that some of his remoteness reflected on his inexperience and defensiveness and not on her. Instead, new defense mechanisms were mobilized to remove a painful affect rather than to think about it.

The new defense mechanisms included: denial of dependency, devaluation of the object, projection of contempt—allowing for the total reconstruction of the encounter and the generation of a "new" object relation under the activation of a new affect: rage. Nor was this change thought through; indeed thought had been preempted. By the end of the interview she was furious with the therapist who, she was convinced, felt nothing but contempt for her.

Rage, now activated by her transformed view of herself and of the student, organized her thinking and mobilized her behavior; rage was in her voice, in her face, in her posture; it was evident in her expressions (as Darwin and Freud would have predicted). This affect reorganized her view of the interpersonal environment, and changed what she offered to it. Because this rage was defensive (trying to frighten away the bear in the zoo), it further clouded her reality testing and made it that much more difficult for her to think about the validity of the underlying emotion, her fear of abandonment. The original experience of dependency and the expectation of shame (which was to a degree generated by the therapist's passivity), were defended against by the total reworking of the encounter and the activation of a new affect in a new object relation. What is crucial to recognize is that this reorganization was done below the level of thought at the level of affect and instinct. It was this new affect that generated a new perspective, a new relationship to the object, supported by yet another defense mechanism, splitting. It was not thought that led to a new appraisal, it was new affect that demanded a new perspective.

If this pattern endured, that is, if data emerged demonstrating that this behavior was structured in the patient's life, then one would formulate another hypothesis, namely, that the patient had become so sensitized to the experience of pain in dependent relationships (mother, father, doctor) that she approached every relationship of this type (or indeed every relationship) with the expectation of pain. At a certain point this expectation would become so certain that rather than openly approach new situations she would actively shape the situation to fit the anticipated results based on a very limited range of affect, and thus more often than not, she would create the outcome she most dreaded. In the context of primitive affect, the outcome is more often the result of limited internal options rather than a response to limited external options.

This reaction can be compared interestingly to an animal model. In 1985 Mitchell, Osbourne, and O'Boyle found that the response of mice to novel situations depended on antecedent exposure to stress. Those mice that had not been previously exposed to high stress reacted with curiosity and investigated novel situations. Under normal conditions, given a choice a mouse would choose the most pleasant option, regardless of whether it was novel or familiar. But a mouse that had been highly stressed avoided novelty and returned to the familiar. What Mitchell and his colleagues discovered was "that mice that had been locked in a box in which they were exposed to electric shocks, and then released, returned to those boxes when they were subsequently stressed" (Mitchell, Osbourne, & O'Boyle, 1985, pp. 212–217). The mice were unable to realize that there was a new path that offered a way out.

The refusal to explore the novel may be a factor in the object relations of those who, like Grace, have had to function with intense, primitive affect dominated by lower-level processing of perception. Choices seem to be organized around an array of very intense but limited affects. What tends to be lacking are creative, novel explorations in the interpersonal context. Indeed it is as if the person, like the mice in Mitchell et al.'s experiments, had some internal set or memory to which it felt compelled to return. This appraisal seems to be influenced hardly at all by subsequent experience, as if removed from the influence of learning or new conditioning. In psychoanalysis this has been described as the compulsion to repeat, but perhaps what is being expressed is not so much the compulsion to repeat as the lack of awareness that choice is available because of the way affects are remembered and stored. Because affects are organized at different neurobiological levels, the memories, instincts, associations available at one level may not be available at another. Making a bad choice may reflect the fact that alternatives may not have been known, or were known but at a different neurobiological level of integration from where decisions were being made.

When integration of these factors occur at neocortical levels, it is generally external influences (reality testing, memory, and perception) that determine the affect. But when integration is below the level of the neocortex affect imposes. Primitive affect is less an experience of the external than an immediate reaction to a sense of danger. Whether due to operant conditioning, systemic illness, genetic transmission, or external crisis, primitive affect delivers its perspective of and on the world without waiting for confirmation. Boundaries are broken down at least in part because once begun the intensity of the internal reaction—autonomic, endocrine, behavioral, cognitive—demands that something momentous must be going on externally. If one's heart is racing, one is breathing hard, the eyes are vigilant, then something must be happening. Seen in this way the loss of boundaries so often described in clinical situations with primitive patients does not occur because the boundary between self and other is collapsing into the self, but rather because the boundary like a net is being thrown out over the object. When someone discovers that, "My heart is racing, and thus I must be frightened, which must be because you are there in front of me; you must be dangerous; and thus I will watch you like a hawk, question your every move, and in the process make you worry about me until you become afraid of me, vigilant yourself, and soon when your heart begins to quicken, then will my boundary have included you." It is not a merger so much as an annexation of external space and freedom by affect.

To undo the effects of ongoing and well-established primitive affect is not easy. It requires patience; it often requires medication; it requires the establishment of safety; it requires neocortical intervention.

In a series of experiments done by LeDoux, Romanski, and Xagoraris (1989), it was demonstrated that rats were resistant to unlearning (extinction) of conditioned fear responses and that the resistance was all but absolute when lesions have been made to the neocortex. When the neocortical influence was eliminated, patterns of response learned through the thalamo-amygdala projections persisted even when the situation was changed making such behavior unreasonable. "Emotional memories established in the absence of the sensory cortex, probably by way of the thalamo-amygdala projection are relatively indelible" (p. 241). The rats refused to unlearn. The importance of this is tremendous. For one it adds data in support of the observation first made by Pavlov in his original experiments that primitively encoded memories persist in an inactive but indelible state waiting only to be rearoused (1927). And secondly, it established that neocortical influence is essential to prevent subneocortically encoded learning and memory from operating. Subneocortical extinction is not so much a matter of a memory wearing away as it is synaptic suppression by descending neocortical pathways. And thus, memories that persist do so for at least one of the following reasons: a lower order pathway has been established with amygdaloid dominance; or a higher order pathway (especially from the ventromedial prefrontal cortex [Rogan & LeDoux, 1996]) has been weakened. The former may account for the persistence of more primitive memory, cognition, and behavior while the latter may account for the return to more primitive memory, cognition, and behavior (a neurobiological explanation of Freud's concepts of fixation and regression). For either or both reasons, lower order pathways of behavior once initiated will continue to their conclusion. There is no point where reflection or delay intervenes as these are neocortical functions. Thus the rats in Mitchell et al.'s experiment ran back to a "wired box" because they had learned such behavior under stress, and when stressed repeated what they had learned. It wasn't so much that they could not learn the new conditions; it was that under stress the old memories returned with all of their original, uninhibited force. So too Grace had to defend herself against a hapless, unresponsive young therapist because under this stress, indelible subneocortical memory was aroused indicating extreme danger. Neocortical influence (inhibition) could not be brought to bear on the process.

The following is an example of such a situation where affect was primitive, memory was absolute, freedom was minimal, and where responses were determined before they were experienced. The patient was a 33-year-architecture student who had made a suicide attempt after finishing his final exams. He had crashed a red Corvette his father had given him into a bridge pylon. The car was demolished. The patient, who was drunk at the time, walked away from the wreck unscathed. Alcoholism, cyclothymic disorder, narcissistic personality disorder, family chaos, a domineering father, and a passive, chronically intoxicated mother, were factors of this man's life and third attempt at death. The suicide attempt, which was rich with psychodynamic data and aggressive intent, had been partially explored. Medication had been begun.

The context of the session was an inpatient unit one week before the therapist was to go off service. At this point, the patient had been hospitalized for nearly a month. He entered the room ahead of the male therapist and sat down. The patient began by saying, "I have nothing to say." "What are your feelings about my leaving?" asked the therapist. "I feel like shit. That's everything, okay? Oh, I need some medication. You better get me some."

Right from the start the patient was threatening the doctor. That threat should have indicated a high level of danger, a low level of safety, and a marginal capacity for thought. Primitive affect ruled. One hypothesis was that given the stress of the doctor's upcoming departure, the more primitive brain centers were in ascendance, and processing of affect was passing more and more through subneocortical structures. The doctor asked, "You need the medication for what?" "What do you mean, For what? For my nerves. For my head. Forget what for. I need some medication. Are you going to give me some? I want an answer now!"

The patient was almost in crisis and his loss of safety and terror needed to be addressed. It should have been clear that the patient did not feel safe enough to explore meaning. The doctor responded, "You want the medication to make the feelings more tolerable?" "You didn't answer the question" said the patient.

Therapist: What are the feelings? Feeling "like shit"?
Patient: No more of that crap. I need medication and if you won't give it to me, I'm gonna create a psych emergency right here. Right now.
Therapist: You're trying to control me.
Patient: I'm sick of talking. I'm sick of therapy. I'm sick of—. Did you call Dr. Giles (his outpatient psychiatrist)? He said you hadn't returned his call. Why not?
Therapist: It's easier for you to get angry at me for not calling Dr. Giles, for not getting you some meds, than it is for you to deal with my leaving.
Patient: You've already left.
Therapist: I'm right here.
Patient: I don't care.
Therapist: Over the past 2 weeks you've been controlling your impulses and feelings. You've recognized your need to go to A.A. You've dealt with some pretty upsetting issues in family therapy. You've known that I was going to leave since the first week.
Patient: Well I'm gonna cause a scene today.
Therapist: I think you're trying to control me rather than trying to deal with your feelings about my leaving.
Patient: Is that so?
Therapist: I think it is.

The biologic background to the understanding of this material included the instability of cyclothymia and alcoholism. But the threat of abandonment had obviously added to that instability. Why? And more importantly why was the threat so intense as to generate such an extreme reaction?

The patient was expressing terror and rage. This intensity of affect had been reflected in his behavior before admission;

he had made a serious, aggressive suicide attempt. But this level
of impulsivity and terror had not been witnessed during his
hospitalization. Indeed if anything this man had displayed
nothing but quiet contempt for the hospital, his treatment, his
parents, himself. Displays of emotion had been conspicuously
absent.

But affects are not understood in isolation. They are understood in a context. Just as when a story is told there are
multiple perspectives to the hearing, so too with affect, there
are multiple loci to the experience. So when looking for affect,
one looks at the interpersonal context of the affect, one looks
into the person expressing the affect, and one looks into oneself, the person receiving the affect. One seeks as many perspectives as are available. The countertransference is obviously a
valuable source of data.

The patient made the resident feel frightened. The resident, at least for the moment, didn't know what to do. "I'm
gonna create a psych emergency," was real enough to increase
the resident's pulse and respiration, create a tightening in his
stomach—noradrenergic release from the autonomic nervous
system mediated by the amygdala, the hypothalamus, and the
pituitary. At this point the resident in his response to his "gut,"
should have acted, either by limit setting, getting help, or standing up and walking with the patient to get him some medication. It was a request that was reasonable given the patient's
internal instability and lack of safety. It could have been
granted without full exploration because the resident should
have realized from his own internal experience that construc-
tive thought had been severely compromised by primitive
affect.

The patient in response to the last intervention leaned
forward in his chair, and smiled,

Patient: Well, somebody better get me some medication
              or I'm gonna cause one hell of a scene today.
Therapist: Why are you trying to control me?

Primitive affect speaks plainly: an eye for an eye. The
boundary between self and other was extended outward,

"Since you have robbed me of my ability to control my internal calm by leaving me, I will take control of yours by taking control of you: Gimme some medicine."

Primitive affect demands immediate attention, and because of that pull, it imposes immediate reactions on the basis of immediate perception. Memory is more or less obliterated by the affect, and thus primitive affect distorts all history past and present according to the most recent perception. Relationships, most notably the doctor–patient relationship, become ahistorical. In the context of primitive affect, confidence, trust, gratitude, cannot be built because they all depend on ongoing assessment, and primitive affects reduce perspective just as noradrenalin compresses time.

Through the countertransference, the patient's intrapsychic world is discovered in oneself. And if one finds in oneself a rapid heart, increased respiration, and a fleeting sense of control, assess for one of two possibilities: There is real danger and action is required: now! Indeed, when with a patient who is not well known, this assessment may be very real, imperative, and potentially life saving.

Or if one is *very* confident that there is no immediate danger, then and only then, conclude that what is being experienced is the patient's affect and intrapsychic world (projective identification), and from that make hypotheses because at that point one has data from multiple sources. One has the data of the interpersonal: An architectural student after working with a therapist for one month is losing that therapist. It is sad because the two have worked well together. The data of the intrapsychic: An architectural student after working with a therapist for one month is losing that therapist. It is tragic because without the loving presence of the doctor, the student will die.

Empathic understanding does not come from one or the other perspective, it comes from holding both and containing the resultant tension. The tension is between affect and primitive affect, between self and primitive self, between object and primitive object, between reality and defense mechanisms, between neocortical control and subneocortical demand. By containing all of that, parallax is generated and hypotheses can be made.

Hypotheses: A patient operating with primitive affect needs a response and sometimes that response in order to be heard needs to be concrete. The dominance of primitive affect can be caused by environmental, biogenetic, traumatic, or conditioned factors. Primitive affect selectively obliterates memory; part self and part object paradigms are the currency of primitive affect with little or no recourse to history or time. Inconsistency and illogic are embedded in these object relations because a false reality is being supported. Primitive defense mechanisms are supporting the false reality.

Specific hypotheses should be formulated about each of these distortions and the specific distortions of reality testing. All the distortions begin with the psychological, traumatic, neurobiological, and genetic distortion of affect. Speculate as to the relative contributions of each. There is less intrapsychic freedom as one progresses from cognitive affect to primitive affect. Degrees of freedom determine the nature of the therapeutic alliance and reality testing. If the patient is under the control of primitive affect, then there is no real therapeutic alliance, no real freedom, and interventions must be aimed at increasing the immediate safety, and thus the therapist should have said, "I will be happy to go with you to get some medication. I think you could use some relief because of how troubled you are about my departure next week." And he should have said this as soon as he was aware that the patient was being controlled by the primitive affect of rage and was not safe (was not in neocortical control).

Safety. In order to allow for the possibility of change, the dominance of primitive affect must be reduced as much as possible. So long as one is in the domain of primitive affect, that is, affect largely mediated by the amygdala, there is little possibility for insight. So long as one is in the domain of primitive affect one is also in the domain of emotional (nondeclarative) memory. It is very difficult, perhaps impossible to "talk" over the influence of primitive affect and emotional memory. New learning does not tend to occur under such circumstances; the mouse will return to the box where it has learned it will be injured; the patient will threaten the doctor whom he has learned he needs. Instinct and action will rule; old patterns of behavior will return; inhibition will be lost.

Emotional memory, that memory that is laid down with amygdaloid predominance, is hard to extinguish. Those attachments and conditioned responses that have been made via communication from the sense organs to the thalamus and then to the amygdala with little neocortical influence tend to persist over long periods of time. Perhaps they never really extinguish. What LeDoux and others have demonstrated with animal models is that memory laid down under certain stressful conditions is encoded in subneocortical circuits and can be quieted by neocortical influence but never wholly removed. "Extinction . . . may represent a process of behavioral inhibition, regulated by the cortex, rather than a process of emotional memory erasure" (LeDoux, 1993b, p. 155). Under stress (the resident is leaving) these subneocortical, primitive patterns of memory and behavior push through cortical inhibition and return to dictate the terms of engagement even when declarative memory has in the interim shown a better way. The "better way" is lost, or more correctly cannot be assessed because primitive affect is leading cognition through lower order pathways. Primitive affect by establishing subneocortical memory overrides the neocortical. Until neocortical control can be reestablished there is little hope that primitive, emotional memory will give way to new learning. This is then a form of regression that while psychologic in its form, is biologic in its etiology, reflecting the shift to lower order pathways of affect regulation and assessment.

It is more than just intuitive that effective psychotherapy requires safety. Without safety primitive affect and emotional memory will dominate, no learning will occur because there will be little or no appreciation of new possibilities. Old choices will be made, old patterns will predominate, and appraisals of the external world will be made on the basis of projection, not just psychological projection from self to object representations in the environment but also biological projection from the amygdala to sensory processing areas in the brain creating a specific background for perception, and thus increasing the likelihood that the background will be what is perceived.

12.

Trauma and Affect

> *That was the year*
> *I started to bleed,*
> *crossing over that border in the night,*
>
> *and in Social Studies, we came at last*
> *to Auschwitz, in my ignorance*
> *I felt as if I recognized it*
> *like my father's face, the face of a guard*
> *turning away—or worse yet*
> *turning toward me. (Olds, 1980, p. 6)*
>
> *Here I stand; I can do no other.*
> *(Martin Luther)*

Trauma touches the psychological and the biological. It is in the past, the present and the future. It organizes and disorganizes. It shapes and distorts. It lies in body and soul. Trauma affects object relations, sense of self, identity, defense mechanisms, conditioned reflexes, affect, the ability to think, perception. Its influence is pervasive.

> I remember feeling this way when I was a little girl. I would wake up at night, terrified of the dark. I'd think sometimes my bed was on the ceiling, and the whole house was upside down; and if I didn't hang onto the mattress, I might fall outward into the stars. I wanted to run to my father, and have him tell me I was safe, that everything was all right. But I was always more frightened of him than I was of falling. It's the same way now. (Lawrence & Lee, 1960, p. 48)

223

This chapter specifically addresses how trauma affects the overall functioning of the individual and thus its influences on the data of the formulation. Consider the following: Cindy was a 28-year-old woman with a history of physical and sexual abuse at the hands of her father extending from when she was 2 months old—verified by a review of emergency room records with findings of frequent urinary tract infections, anal bleeding, and vaginal dilatation. She had little memory of the specifics of the abuse even though it continued into her midteens. She began to self-mutilate from the age of 4. Alcohol abuse began at 11. Drug abuse began in early adolescence. She dropped out of school after the first year of college and had been able to do little with her life ever since other than to take drugs and alcohol while supporting herself as a prostitute. Her adult relationships were mostly with other alcoholics and prostitutes, many were abusive.

The patient had been slowly recapturing some memories of the abuse inflicted on her by her father. Often these memories were followed by episodes of self-mutilation that she experienced in a numb, zombielike state of mind (the psychobiological defense mechanism of dissociation). She had just the day before hit herself until both arms had raised welts and extensive areas of discoloration. In discussing this behavior, she remembered another incident of abuse. She stopped talking and looked at the floor,

Patient: I don't like to say bad things about my father. He hit me. I must have been bad or he wouldn't have hit me. (She was silent.)
Therapist: Are you thinking about what happened?
Patient: No.
Therapist: What are you thinking? (She looked up.)
Patient: What did you say?
Therapist: Are you having any thoughts? (Another silence)
Patient: I deserved to be hit. (matter of factly)

This certainly was evidence of severe superego pathology (guilt that her incestuous longings for her father had been met) that prevented her from seeing alternative views of what had been happening (denial). But the psychological explanation in the context of severe abuse is rarely if ever sufficient, and therefore making this conscious to the patient is usually ineffective at best, and at times destructive.

Several sessions later, she recalled how she used to cut her legs, thighs, and abdomen, smearing blood on herself to prevent her father's advances. In that same session she told how she used to obsessively play a game whereby she had to "keep a rod separate from a circle" indicating the motion of a rod and circle with her fingers. When asked how she understood the game of the rod and circle, this woman of above average intelligence replied, "I don't know." "Are you sure?" the therapist asked. "Yes. I don't know."

One might ask how is it possible that this woman who had suffered sexual abuse from the age of less than one year could not know the meaning of this "game"? Is she concealing? Is she so concrete as to be unable to make sense of even the most basic of symbols? Or is it just too "unsafe" for her to explore meaning at all, unsafe not just from a psychological but from a biological perspective as well? If the latter is the case, which I think it is, how can it be that a thought is not just psychologically unwelcome but biologically unsafe? How does internal biological homeostasis relate to psychological safety? How does a memory threaten biology?

"The medulla oblongata is a very serious and lovely object," Freud wrote in his *Introductory Lectures on Psychoanalysis* (1916–1917). He went on, "I remember quite clearly how much time and trouble I devoted to its study many years ago. To-day, however, I must remark that I know nothing that could be of less interest to me for the psychological understanding of anxiety than a knowledge of the path of the nerves along which its excitations pass" (p. 393).

From this statement it is reasonable to say that despite (or perhaps because of) Freud's earlier work on nerve conduction and synaptic transmission, he failed to recognize the possibility of structural changes that intense, ongoing anxiety and terror might bring to the central nervous system.

What is now clear about anxiety and fear is that if it is of high enough intensity and repeated often enough, not only

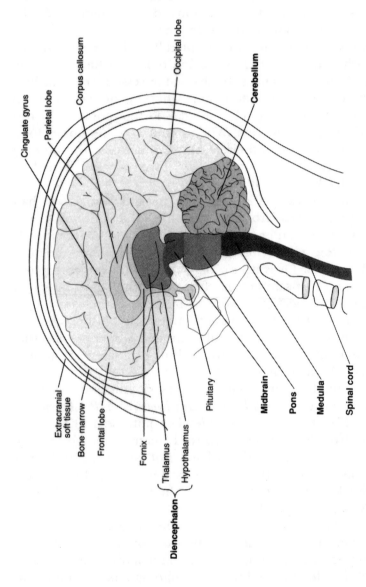

Figure 12.1. A schematic drawing showing the relative positions of the medulla oblongata and pons. (From: Kandel, Schwartz, & Jessell, 1995, p. 80)

will there be acute biological changes when danger is present, but that specific structural changes in synaptic connections will develop in the brain—perhaps not in the medulla oblongata, but in the amygdala, the pons, and other lower order pathways (see Kandel, 1983; Krystal, 1984; LeDoux, 1996; van der Kolk, 1996c). The answer then to how does a memory affect biological homeostasis has to do with the fact that once underlying structural changes in the brain are brought about by trauma, they are enduring. They influence not just the reaction of danger and to the memory of trauma, but have a more or less permanent impact on thought and function in general.

In recounting another episode of her history, Cindy described how the family dog had once urinated on the floor and barking all night had awoken her father from sleep. He dragged his daughter from her bed and beat her. He then smeared her face in the dog's urine. After hearing this, the therapist asked for her reaction. Cindy said, "I deserved it. It was my dog." Again on one level, there was evidence of severe superego and ego pathology with massive denial. In frustration perhaps, the therapist said, "Hearing this just makes me mad at your father." The patient said nothing, stared at nothing, did nothing (dissociation). The session ended. That night Cindy cut both of her wrists with razor blades.

She had experienced no safety in the notion that she was not to blame, that there was an alternative way of looking at her history, that rage and disgust with her father were not unreasonable given his sadism and abuse. "Trauma, especially prolonged trauma at the hands of people upon whom one depends for nurture and safety, can significantly shape one's ways of organizing one's internal schemes and ways of coping with external reality" (van der Kolk, Hoestetler, Herron, & Fisler, 1994, p. 719)

There was no freedom, no capacity to explore new ideas, no capacity to "play" on any level, no capacity even to examine her notion of safety. The danger was primitive and biological. Putting it into words just made it more dangerous. Telling her that she could discuss her memories about her father made her feel more unsafe because it showed her that the therapist was not sensitive to the level of danger that she was experiencing—both psychologically and biologically. It showed her that she was alone with her father and her aberrant psychobiology. But if language and understanding sometimes make things worse by resubjecting the patient to the terrifying affects, how does one integrate the data of trauma into psychotherapy? How does one proceed when each step seems to make matters worse? The answer must be that such data need to be integrated into a formulation that may or may not recommend exploratory therapy with its emphasis on verbalization of meaning. Because if the purpose of psychotherapy is to make the unconscious conscious, then there is ample evidence to support the claim that some thoughts are best left unthought—or at a level below verbal, symbolic awareness. There is the danger that these thoughts once on the surface of consciousness will take over consciousness.

Cindy's evaluation continued the day after she had cut herself. She entered and stated rather matter of factly, "Last night I just wanted to hurt myself."

Therapist:	Do you know why?
Patient:	It was just a feeling I had. I felt like—(She stopped talking.)
Therapist:	Cindy? (She did not answer, just looked around the room. Seemed to drift off—again a dissociative reaction). What are you thinking?
Patient:	It made me relax to cut myself. I knew that if I saw my blood I would feel at peace. It's like an activity that relaxes me. When I cut myself I don't feel anything. The last time I was admitted to South Orange Hospital, I had a razor hidden in my purse. They took my purse. And when they gave it back, the razor was still there. There was nothing else I could do. They left me with one razor and one thought.
Therapist:	Which was?

Cindy stared straight ahead at the white wall that may have been playing a memory, as if she were seeing, as in a movie, what it was that she had done (the highly visual and powerful memory of the amygdala called eidetic memory). Cindy finally looked at the therapist,

Patient: When I came out of the bathroom all cut up, the psychiatrist said she'd admit me this one time, but never again. I was sent back to the E.R. They stitched me without novocain. I was crying. The surgeon kept sewing. He must've thought, "This'll teach her a lesson."

Therapist: What lesson?

Patient: I don't know. (She looked at the wall, at nothing, or perhaps she was seeing the memory again.)

Therapist: What are you feeling now?

Patient: Guilty.

Therapist: Why?

Patient: Because I'm not feeling anything and I know you want me to feel something.

Therapist: Do you feel you're disappointing me?

Patient: No. I don't feel anything about you.

She pulled her knees to her chest and just stared. Not in sadness but in emptiness. It was a blank stare.

What are the data? The patient has a horrific history of abuse. Significant ongoing physical or sexual abuse is, from a psychobiological perspective, more damaging than acute trauma. Specific biological abnormalities are frequently found as a result of ongoing trauma, including changes in adrenocorticotrophic hormone, cortisol, and noradrenaline, and central nervous system changes affecting the locus coeruleus, postsynaptic supersensitivity to noradrenaline, and changes of the function of the amygdala and the function and volume of the hippocampus (Bremner et al., 1995). These biological changes affect psychological function in ways that go beyond the memory of the abuse.

When the issues of blame and reaction to blame were approached by the therapist, the patient responded by becoming unresponsive (dissociation), and then by cutting herself the same night (acting out as a psychobiological mechanism to

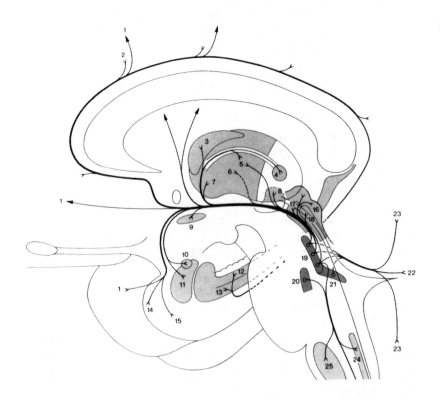

Figure 12.2. The locus coeruleus (blue spot) is the dominant source of noradrenaline in the central nervous system. When it is depleted due to ongoing trauma, post-synaptic supersensitivity results. In such a state, there are heightened biological reactions to the neurotransmitter. This diagram shows the extensive connections from the locus coeruleus to other parts of the CNS. (From: Nieuwenhuys, Voogd, & van Huijzen, 1981, p. 228)

restore internal homeostasis). Her affective responses were either nonexistent or overwhelming. It was as if there were an on–off switch to emotion: nothing or flooding. Impulsivity in the face of overwhelming affect was high (a possible supersensitivity response). Asking this patient to explain her behavior, asking her "why?" led to blank stares or verbal responses that contained blatant internal contradictions that the patient accepted unambivalently. In response to the gentle confrontation, "Don't you think it might be reasonable to be angry with your father given what he did to you?" The patient responded, "No. He was my father," which left the therapist with nowhere to go because the patient was saying that she was not safe questioning the illogical, unstable basis of her stability.

Is it meaningful then to discuss transference, defense mechanisms, countertransference, object relations in this context? Yes, but the discussion must be framed not just in the psychological response to trauma and safety but also within the biological response to trauma and safety. Therefore the formulation must address issues of biologic safety first and foremost. "The first task of recovery is to establish the survivor's safety. This task takes precedence over all others, for no other therapeutic work can possibly succeed if safety has not been adequately secured. No other therapeutic work should be attempted until a reasonable degree of safety has been achieved" (Herman, 1992, pp. 159–160).

Whenever there has been significant ongoing trauma and evidence of significant structured, character change consistent with trauma (posttraumatic stress disorder [PTSD], complex PTSD, dissociative disorder, multiple personality disorder, some forms of borderline personality disorder), the evaluation and formulation must focus on safety. All other psychodynamic interventions must wait—sometimes years, sometimes forever—until safety can be formulated, defined, established. Where there is no safety, there is no meaningful communication. When communication itself is the danger, then the establishment of safety is indeed very hard. Psychotherapy fails, frustration becomes acute, sutures are made without anesthesia.

What was safe for this woman? What does it mean when someone honestly says, "I knew that if I saw my blood I would feel at peace"? The data of trauma, including self-inflicted trauma, may have interpersonal and intrapsychic meaning but they may also be overwhelmed by the biologic, and if this is evident, then it is the biologic that must be addressed before the interpersonal or the intrapsychic. What this woman was probably doing by dissociating had to do with something like this: "I know that if I talk to you about my father, it will bring back memories which will bring affects that I cannot control because they set off a chain reaction that once begun works at a level I can't control. They run a course and I am dragged along like a fallen rider, my foot caught in the stirrup." This form of reaction to "insight" is not infrequent when there are attempts to apply meaning to experience before safety has been established.

The patient was telling us then that certain thoughts, memories, experiences set off biologic reactions that are self-sustained. Once begun the only way to stop them was to flood them—with drugs, alcohol, sex, terror, pain, rage. These biologic reactions don't respond at the symbolic or verbal level because these are at the level of the neocortex and thus do not directly touch where the problem lies. These states respond at an affective–experiential level. Because these memories are state dependent, words, by recreating the story that recreates the emotional state in which the memories were laid down, can be extremely dangerous. This is because words, which provide one way of gaining access to memory, can start the process off by initiating an emotion, but then offer no way to control the emotion. So the patient dissociates (self-mutilates and acts out) in an attempt to remove herself from the assault of words (the stimuli to memory).

Psychotherapy can in this situation go to the core of what is unsafe, and the invitation, "Tell me what you are thinking," can be threatening, even toxic because it misses an essential point. The tyranny that was once external and interpersonal (terror of an abusive father) has been replaced by a tyranny that is internal and synaptic (state dependent supersensitivity to certain neurotransmitters, especially noradrenalin). The former tyranny was etiologic to the latter but once established the biological reaction functions independently from "real" danger. So how does one gather the data of trauma and integrate it into a formulation?

This is an example from another patient who was not as damaged as Cindy.

Patient: I had an eating "problem" when I was younger. Then a real disorder when I got to be 14.

Therapist: Tell me a little about that.

Patient: I felt I was overweight. Other things were going on. Hard to put them all together.

Therapist: What do you feel now?

Patient: Hopeless. I feel "hopeless" is as good as I'm ever gonna get.

Therapist: What are the things that keep you from recovery?

Patient: I wish I knew. Nausea mostly. . . . Things are unsettled at home. I don't want to go into that. But—some decisions I need to make back home. I can't make them here. A lot's going on. I don't know . . . I have all these other problems that need to be worked out, but they can't be worked on here. I have dissociations. Flashbacks. Things like that.

Therapist: Like what?

Patient: I don't want to get into it. Problems at home. When I was younger. Remembering things that I don't want to remember.

Therapist: Do you feel more hopeless now?

Patient: I think these things were inevitable. They were always bothering me. Things—I didn't know what. Now I know.

Eating disorder, flashbacks, dissociative symptoms, "remembering things I don't want to remember," a sense that things are inevitable—all of these taken together begin to suggest (but do not prove) the possibility of biological, structural pathology in the locus coeruleus and other subneocortical structures of the brain, and a possible history of abuse. Possible.

When the patient said, "I have all these other problems that need to be worked out, but they can't be worked on here," she may indeed have been accurate, that until she felt more safe, those issues would have to wait. The task of the evaluation, having identified these issues, would be to proceed slowly and cautiously and to establish safety. One would not want to begin addressing areas of abuse until both the therapist and the patient had some sense that the patient felt safe. One would predict then that if one were moving too quickly in the history (provoking memory), or in the transference (either provoking memory or affect), the patient's condition would deteriorate—evidenced by acting out behavior, dissociative symptoms, withdrawal. The therapist's frustrated, "How can you do this to yourself?" should be an indication to the therapist that he was moving too quickly to establish a coherent past when the patient was still unrooted in the present.

One must go slowly then in dealing with traumatic history because in that context, memory, and particularly state dependent memory, can come back with awesome biological force. An example of the return of such memory is taken from the work of Joyce Carol Oates (1991):

> Kathleen was never to see her father again but she remembered him vividly for years: at night in her assigned bed . . . waking suddenly to see that swollen face descending upon her, the pop eyes, the wormy veins in the forehead, the fists bearing down upon her like horses's hooves—"Where is she? your mother? filthy lying cunt of a mother"—and Kathleen smelled whiskey and puke catching her father's blows full in her face and in the soft cringing parts of her body unprotected inside her pajamas, like a baby she tried to crawl down beneath the covers to escape, burrowing headfirst beneath the covers but that only made Daddy madder, resisting only made him madder, Mommy had said "You'll learn: better now than later" but still Kathleen tried to escape and Daddy yanked her back by her legs almost lifting her he was so strong . . . crying now knowing not to expect mercy from those hands—. (pp. 20–21)

While this may be a work of fiction, it is a reasonable approximation of fact. Indeed a patient with a history of suicidal behavior, intense emotional lability, alcoholism, and who had suffered through years of child abuse, when asked more specifically about her past, came the following session and presented Oates' book with the comment, "Read this. Then you'll know about my past." Ironically the patient's name was also Kathleen.

Affect connects self to object offering the possibility of safety. Primitive affect leads like a fire to whatever burns. There is little or no safety in the connection when the bond is made by primitive affect because there is little internal control.

Where there has been abuse, what should one expect in the transference, the object relations, the defense mechanisms, the countertransference? How do abuse and primitive affect distort the data of interpersonal communication and safety? Stone writes, "Although even a solitary episode may have a lasting effect, episodic or continuous incest is especially likely to engender lasting problems with impulsivity, guilt, sense of betrayal, simultaneous adoration and vilification of the abusing relative, and craving for revenge" (1991, p. 193). All of these should be expected in the therapeutic context.

The following example is taken from a session with a woman who had suffered from many years of child abuse and from dissociative identity disorder (multiple personality disorder). After a long phase of desensitization and stabilization that made use of medication, relaxation techniques, and hypnosis, she was able to benefit from more traditional, verbal psychotherapy. At this point in the treatment she was able to describe the distortions, without falling prey and losing control to the psychobiologically triggered affect that earlier had tyrannized her life, the way her father had once done.

She entered and sat down opposite me. She didn't speak for a moment. "There is this Emily Dickinson poem I read, years ago. It described a woman standing outside of someone's home and looking through the window into this house." She looked at me, observed me for a few seconds, then went on,

There was a table with chairs all around, set for dinner. A wonderful table with candles, food, everything you could possibly want. It was like Christmas inside, but I was outside, cold. That's how I feel

when I come in here and look at you. It's like seeing something I
want, through a window.

   The data included data of transference and defense mechanisms. There was primitive idealization of the object (transference); devaluation of the self with intense longing (envy) as
the affective bridge. Despite the distance she described, I felt
very close and protective toward her—rescue fantasies as part
of the countertransference and up to a point as part of the
necessary, real environment of safety. The treatment requires
that one is ready to take heroic measures, and at the same time
not violate boundaries which the patient will invite you to cross.
Gabbard's statement, "The patient's demands for reassurance
that one really cares and is not simply a prostitute who receives
a fee in return for time and attention may lead therapists to
go to extreme lengths to demonstrate their sincere concern"
(1994, p. 132), is not a statement about sincere concern, but
about the dangers of boundary violations when working with
the abused. In order to be reassured that her feelings are valid
and safe, the victim of abuse demands that her feelings be
replicated in the caregiver. The patient doesn't so much collapse into you as she will attempt to pull you into her (the
boundary does not collapse; it is pushed outwards).
   The patient went on, "I never felt I belonged anywhere
or to anyone except to him, except to my father. Never. He
made me feel like an object, a thing. Like I was his. That I
belonged to him." "Like a table or a chair?"

> Exactly. I felt like he could do anything to me. I was just his. I
> tried to fight that feeling. I did everything I could to feel separate.
> I pretended that I wasn't part of the family. That I didn't belong
> there. I invented a new family that I belonged to. I was just waiting
> for my new family to come and take me away. I knew that I didn't
> belong, that I was different because I saw that they were all stained
> and tainted by my father, in the same way that I'd been stained
> and tainted by my father. But no matter how I tried, it always came
> back. That feeling. That I belonged to him. I was, like you said,
> his chair.

She looked around the room as if she were remembering something very clearly (possible eidetic memory). She went on,

When I think about him, it's as if it's happening all over, the same smells, the layout of the room, the color of the walls, I can even smell the tobacco on his hands and the alcohol on his breath. And I can see his mouth turning all tight with anger. It all comes back so clear.

Boundaries, state dependent memory, self and object, primitive affect; the invasion of the self by the object. The once and still valued object's physical possession of and use of the self in any way that it wanted. Because a valued and needed object was simultaneously an abusive and dangerous object, going to that object for relief and soothing was not, could not be, abandoned.

Because the sexual abuse may offer some degree of pleasure and comfort even at the price of humiliation and helplessness, a facet of the abusive relationship is not infrequently maintained by the victim. It is as if the attempt to maintain some form of tenderness and normality is supported within the realm of the perverse and sadistic. This "bargain" requires more and more primitive defense mechanisms in order for the girl to cope with her intense ambivalence and terror. Dissociation, denial, primitive idealization, projective identification, splitting are all common sequelae leading to the further destruction of healthy self and object relations.

With the corruption of internal self and object representations and of healthy boundaries, it is tragically easy for the abuser to project guilt and the sense of responsibility into the child.

My father came into my room one night and took away all of my dolls. The next morning he came back and said that I could have my dolls back if I would have sex with him. I missed my dolls. I loved them. So I agreed to have sex with him. I bargained my sex for a doll. I'm so disgusting. I'll never forgive myself for that.

Self-esteem is lost, leaving the patient feeling that she should be punished for her moral depravity. I said,

It wasn't as if there was a bargain for you to make. He was going to do what he wanted with you whether you said yes or no. Offering the dolls was his way of making you feel like what was happening was your doing. It wasn't your doing at all. It was his.

Because the object is ultimately so unpredictable and dangerous, there is the corruption of the capacity to receive comfort from any human relationship, which leads to the further corruption of affect, and to the further corruption of safety. "I was afraid to go out. I was afraid to go to school. The only place I felt safe was alone in my room. Because it was the only place where I felt in control of anything."

Where affect is controlled by a needed, sadistic tyrant then control of affect is lost. The only response is to try to establish absolute control over whatever is left. Sometimes this means control over a more and more limited world rather than risk venturing out into a physically and biologically dangerous universe. Outward curiosity is restricted or destroyed.

> Sometimes I can't stand to go out. It makes the past more present. The crowds frighten me when I've been bombarded by memories. And the open spaces frighten me (the association of agoraphobia, panic attacks, and child abuse). I want to be in a small, closed space—that makes me feel safer. And being surrounded by things that I know. I like to have the closet door open so I can see my clothes. Does that make any sense to you?

She asked me and I answered, "That having lived with the terrifying unpredictability of your father's cruelty and rage, you want order and dependability? Yes that makes sense to me."

The clarification of the patient's chaos. The goal of safety is not to interpret conflict but to clarify chaos. When the patient can safely describe her abuse, it is important to give meaning to her reactions and to her defenses. Or to allow her to discover her own meaning, "That's why I sometimes don't want to leave my apartment. I feel safe there. That's why I don't want to leave here sometimes. I feel safe here."

Safety comes under extreme threat in any and all situations where affective links have been refashioned by abuse. One can predict that in this context, the establishment of connection in the doctor–patient relationship can be traumatic, and may very well lead to increased dissociation and acting out behavior as an attempt to destroy the threat of connection. It is as if the patient is saying that connection on any level is dangerous because it reestablishes the bond of a primitive unpredictable affect.

> One of the most consistent features in the transference dominated by the acting out of severe hatred is the patient's intense involvement with the therapist, the extraordinary dependence manifest simultaneously with the aggression to the therapist, an impressive demonstration of the "fixation to the trauma." . . . The total situation illustrates the intimate link between the persecutor and the persecuted, master and slave, sadist and masochist. (Kernberg, 1991, pp. 227–228)

The transference becomes fraught with contradictions that one should anticipate when trauma is suspected. The patient will vacillate from hollow detachment (reflecting dissociation), to paranoid withdrawal or rage (projection), to intense dependency (primitive idealization), shifts derived from both biological as well as psychological distortions of affect and thought. In some ways the idealized transference is easier to work with because the patient may see you as a safe object who can help her deal with past trauma. Up to a point this may be the case, and because this is how one feels about oneself and what one is offering the patient, it is easy to agree that this represents the "truth." But it represents only a *part* of the truth.

One should approach these treatments with the hypothesis that all of these transference paradigms, including the idealized transference, are distortions, and that they all reflect the patient's basic lack of safety, and not some newfound haven in the treatment. The rapid establishment of safety in the transference via primitive idealization is just that, primitive idealization. Safety takes time to establish, and in the context of child abuse, it may take a very long time. The idealized transference should be used if it is there but used cautiously because it too is unreliable at its core; it aggressively demands the therapist's near perfect empathy, availability, and compassion. When those fail in any way, as they must, safety fails.

The hypothesis must be made that even when primitive idealization is nourishing a positive transference, the underlying affect is terror, and that the goal of the treatment still remains the creation of a safe, inner place. The danger is that the therapist assumes (countertransference) that the patient's proclamations of comfort in the object relation are real. One starts to believe that one is as good and valued as the patient says, and that the patient really is as lucky to have found you as she says she is. You then proceed as if real safety had been established, gathering more and more history as you anticipate a direct path to real intimacy, gratitude, object constancy. Then you react with a certain amount of surprise and wounded pride when the patient acts out sadomasochistically.

The telling of the story of trauma is dangerous. ("The discontinuous 'form' of oral testimony often duplicates the disjunctions of the . . . experience itself, thus exposing the witness once more to the status of victim through the very process of overcoming it via narration" [Langer, 1991, p. 104].) It is dangerous for two basic reasons: First, telling touches violent memory which touches primitive affect (state dependent memory). Second, the telling reestablishes primitive object relations where the object is primitively idealized and the self is massively devalued. The therapist is so idealized that the patient is reduced to an object to be used. A sadomasochistic object tie is established. Connection undermines safety. Or in this woman's history, connections were destroyed in order to stay alive and remain safe. She related how,

> Sometimes I felt like God. I made up elements in my head when I was a child. I made them up and then they came to life (dissociative identity disorder). Just like God. And like God I felt frustrated with what I had made because there they were, running around doing what they wanted to do and all I could do was watch them.

Grandiosity, primitive idealization, but now with the self as God and the objects, parts of the self, dissociated and "free," no longer controlled by some external object, nor by an internal executive self. Freedom came from severing the connection to the external object by severing the affect.

Patient: I remember when I was in college, the first time I ever told anyone what had been done to me, a psychiatrist, I told him about what my father had done, had been doing. I had to get to the point where I didn't care about myself. I had to make myself the same as what he had done to me. So I didn't care, at all. . . . About anything. I had to get myself. . . .

Therapist: Drunk?

Patient: Yes. Drunk. I got so drunk I couldn't stand and then just whatever happened happened, didn't matter. Because I didn't matter. I had to get there, like that, before I could talk. It had to be that everything was the same, inside, outside, past, present. I had to be what I had remembered. And when I felt that what I had done was the same as what he had done, I could talk. When I didn't matter.

It was as if in order to access the historical, declarative memory of her childhood, she had to first go through the emotional memories and behaviors that had framed it and that took over whenever the memories of the one recalled the memories of the other. Another way of stating this is that declarative memories were being recalled without having first established the safety necessary for emotional memory and in consequence the corrupt attachment behaviors of childhood incest were being repeated.

> In a process that may be somewhat analogous to the learning of motor skills, people proceed in later life to enact attachments in accordance with the "rules" or prototypes they have extracted based on their prior experience. If this early attachment experience contained aberrations, they will proceed to extract aberrant rules and generalizations, and they will enact them later without being able to have conscious knowledge of why they do so. (Amini et al., 1996, p. 230)

When this patient was asked why she did what she did, her response was "Because I had to," which was the psychological and biological truth that she was victim to.

Trauma affects all psychodynamic data because it pollutes the interpersonal and biological foundation of safety. Attachment behavior, that which is biologically so primitive and basic, becomes biologically and psychologically unstable. The consequences are far reaching. There is no longer such a thing as pleasure; there is only freedom from pain. "A good deal of pleasure . . . is exploratory, expectant of novelty, stimulus seeking, often linked to a variety of specific sensations, and it is organizing in its functions. . . . There is pleasure not only in finding relief from tension but pleasure in finding and making new insights."

But when creative explorations consistently lead to terror, then there are massive shifts in outlook, massive impediments to curiosity. Pleasure is no longer sought; the absence of pain becomes the principal motivating force when motivation has been corrupted. "Piaget . . . considered assimilation to be the 'basic fact of life.' The motive of cognitive assimilation refers to the biological propensity to process information, to structuralize such information according to what is familiar, and, more broadly, to seek out novelty" (Emde, 1991, pp. 35–36).

This "biological propensity" to understand and assimilate one's environment, is then to a greater or lesser degree crippled by abuse. The child's researches are brought to a premature end. Curiosity, linked as it is to affect and the "expectation of pleasure," is severely curtailed, and the will to explore and make sense of the new is lost. Little or no cognitive exploration will occur until such exploration has once again been made safe.

This leads to new distortions: As the child is less able to explore and assimilate, he or she has less information available to compare, to contrast, to work or play with. Over time there is less rather than more data to offset the distortions that have already been laid down. Thus Cindy was unable to explain the "game" of the rod and the circle that she had been playing not because she wasn't smart, but because all research and curiosity had been drastically foreshortened by the expectation of painful and frightening affect.

As with all other psychological domains, cognitive assimilation operates according to the principles of regulation. Affects are central mediators in this regulatory activity. . . . If the environmental event is mildly or moderately discrepant from what is known, it is experienced as interesting; if it is extremely discrepant, it is experienced as frightening. (Emde, 1991, pp. 36–37)

What one is able to understand is narrowed. When presented with information that one should be able to assimilate, the victim of abuse is overwhelmed and frightened. Life then is lived within a very narrowed range and according to specific distortions.

The limited range within which a patient of abuse is able to safely operate creates consequent deficits. The transference of the abuse victim reflects this deficit state. Very often the patient will present a situation that is emotionally confusing, and like the Auschwitz survivor quoted at the outset, the abused patient will know that there was a truth somewhere in what she was experiencing, but she will be unable to locate or articulate that truth. In such circumstances, the therapist must be active in helping the patient deal with those deficits and in locating emotional truth from the mass of ambivalently presented material. "You weren't having sex to get your dolls back. You were having sex because you were forced to have sex," is such a clarification that can be made once safety has been established.

The hypothesis that emerges is that in the treatment of patients who have been abused, the patient will not only rely on the therapist for emotional clarification, but that she will *need* to rely on the therapist to clarify things for her. If clarification is not offered, the patient herself will be unable to find a way through and will become more confused. There is not just a conflict that opposes understanding as in the more traditional psychodynamic model; in abuse victims, there is deficit. One should expect the patient to depend on you absolutely because she has real deficits, and then to hate you with passion because she has limited safety.

Because the patient of abuse comes to the therapist needing direct help and clarification, one feels (countertransference) that the patient *really* needs one's direct help to save her. This is both true and untrue; that complexity should be underscored. The patient will really need the therapist to save her, and this fact is fraught with danger because the patient's real need does not change the fact that the patient is still conflicted. Both despite and because of the need, the patient will have to act, either through sadomasochistic seduction or defensive rage, as an expression of that conflict. When these behaviors happen in the transference, the therapist should not be surprised, flattered, or annoyed. These behaviors should be anticipated. "Basically, what the patient is enacting is an object relationship between persecutor and victim, with alternating identifications with these roles while projecting the reciprocal role onto the therapist" (Kernberg, 1991, p. 228).

The fact of deficit and direct need in the abused patient does not eliminate conflict or the need to "slap the hand that feeds." Knowing that trauma has occurred one can predict the interpersonal sequelae of these distortions. Or by identifying the sequelae, one can hypothesize antecedent trauma. In either case, having identified trauma or the consequent corruption of attachment behavior, one can predict at least some of the changes and the forms that these changes will take by understanding the affective base on which attachment rests. The base in abuse is corrupt, "He used his authority as my father to get me to submit to him when he wasn't really in the role of my father."

Because of the corruption of attachment behavior, there is a distortion of the mental status, of defense mechanisms, transference, and countertransference that should be anticipated and accounted for in the formulation. Because the traumatic condition creates structural distortions at the biological level, interpersonal connections are subverted at the biological level. Formulation and intervention therefore cannot be aimed at addressing psychological conflict without first having addressed the underlying psychobiological deficit and safety. Most of these deficits have to do with the lack of control of affect, and the consequences that this brings: poor or nonexistent understanding of human motivation, restrictions to curiosity, impairment to cognition, and reliance on external factors to regulate internal forces.

An example of primitive affect's control over cognition and the consequent reliance on external factors to provide safety is demonstrated in the following exchange between a 35-year-old woman with dissociative disorder in the context of a history of child abuse, and her therapist. The patient, who had been able to attain a good level of safety with her female therapist, described what it was like to leave the therapist's office on Thursdays, her last appointment of the week.

Patient: It's awful. I just can't imagine Monday [her next appointment], that I'll ever see you again.
Therapist: What gets in the way?
Patient: That anything can happen to you. That I'm such a bad person that God would punish me by taking you away from me. That He'll take you away or that you might not want to see me anymore. My father used to tell me that no one would care about me or love me the way that he did. He said that as if his "love" was a gift or something. That I really didn't deserve his love at all. I think he said that to make me depend on him more and it went hand in hand with his warning me never to tell anyone what he'd done because then I'd really be alone. I can't believe that I'll ever be loved by anyone.

The therapist was mindful that this memory had been aroused by data from the transference.

Therapist: What you seem to envision is that I'll just "wake up" over the weekend and not want to see you anymore.
Patient: Yes. That you'll decide that you've had enough of me. That you really hate me.
Therapist: Where is that thought coming from?
Patient: It's coming from my father. From that part of my mind that's still his. I can hear his voice even now. I know it's crazy, but I want to believe him even now.

The therapist by bringing the history and the transference together was aware that it was primitive affect aroused in the transference, the expectation of loneliness, that was driving the patient's thinking by eliciting state dependent memory. It was the affect from the transference that was hypothetically touching on primitive affect and thereby limiting neocortical and hippocampal recall and reaction. "It is also possible that the early arrival of inputs from the thalamus [the therapist is going away for the weekend], might allow the amygdala to inhibit descending inputs from the cortex [she has worked with me for over a year], thereby allowing the thalamo-amygdala system to control emotional responses and establish emotional memories unchecked by descending influences from the neocortex" (LeDoux, 1992, pp. 276–277). Thus the fact that the therapist had demonstrated dedication and commitment to the patient, the neocortical influence, was lost. The stress of separation and the accompanying affect released primitive memory that had been under cortical control and so, "I can still hear his voice," was perhaps a memory not that dissimilar from the memory, "I can still smell the oatmeal." She was hearing a voice then that was not a schizophreniform reaction but a manifestation of the indelible power of primitively encoded dependent memory when released from cortical control, leading to the patient's primitive association, and overvalued idea, "I want to believe him even now. I don't know why." The therapist, well aware of the long history of abuse that the patient had suffered at the hands of her father, said,

> I don't know if you're believing his voice [history] or believing the affect that you feel when you are facing the prospect of time away from me [transference]. Because it seems to me that once you start to feel lonely [association of the father's prophecy and the affect of loneliness], the affect you feel gives his voice a "head start" over what you know, over what you have learned about me and about our relationship. [Memory from the amygdala once aroused projects to and thereby influences neocortical memory.] You are not alone. I won't suddenly turn against you. I will be here on Monday, and our work together continues and will continue [attempts to reinforce neocortical and hippocampal learning and control over subcortical memory].

The patient smiled, somewhat comforted and said,

When we talk about him, I can hear him. His voice. I think I was
6 when he first told me that. No, I was 5. When I'm lonely that's
when his voice is the strongest. It makes his statements seem true,
that I'll always be alone, that no one will ever love me.

The therapist repeated what she had said, especially reinforcing how it was the feelings that the patient was having that
were making his words seem so true. The therapist emphasized
that it was the affect that was true (she was lonely), not what
he had said (you will always be alone) to support neocortical
suppression of primitive memory. The patient added, "I get
my thoughts and my feelings confused. I can't always tell the
difference between the two."

The therapist was able to deal with the patient's loneliness
and fear, her need for clarification, and the reestablishment of
safety in the context of a dependent transference. The therapist
was as effective as she was because she understood the primitive
quality of the patient's affect and state dependent memory,
and was also aware how these would reverberate in the transference.

Therefore in the context of trauma one should hypothesize and anticipate extremes. The transference will be some
combination of dependent, flat, paranoid, erotic. Countertransference will reflect the transference with shifts from hopeless frustration and resentment to fantasies of heroic rescue.
Defense mechanisms will protect gross distortion and inconsistency. Hope and freedom will be attacked. Affect will swing
wildly.

The shift from affect to primitive affect is quickened by
trauma, and brings about a shift from relative neuropsychologi-
cal freedom to patterns of fixed responses. One can then understand Cindy's response if one understands it from the
perspective of primitive affect: "There was nothing else I could
do. They left me with one razor and one thought." She had
no freedom.

Martin Luther may have also lacked freedom when he de-
clared: "Here I stand; I can do no other." But this is another
kind of servitude from another point of reference, with input
from other parts of brain. The doctor who stitched Cindy

judged her behavior from his perspective. His choice showed that he neither understood her, nor the lack of real choice available to her. He mistook her action for freedom.

Freud understood freedom and tyranny, "I believe in external (real) chance, it is true, but not in internal (psychical) accidental events" (1901, p. 257). His sense of psychic determinism where events were driven by powerful unconscious factors in a way reflected the power of subneocortically encoded memory.

To understand freedom then, one must understand affect. One must investigate and understand where it comes from psychologically and where it comes from neurobiologically. From an understanding of where it is, where it began, how it got there, one has a better sense of where it is going, and how free it is to chose its path.

13.

Affect and Medication

One pill makes you larger
And one pill makes you small,
And the ones that mother gives you
Don't do anything at all.
(Grace Slick)

What has happened to the prognosis of
affective disorders? It has been steadily
worsening. . . . We now recognize that
some mood disorders may be quite
chronic.
(Andreasen, 1994, pp. 1405–1406)

Sometimes psychopharmacological intervention is curative, sometimes it is not, and as Grace Slick and Dr. Andreasen remarked in very different contexts, sometimes things just stay the way they are. In this brief chapter, I will address these issues of chronicity and change. The chapter will not discuss the choice of medication for a patient; reference should be made to journals and psychopharmacologic texts for this information. Rather the chapter is about the approach to a patient when psychotherapy and psychopharmacology are both indicated.

Obviously when assessing a patient, symptoms should be identified, a phenomenological diagnosis, or diagnoses, should be made, and then where indicated, psychopharmacological recommendations should be offered. Indeed every patient presented in this book was on psychoactive medication with the exception of the woman who had been actively trying to conceive. Treatment, however, does not begin or end with medication. Indeed there is an increasingly large patient population where medication alone is clearly insufficient, and, as Thase points out, "A number of studies have examined the relationship between DSM-III or DSM-III-R personality disorder and antidepressant response. . . . Although no study is definitive, the weight of the evidence indicates that depressed patients with personality disorders are less responsive to pharmacotherapy than patients with no Axis II comorbidity" (1996, pp. 292–293). And a somewhat similar comment about a different disease. "Panic disorder has extreme ramifications throughout our society beyond the health care systems. . . . 73% to 93% were symptomatic when followed for up to 20 years" (Marshall, 1997, p. 37).

One of the greatest burdens that operates is duration; the longer the symptoms persist, the more likely are they to infect multiple areas of psychological and neurobiological functioning leading to more widespread damage. And thus not surprisingly the corollary: "Antidepressant treatments are generally more effective for individuals with circumscribed episodes of depression of moderate severity" (Thase, 1996, p. 293). Where symptom reduction can be obtained it should be aggressively sought in order to prevent chronicity and to realize the broad based improvements that such measures can bring. The belief that symptoms should be left unmedicated so as not to reduce the patient's motivation for a deeper cure is now known to be wrong. "We used to believe," Cooper wrote, speaking as a psychoanalyst,

> that symptoms were surface manifestations of deep disturbance . . . and that the symptom was not the target of our ministrations. In fact we thought that too easy symptom removal would confront the patient with the task of constructing a new symptom. . . . Contrary to expectation, symptom removal, in many although not all instances, may lead to enhanced self-esteem and possibilities for new experiences and renewed characterologic growth" (1985, p. 1399)

The hope that the introduction of medication will lead to broad based improvements for patients whose symptoms have been chronic may not always be borne out. Indeed in such patients the psychobiologic, genetic, and environmental factors that initially caused specific symptoms may have gone on to effect structural change in multiple brain systems that then begin to interact and to reinforce biologically and psychologically. Thus a patient with an overly active subneocortical system may generate anticipatory fear responses in not just lower order but in neocortical and hippocampal systems as well that would then feed back to the arousal system reinforcing the initial pathology (adding agoraphobia to panic disorder). The patient might turn to drug or alcohol abuse as a means of quieting the fears. Cycles of pathology would have been established, and the patient's sense of him- or herself as frightened and dependent (dependent personality disorder, substance abuse disorder) would have been reified in behavior and in memory. So too with ongoing child abuse, changes in the locus coeruleus lead to increased vigilance and subneocortical arousal as well as postsynaptic supersensitivity in central noradrenergic receptors. Structural changes in the hippocampus will affect memory. Changes in cognition and impulse control would lead to further changes in the personality and to the sense of self (chronic PTSD, dissociative disorder, substance abuse disorders). The relationship of dysthymia as a genetic illness and learned helplessness as a conditioned response to environmental stimuli are separate but potentially interdependent sequelae. Here the experience of chronic dysphoric mood would begin to reinforce and self-sustain through the chronic, subjective experience of failure and helplessness (see Miller and Keitner, 1996). Genetically transmitted anxiety disorders (panic disorder, generalized anxiety disorder, obsessive–compulsive disorder) and the subcortical systems that regulate fear and arousal have been shown to interact and reinforce patterns of response where systems find what they are looking for (Le Doux, 1996; Marshall, 1997).

In these and other scenarios, systems in the brain have been affected at multiple points, and as with the interaction of affective disorder and personality disorder described by Thase, or anxiety disorder and personality function described by Marshall, deficits in the one establish and perpetuate deficits in the other. In particular, genetic biological disorders may establish disorders of, or patterns of conditioned response that then reinforce the genetic disorder until there comes a point in time when the distinction between the two blurs. In patients such as these, psychopharmacological intervention, while indicated, may not be sufficient as it may address just one of several systems that have been damaged as a result of the biological, genetic, and environmental cascading of central nervous system pathology.

Because a deficit may have become neurobiologically structured, does not mean that the intervention should be exclusively pharmacologic. Expressed another way, just as thinking, feeling, and behavior are influenced by neurobiology, so too neurobiology is influenced by thinking, feeling, and behavior. "Contrary to some expectations, biological analysis is unlikely to diminish the interest in mentation or to make mentation trivial by reduction," Eric Kandel wrote in 1983. "Rather cell and molecular biology have merely expanded our vision, allowing us to perceive previously unanticipated interrelations between biological and psychological phenomena" (p. 1278).

The following is an example of such a complex interaction. The patient is a woman with a long history of dysthymic and anxiety disorders treated with multiple antidepressants and anxiolytics. Her mood, while improved, has remained dysphoric, and her outlook remained fiercely pessimistic. She tended to be socially isolated, left home reluctantly, and usually only to go to work or to fulfill social obligations. She was in treatment with a psychiatric resident, a woman about 10 years her junior. Her mother had died in an accident when she was 8, and her father, a chronic alcoholic, had become increasingly depressed and withdrawn after his wife's death. He probably suffered from major affective disorder, depressed type as well as chronic alcoholism. The father was in the habit, when intoxicated, of referring to this daughter, his only child, as his "only burden," and to his bourbon as his "only son."

> I hate going out [agoraphobia? social phobia?]. Hate it. I go to the supermarket and I feel that the checkout girl is thinking, "Oh here comes that lonely, pathetic woman again" [projection and

perhaps displacement from the transference]. I didn't want to mention this, but I'm seeing Dave on Tuesday. I invited him to a movie after work and he accepted, probably because he feels sorry for me [again possibly displaced affect from the transference]. It's embarrassing. I wish I weren't hoping for something more because of what it will be like for me when I realize there won't be anything more [anticipatory anxiety]. I don't even like the movie. What am I hoping for—love? romance? Shit. Hope is the worst. I just want to get it over with. I know what's going to happen. It's such a joke, my fantasies. All I want to do is get the humiliation over with now instead of having to let them build. And then have it all come crashing down. I'm always going to be alone. I despise this feeling, this hope.

The therapist offering something of a clarification and perhaps support said, "What you're describing isn't hope. It sounds more like what you're feeling is anxiety in anticipation of what you feel is inevitable shame."

Well it's the way I see it. Like the party I went to on Saturday. I left after 15 minutes. I just wanted to get it over with. There's no point to put off the inevitable. I knew how it would end, me alone in my car. Crying. So I just left, went to my car, alone, and cried. What's the point of pretending anything will ever end differently, of "hoping"? It just makes it worse because if I start to hope, start to think maybe I won't be alone, I'm just left that much more empty and depressed. I'm not going to hope because whenever I do, I get slapped for the "chutzpah" of having dared to ask for more. It's humiliating knowing that I'll be told that I have no right to have thought that I'd ever be anything but alone.

A patient who probably had genetically transmitted affective and anxiety disorders, continued to suffer from chronic despair despite aggressive psychopharmacologic treatment. Psychopharmacology is one of the very important tools that must be integrated into a formulation. In one's assessment of psychopharmacology one should anticipate not only those symptoms that medication may benefit, but also anticipate those symptoms where there may be limited benefit. The formulation should address how medication may help psychological therapy and how psychological therapy may help medication.

In the clinical example just described, hopelessness, anxiety, and shame were only partially improved by psychopharmacologic intervention. "Simply put, individuals with personality disorders may have a greater 'burden' of factors that mitigate against a robust antidepressant response" (Thase, 1996, p. 293). Another way of conceptualizing this statement is to realize that in many clinical situations, the individual whom one is treating may suffer from pathology in multiple systems that are not clearly demarcated, and therefore the treatment of one does not necessarily lead to the improvement of the other or to the recovery of the whole. "The boundary between behavior and biology," Kandel wrote, "is arbitrary and changing" (1983, p. 1278). In one's formulation one must hypothesize the likelihood of these affective burdens operating on both sides of the boundary.

The burden of this woman's illness may have affected many boundaries. Hereditary affective illness is heterogeneous and probably disturbs multiple neurotransmitter systems, including but not limited to monoaminergic and serotonergic systems of mood regulation (Weiss & Kilts, 1995). After many years of biological illness, the subcortical thalamo-amygdala system may have additionally begun to be conditioned by this internal dysregulation of mood by reacting with increased fear responses based on the ongoing, internal experience of dysphoria and pain. Maternal loss coupled with paternal despair, neglect, and verbal abuse may also have increased the subcortical conditioned expectation of dysphoria and pain but based now on external sources. The dysregulation was crossing boundaries and so the treatment, to be effective, would have to do the same. The transference is one of those vehicles with which one can cross boundaries—both psychological and neurobiological.

14.

Affect and Formulation

In order to find the patient,
we must look for him within ourselves.
(Bollas, 1987, p. 202)

This chapter will demonstrate the progressive construction of the formulation. A great deal has been left out in order to more clearly show how one gathers data and shapes questions and hypotheses into a formulation. The discussion is not intended as a guide to working with a difficult, suicidal patient.

The patient was mentioned earlier. She had been referred to me by her therapist and psychopharmacologist. The therapist had confided that she, the therapist, was being admitted to hospital for a workup of a possible cancer, and that given those circumstances the patient was more than she could manage. "She really needs more time than I can give her," she had told me. She added that she thought the patient's suicidality and depression indicated a need for "more medication."

The main affect communicated was anxiety. I soon came to realize that the anxiety reflected the therapist's concern lest I not be willing to accept the referral. When I asked for more data about the patient, the therapist told me more about herself, about her own illness. When I did agree to see the patient, I was struck by the sudden disappearance of anxiety in the therapist and by her desire to end the conversation. It seemed that the therapist wasn't so much planning an orderly referral, as she was desperate to get rid of the patient, and once the means to that end had been identified, me, she was eager to be gone. (A year later I learned that the therapist had had an infection, which was treated routinely, and that there had been no cancer.)

After hanging up the phone, I became anxious. After all I had accepted a suicidal patient about whom I knew very little except that she suffered from some form of depression, she drank to excess, and was in the midst of a therapeutic crisis (all significant risk factors for suicide). The appearance of anxiety in me identified the first affect and the first hypothesis as to defense mechanism, projection. Anxiety had been projected from the therapist into me. I further hypothesized that the intensity of the anxiety—the therapist had sounded frightened for herself more than worried about the patient—indicated that the projection had to do with primitive affect probably from the patient. There was something noxious about the patient and about what she contained and communicated.

The other hypothesis that I entertained was the possibility that the therapist felt overwhelmed, and that her anxiety reflected her concern for an increasingly suicidal patient in the context of a failing treatment. Afraid that the patient would suicide, she wanted to refer her to someone else.

When I spoke to the psychopharmacologist, he indicated that the patient was "a severe borderline" who suffered from chronic depression. He did not feel that the patient was any more suicidal now than at baseline, and that her affective illness and psychopharmacologic treatment were "in adequate control given the severity of her character pathology." He felt that she needed "more therapy."

This data added weight to the first hypothesis. Both the therapist and the psychopharmacologist were trying to establish distance from the patient by directing the responsibility of her care elsewhere. I hypothesized that there was something deeply unattractive or disturbing about this woman. She was suicidal, that much had been made clear, but doctors don't usually run from a patient just because the patient is sick.

I was also struck by how little communication there was between the therapist and the psychopharmacologist. They seemed to be avoiding, as well as blaming, one another. I hypothesized that they both must have been quite frustrated by the patient's lack of progress, and wondered whether the patient might be feeling some of their blame as well. The patient called the next day. She was cordial and to the point. When asked she indicated that she was in no immediate crisis. She seemed eager to see me. We set up an appointment for the first evaluation session. I felt calmer. When I first saw the patient, I was surprised at how physically attractive she was. I was also impressed that she hardly looked at me as I introduced myself; hesitated when I offered my hand in greeting; stared at the floor when she talked; brought her own tissues to the session. When asked a question, she answered as if she were reading from some book. It was as if she wanted nothing to do with me and was offering no more emotion than was necessary.

I hypothesized that attachment was conflicted, affect was dangerous, and that safety was the capacity to maintain distance. A response not more than a few minutes into the interview—"I'm always alone. I hate it. That's part of the reason I want to kill myself"—indicated that my hypothesis was either wrong or incomplete. Not surprisingly I needed more data.

The data available to me at the start of the first interview included: evidence of depression, anxiety, suicidal ideation, a history of suicidal behavior, alcohol abuse, a therapist who wanted nothing to do with the patient, mutual accusations by the therapist, the psychopharmacologist, and the patient, anxiety in the therapist, the patient's calm voice on the phone, a mixture of anxiety and curiosity in me. Finally, there was the punctual arrival of a slender, attractive, stylishly dressed woman who had eagerly established an appointment with me and then avoided me as best she could.

Thoughts about anxiety, rage, contradiction, despair, suicidality, projection, and avoidance were all in my mind by the time I sat down with the patient and said, "I have talked with your doctors so I know a little about you. But could you tell me in your own words what brings you to see me?"

As the patient began to elaborate the symptoms and issues that brought her to me, I was listening for answers to my one spoken question as well as the many unspoken questions. These questions included:

Why was your therapist running from you? Why was there so much antagonism between your care providers? Why do you never look at me? Are you acutely suicidal; will you need to be hospitalized? Will I need to adjust the medication? Will I be able to make these adjustments on an outpatient basis? Why is anxiety so prominent an issue? Is your affect constricted or do you fear affect? What are you projecting? What are you avoiding? Suicidality had become the central issue. Is it the only issue, or is it one of several issues? Is your suicidality a resistance? Is it affective illness? Is it characterologic? Is it all of these? How will your suicidality enter the transference, the countertransference? How will it influence my ability to think and act? The risk factors are significant: depression, anxiety, alcohol abuse. Will I have to hospitalize you?—came up again.

The first question guided the patient's response. The other questions guided mine as I listened to this woman speak.

I've been depressed for years. I've tried just about everything. Nothing seems to work. The depression is awful. There's nothing in my life that makes me think it will ever end—I get suicidal—I'm suicidal all the time. Sometimes it's worse, sometimes it's better. But the thoughts are always there.

The "chief complaint" then included depression and suicidal ideation. It also included an issue of transference: "I need your help and I will not let you get close to me." There were contradictions between the words and the way she spoke them. I was faced with a choice. I could ask her to elaborate on the content of the material (suicidality) or on the transference (fear of affect and attachment). At this early stage of treatment, it is very, very rare to choose the latter, and with a potentially suicidal patient, one almost never addresses the transference before the content of the material is clarified. I asked her,

Therapist: Are you feeling suicidal now?
Patient: It's always there.
Therapist: Can you tell me more about it.

Patient: I want the option to kill myself. I mean if this
              treatment doesn't work, I want to have somewhere
              to go. I have nothing. I feel hopeless. Suicide is
              someplace to go.

From the perspective of transference, her response contained a threat. She would sit back and wait. If I didn't get
her better, she would suicide. Threat was something she was
comfortable with; it was strangely safe.

I asked her more about her illness. She told me that she
lived in her own apartment, had a few friends, drank alone. "I
drink to ease the pain." She denied any current neurovegetative symptoms of depression other than her suicidality. She
kept a store of razor blades, an Exacto knife, plastic bags, a
cabinet full of pills, and a suicide "how to" book by her bed.
These had been there for years. She assured me that she was
not any more suicidal now "than usual," but admitted that she
had cut her wrists 2 months ago (no sutures had been required). She had not reported this to her therapist, and added
that she frequently concealed things from (lied to) her therapist. She had also made other, more serious, suicide attempts,
had been psychiatrically hospitalized twice, and was unwilling
to stop drinking. It was as if she were restating her refusal to
engage the treatment or me. "Are you suicidal now?" I asked.
She answered with some impatience. "I'm always suicidal. I've
already told you that." I had in the course of 5 minutes asked
her the same question twice. I was anxious. I found that I was
having trouble thinking, almost imprisoned with anxiety. When
I realized that, I thought about the therapist who had wanted
to get rid of this patient. I wondered whether she too had felt
trapped by this woman's—fear? rage? suicidality? hopelessness?
I wasn't sure. My mouth was dry. This data from the countertransference indicated that much of the affect that was being
contained was primitive and was affect at the level of the biogenetic or conditioned response, or most probably both. (Patients who are struggling with biogenetic illness alone may feel
imprisoned by their illness, but do not usually project that into
the doctor, and thus the transference may communicate helplessness, but in the countertransference one does not usually
identify with or experience that helplessness.)

I asked questions about her depression, her alcohol abuse, her medication. At one point there was a brief silence. She turned to me, looked at me for the first time and said, "Why would I have kept this appointment with you if I were planning to kill myself?" I thought about that. What she said had made sense, and it had been said to my face, not to the floor. Her logic left me feeling a little safer. I felt able to think.

I wondered why she had decided at that moment to help set me free. My provisional hypothesis: I was offering her some hope, some safety, and thus some neocortical freedom which she was giving back to me. But as her former therapist had felt the need to escape from the patient, I anticipated the issues of rejection and imprisonment would recur in the history, the transference, the countertransference.

I asked her to bring the razor blades, the pills, the book, the plastic bags to me the next session. She shook her head, "They sell plastic bags at the supermarket and razor blades at the five and dime. I've got dozens of Exacto knives at work. What's the point if I bring them in to you?"

I found that I was able to think. I said, "Suicide has always been your out, your trump card. If this treatment is going to work, you're going to have to take some other risks. Having suicide as an ever present ally takes away the chance of discovering something new." "Like what?" "I don't know," I said, "That's what makes the unknown unknown."

She agreed to bring the objects in. She agreed to see me the following day. After establishing certain conditions and parameters, I felt safe enough to let her leave my office. That night I worried. Had I done the right thing?

Safety. A chronically suicidal patient who has made acute suicide attempts is not safe; indeed the risk for completed suicide is high. And further this patient's definition of safety, do not let anyone close, had kept her in constant danger. After making biological and psychopharmacological assessments, I had decided that her ability to allow me a little closer, to find hope, fragile though it was, allowed me to trust her with her physical safety.

The next session the buzzer rang 5 minutes before her hour. She came into my office without acknowledging me in any way. She had not brought in any of the objects. When I asked, she replied that she had changed her mind. When I asked her why, she said she didn't know.

She crossed her long legs, took out her packet of Kleenex, and made it clear that in no way was she going to cry. She repeated, "I don't know."

The following session she brought in the knives, the pills, the razor blades, the book, and the plastic bags. As she handed me her "stash," she asked without a smile, "Now what am I going to wrap my fruit in?" It was in a way a humorous comment, and yet I felt it would have been wrong for me to laugh. Why? I didn't know. I waited. She went on, "I needed to know that I was making this choice. Not you."

She was entrusting me with trump cards (albeit replaceable trump cards), and yet there was no hint of trust. She remained distant, almost out of touch. I asked her, "Did you feel that I was forcing you to do something against your will?" She said, "It would have been if I had brought them in for you."

"For you." Why was doing something "for me" so threatening? The issues of coercion and rejection came back. They had been established very early as an aspect of the transference. Her not so subtle threat: "If you don't get me better, I'll suicide." Indeed the issues had come up even before, in the referral; I had felt that I had no choice but to accept the patient whom another had rejected. A hypothesis emerged that for her human relationships were a balance of rejection and coercion: to move close was dangerous unless you had superior force.

But she had already taken a step toward that edge, toward what was unsafe in the transference. By giving me the objects, she had allowed herself to approach. She insisted this was done according to her will: "I did this on my time and according to my wishes and not yours." There was nothing wrong with this attitude. I just wasn't sure why she felt she had to be in control of me. She maintained the "right" to drink, refusing the idea of AA or the offer of antabuse. Her assurances of safety were qualified, "I won't kill myself this week. That's as good as I can do. What do you want from me? A guarantee? Forever?" Yes, I thought, I would have felt more comfortable with that. We discussed hospitalization again. "If you hospitalize me, I'll lose my job. Then I *will* kill myself. I don't need to be hospitalized. I know it." I assessed her suicidality and depression; I decided it was reasonable to continue on an outpatient basis.

As I thought more about the treatment, I realized that I was experiencing her fierce need to control her life, her death, her distance from me. I wanted to ask questions that would bring more data about that sense of safety, freedom, and her fear of me. I wanted to ask her why she was afraid, but I realized that asking her "why" would stifle her thought, and that I would have to discover the answer myself. And then I heard myself ask her, "Why?"

I don't remember just what she said because I was caught in the fact that I had gone against my own thinking and was at that moment listening to my own thoughts and not to my patient's as I tried to understand why I had asked a question that I knew she could not answer. As I thought about that, I realized I was angry with her. That I had been working very hard to insure her safety, that I was carefully evaluating each decision as to medication, treatment, hospitalization, and that all I was feeling was distance and her refusal to participate.

I reasoned that some of this was biologic illness and some of it was not. Her suicidality kept me anxious, uncertain, off balance; I didn't like feeling so out of control. I realized I wanted her to feel some of that, which was why I had asked her a question that I knew she couldn't answer that would make her feel uncertain, a little pushed, a little attacked. I wanted her to take some of herself back. Projection. Once I understood that I realized that the data of the referral and of the countertransference were concordant. The reason the treatment had failed was because the therapist had kept trying to force the illness back into the patient just as I had done by asking her "why?"

I heard her say, "I don't know what else to say" and then I asked, "Can you tell me about the previous treatment with your therapist?" because that seemed to be where more data about what I had done, might lie.

My therapist had been late to every session. Every one. I suggested that we schedule the appointments 15 minutes later because she

was always 15 minutes late. Susan said no. So I'd arrive on time
and she'd be 15 minutes late. In session I'd get to the point where
I'd describe what I hated about myself and how I thought I'd never
be happy. She'd just say to me that I was doing it to myself. That
made me feel worse. I'd ask her for guidance; she'd say, "Stop
doing it to yourself." [The therapist's failure to distinguish between neocortical and lower order determinants of behavior.] I
felt guilty. I felt lost. I felt I was doing something wrong. I left
every session feeling bad.

It was as if the therapist were attacking the patient—just
what I had discovered in myself. The data of the therapist's
constant lateness and the critical, "You're the problem; get
better," had been corroborated by the data of my countertrans-
ference-based attacks, "Why?" I asked her, "How did you feel
when your therapist asked you to see another doctor, to see
me?" "I don't think Susan liked me or disliked me," she said,
"I was just another patient in her day. Nothing special." I
wanted to know why, but would not make the same mistake
twice, at least not consciously in one session. I simply asked,
"Can you tell me more?" "The referral upset me but it was
also a relief. I didn't want to upset Susan any more."

The patient felt nothing for the therapist. The therapist
felt nothing for the patient. She was difficult to empathize with
because as one got closer to her, she pushed back. Everyone
was alone. She elicited retaliation, in the therapist and in me.
I still wasn't sure what was being rejected. But I felt certain that
this patient needed to reject in order to feel safe—but from
what? And when she couldn't totally reject the object, what did
she do? Did she have to control the object? If that were the
case, how had she controlled me? How had she controlled her
former therapist?

I recalled Freud, "The emotions are the constituent which
is least influenced [by repression] and which alone can give us
a pointer as to how we should fill in the missing thoughts"
(1900, p. 461). Look to affect. What were the affects? After the
fourth evaluation session, there was a holiday weekend. With
medication, her suicidality and depression had diminished. But
she was a new patient; there were only the rudiments of a therapeutic alliance. I was still concerned about her safety, and suggested that she call me. We set a time. The weekend came. I

waited for her call. It didn't come. I called her and got her answering machine; I left a message. She didn't respond. Her suicidality had diminished but it was, as with all chronically depressed patients, unpredictable. Had I made a fatal error by not hospitalizing her? The affect was powerful and very clear: I felt fear.

Five minutes before her next session, the doorbell rang. I went out; she entered without looking at me. The session began; she didn't bring up the phone call. After a few minutes, I asked her about it. She replied, "I hate to call." "What do you mean?" "I hate the idea of setting myself up, of encouraging an emotion that isn't real. This is a mercenary relationship. After all I pay you to listen. That's all there is to it. Calling you over the weekend just encourages an attitude that isn't real."

She seemed detached, unconcerned. I felt that I knew what she was thinking. I had felt afraid for her life. She had felt afraid to need me. The two had been equal in their capacity to strike terror. "I know what that feels like," I wanted to say, "the fear." I said nothing. I realized that she wasn't ready to accept empathy. I realized that the demonstration of empathy was at the core of what for her was unsafe, and that if I tried to empathize with her in that moment, she would have felt shame. She was too vulnerable to allow me to be close.

Hypotheses: She needed to be remote because of how frightened she was to need; the experience of need through subneocortically mediated pathways lead to the emotions of fear and shame, and to the state dependent conviction (memory) of rejection. Go slowly. Do not force her to feel how well I might know her. That might make me for the moment feel powerful and sage, but it would only arouse shame or anger (resistance).

Two sessions later, she revealed that she had not told the truth. She had called my office but not at the arranged time; at a much later time when she was drunk. She listened to my voice on the answering machine and then hung up without leaving a message. I asked for her thoughts about that. She said that she had none. Her prior association had been to a boyfriend who had left her for another woman. I said nothing. I only repeated how important I felt it was for her to call me if she felt depressed or suicidal. She was silent, stared at the floor. I asked her, "What are you thinking?" She answered, "I'm thinking about work."

I was thinking about empathy and her need to keep me away. I remembered how in her previous therapy she had always felt humiliated. I was conscious that I did not want to inflict shame on her, but no matter what I said, no matter how supportive, she seemed to feel abandoned. I hypothesized that her safety was the capacity to keep others away. Empathy was the danger. She existed in an isolation of intense pain. Coercion was the form of attachment allowed.

"I was married once" she told me when I asked her about intimate relationships. "I thought I loved Joe. What was really stupid was I thought he loved me. After we'd been dating for four months, I was raped. Joe felt so angry and sad—helpless I guess. We got married. It kind of grew out of that. Weird."

Her marriage emerged from a rape. The bond of coercion. It also raised questions about posttraumatic stress disorder, but there was no solid evidence of that. The marriage was "tempestuous." There were constant arguments. Joe would frequently disappear for a night, a weekend. After a year Joe confessed he was bisexual. A year later, he left. "At least the divorce was honest. After that I got into a series of devastating relationships. Each time it seemed to be with a man who didn't want to be with me. I'd get involved, fall in love. And then the man would leave. Just like that."

This was data from the history but also data that helped to understand the transference. She saw me, like other men that she had valued, as someone who would leave her with nothing but pain. Attachment was pain.

> Oh, I forgot the most important one, Henry. We met at a business conference. He was seated next to me at one of those awful dinners. He called me the next day. It wasn't as if we'd said more than, "Isn't this the worst meal you've ever eaten?" We started this relationship going and then about 2 months into it, he called me and told me he was going back to his ex-wife.

This theme appeared in the referral, in the transference, and in her sexual relationships. Shame was the affect she expected; anger was used in defense. And thus when I asked, "Can you tell me about your childhood?" —there was a context within which I listened. There were already specific themes: the danger of attachment, the futility of empathy, the inevitability of rejection, and coercion as a safe way to connect.

> I was miserable. My very first memory was being stung by a bee. I was 3, maybe 4. I have no idea where my mother was. I mean she was there but she was never there. She was more like a baby-sitter than a mother. When I was 7, I wanted to run away. I don't know why. I didn't know where I wanted to go. I remember my mother was in the kitchen cooking dinner, my brothers were out back. I was trying to tell her, I don't know, something. She was cooking dinner. I climbed out of my bedroom window onto the roof. I was going to jump off. I guess she heard me and pulled me back in.

Was this evidence of childhood affective illness, a little girl's desperate and futile attempts to be heard, perhaps both? I didn't know. But associative learning was being laid down. The attempt to be heard was treacherous; it led to indifference, rejection. I asked about child abuse. There was none, except for parental distance and well-fed neglect.

> When I was 9, I lay down on the road. It was during the day. There were hedges on both sides. It was a dead end street so there were hardly any cars. I lay down and waited to be run over. I waited about 10 minutes to die. No car came so I went home. I never told anyone.

She seemed deeply distressed, but the telling seemed to bring her in touch not with sadness but shame. The stories revealed how she could not reach her mother. The mental status revealed that she could not look up. The transference uncovered the dangerousness of her desire to reach me. "Nothing has changed. Nothing ever will."

Shame was the bridge from mental status to history to transference making me feel that any response I made would feel like an assault. The affect was primitive, raw, monochromatic, subneocortical. Attachment seemed so dangerous. Every object tie led to shame and then to fear. I hoped to find some space, some hope in the relationship with her father.

> He loved to hunt. He loved my brothers. I was his bother. When I was 9 I had this pain in my belly. It wouldn't go away. I told my teacher. The school nurse thought it was indigestion. I told my mother; she said to go to bed. My father thought it was for attention. I was in pain and vomiting. I saw a doctor. He thought it was indigestion. My father yelled at me, "Knock if off." It went on for 3 weeks. Finally another doctor saw me and decided to operate. My appendix had ruptured. Only then did my father believe me.

The pattern was pervasive. The desire to be heard led to shame. The affective response was primitive, conditioned and learned. There was no freedom.

> In school I was the outsider. I was ugly; I was left out. I hated school. I'd truant. Just hitchhike to kill time. I didn't care if I got hurt. I don't know why I never was. I'd go to political demonstrations. Just to be antianything. It didn't matter what. I got kicked out of school. I told my father. He just stared at me, "You're going to amount to nothing." I never went back to school. The next month I ran away from home. It was 10 years later before I returned.

In those 10 years she had moved to Chicago and begun work for a clothing manufacturer. Over the course of time, she became one of their principal designers. Her success, however, did nothing to change her view of herself and her basic sense that she could never safely attach.

After father and daughter had reconciled, when he was dying, he called her to his deathbed. He whispered to her, "Come here, let me love you." Her response to her father was, "You can't."

I asked her what she meant. She made it clear that she felt she was incapable of loving or of ever being loved. It was not the fault of others, it was a fault from within herself: "I can't be loved," was her deeply felt response, and beyond that the more primitive, "I cannot attach. I have associatively learned that as I approach others I am increasingly in danger (a subneocortical response). In order to stay safe, I must stay apart." She could not risk the desire to be close; even the desire to be understood was dangerous. I would have to be very careful about showing her that I understood.

The data showed that she was primitively connected to shame and rejection from at least two sources. First there was a biological source of illness. Chronic dysthymic disorder, perhaps of lifelong duration. Intermittent alcohol abuse. Second there was conditioned avoidance of attachment because of the association to shame and fear. Attachment had to be controlled: by distancing from the object (displacement, avoidance), or by controlling the object (projection). But in no circumstance would the subneocortical system mediating this behavior allow her to approach another, or be approached by another, without registering its perception of intense danger.

Suicide joined both aspects of pathological affect. It was harmonious with chronic dysthymic disorder. It was harmonious with the need to restrict freedom. Suicide was a psychobiological comfort, which made working with this woman so troubling. When I felt the depth of her attachment to suicide, it was eerie and repellent. When under its control, I felt sick, as though I had been infected. When I tried to step between her and her illness, I realized how unsafe she felt without that control.

Safety was the comfort of razor blades, Exacto knives, pills, and a suicide book by her bed. The edge of danger was empathy. Usually it is the other way around. This woman was afraid to feel understood because she was convinced she would never be accepted by those she wanted. Her desire for attachment came to be associated with aversive affect through both genetic (dysthymic disorder) and environmental (conditioned) factors. Thus in the transference she would identify me as the one who by understanding her would bring her shame. "This isn't a relationship. I pay you to listen," was for her the sum total of our relationship.

A safe place. I would certainly advise the use of antidepressant and anxiolytic medications. I would not expect her affective illness to completely remit given her past treatment failures, but more significantly the lifelong duration of the illness, the comorbidity of personality disorder, and alcohol abuse.

Because I would not expect medication to provide the comfort and safety of cure, therapy would have to become and provide the safe place, which would take time. Medication would help to gain time. Interpretations would have to wait because I did not want to call subneocortical memories into the transference. Words would need to hold and support without too much focus on the transference. I did not want to bring her shame by reexposing her to state-dependent memory that she was not yet ready to contain. But she continued to avoid me, reject me, project her hopelessness into me. And if I could not interpret this because interpretation brought an acute experience of shame, what could I do? I would have to contain the cancer that the therapist had refused.

The data indicated primitive affect. Therefore the cure would be psychobiological where words and medication would be used to hold, and where learning would have to be unconditioned before new learning could begin. Subneocortical dominance of attachment bonds as reflected in the history, and seen in the mental status, the transference, and the countertransference would have to be contained, and gradually brought into focus in the transference. But the transference would have to be used more for desensitization of these emotional memories than for cognitive interpretation. I hoped primitive emotional memory would in time give way to more even neocortical assessment and control. There would be few interpretations. I would have to keep her physically safe enough until she was psychobiologically safe enough to begin. I would have to contain her illness until it was safe.

15.

Data, Hypothesis, Affect, and Map

> *Canst thou not minister to a mind*
> *diseas'd,*
> *Pluck from the memory a rooted sorrow,*
> *Raze out the written troubles of the*
> *brain,*
> *And with some sweet oblivious antidote,*
> *Cleanse the stuff'd bosom of that*
> *perilous stuff*
> *which weighs upon the heart?*
> *(Shakespeare, Macbeth, V 3 40)*

Can one calm memory? It depends. The integration of inter-personal data in a biological context is crucial for successful psychotherapy. The intent of this book has been to demonstrate how to take the clinical situation, the face-to-face encounter between patient and therapist, and break the seamless experience into its parts. Each piece of data (first data, first meeting, mental status, transference, countertransference, resistance, defense mechanisms, history) must be examined with regard to its origin, meaning, direction, and strength. Decisions are made about the data in isolation, in reference to other specific data, and in relation to the individual as a whole. Hypotheses are constructed about the data, and about what one expects to encounter in the patient and in oneself.

In addition, one must try to understand each piece of data from one of four perspectives as regards affect in order to better understand what areas of the brain are most likely in control

271

of what has been observed. Specifically, it is necessary to try to locate each piece of data in relation to its potential psychological, biogenetic, conditioned, and/or traumatic origin. One does this in order to better understand how free the data may be of their own consequences. The relative balance of the parts of the brain from which the data and affect spring determines the power of its inevitability.

The following examples demonstrate the clinical use of the integration of data and affect; the first example is where the origins are hypothetically neocortical; in subsequent examples the origins are predominantly below the level of the neocortex. The first example involves a treatment that I supervised between a therapist, a resident in his early thirties, and a woman in her midtwenties, a graduate student in anthropology. She had presented for treatment because of difficulties with intimacy, and mild to moderate dysthymia. She came to a session anxious and pressured, a little late, a little breathless, and said to her therapist,

> I have this major decision I have to discuss with you. Jack invited me out for New Year's Eve. I accepted. Then I got a phone call from Frank Leeds—you know he was one of my teachers last semester. Well he invited me to go skiing with him to Vail—all expenses. I'm not sure what I think about Frank but I love to ski. I guess I'd have to sleep with him if I went. I don't really want to sleep with him. I mean he's not my teacher any more. It's okay on that level. But I don't know what I'd tell Jack. I really do love to ski and I could never afford a trip on my own. I told Frank I'd tell him after I saw you today.

I asked the therapist what he did next. He mentioned that he felt anxious because of how much the patient had come to rely on him. He said that he asked the patient, "Do you feel it's realistic that you could go off skiing with this man, share the same bedroom, all expenses paid, and expect that there wouldn't be sexual expectations?" I thought this was a reasonable question. It was one that focused primarily on the extra-transference. But as he related the patient's response to his question, I found myself drifting back to something else. I said to the therapist, "It's odd that you'd be feeling anxious."

He laughed a little self-consciously, and then said, "You're right. I thought about that, sort of. I think there are two things. First I don't want to push her toward a decision. I think it's real important that I stay neutral." That seemed reasonable enough given the woman's intelligence and the fact that she had functioned and lived independently for over a decade. "And then second, well, she's expecting this from me as someone who will help her, a parental figure who will guide her through life. I don't want her to leave the session disappointed with me."

I wasn't sure why he wanted the patient to like him. I asked him about that. He answered, "It's a big deal for me getting the patient to like me and be comfortable with me. I don't want her to be angry or disappointed with me. There is this approval thing in me, I know it. It's core to me as a human being, and I see it as being at odds with being a therapist. It's something that's definitely there."

I had known and worked with this therapist as his supervisor for 5 months; I was impressed with his intelligence, stability, and honesty. I felt that he could explore the issues of the inappropriateness of his affect (his anxiety) and the data of the countertransference (the desire to be liked) without being threatened or overwhelmed. I felt there was enough safety and freedom to go further. I said to him, "Do you have any sense of where the need to please her is coming from because I think it has more to do with you (countertransference) than with her (transference)?"

He became a little tearful and related that he had had an older brother who was killed in an automobile accident when he, the therapist, was 8 years old.

> I always felt that I had to make it up to my parents that Joey had died. That somehow I had to be as good as he had been, or better. I think it was really about how I wanted my parents to love me the way they had loved him. But they never did. I could never be my brother. Because of that it seemed I could never win their real love.

He continued to say that he realized that some of the anxiety he was feeling must have been related to his need for the approval of others—his parents, his patient, friends, me. There was a countertransference issue that the therapist had understood; one that he would have to work through separate from his work with the patient.

The understanding of the therapist's anxiety was mainly accomplished by the therapist himself, was not rigidly fixed in the transference (between him and me or between him and his patient), and was reasoned through once the data were identified. The transference and countertransference were thus used as sources of information, in this case about affect, and when confronted was responsive to language and reason. This is an example of data, hypothesis, and affect at the level of cognitive identification and interpretation.

The following is an example of integration of data and affect at another level. It is taken from a session 6 months into the treatment with the woman described in the previous chapter, who had been referred to me by her psychotherapist and psychopharmacologist. She began by saying, "My friend Sally's mother was diagnosed with cancer. The doctor said he was 90% sure that she would be cured by radiation—I'm not sure what that's supposed to mean."

From this beginning, it wasn't clear what the data meant except that she was expressing several things at once: disease, decline, hopelessness, distrust. This could represent information pertaining to biological illness, a sense of hopelessness in the context of biogenetic illness. It could represent a biological and/or conditioned response of paranoia to authority figures. It could represent a reasoned and cautious distrust of authority figures. It could represent a traumatic and/or conditioned response on the basis of long-standing rejection and neglect. Obviously, at the beginning of the session, I did not know which of these factors were contributing most, and similarly what level of the central nervous system was dominant. I would need more data, but guided by my formulation, I anticipated that I would discover data in support of more primitive organization. As I listened, I would be listening for data that would help identify the level of the communication. I would be listening for freedom and safety, and would want some sense of how far I could push the issue of safety based on how much freedom I felt that the patient was operating from. The more freedom there was in the response the more I would assume that the integration was at the neocortical level. The more the responses seemed out of the patient's willful control, the more I would assume that the integration was biogenetic or more psychologically primitive—at a conditioned or traumatic level of integration. The data I would be looking for had to do with freedom. She went on,

> Anyway there's this woman at work, Dawn, she's about my age. They didn't fire her but they're threatening to. They treat her like shit. They just don't understand what she's worth. I mean they think they can just let her set things up and then after she's done all this work for them, fire her. Use her and then get rid of her. They feel they can treat her like shit and it doesn't matter. It scares me. The whole place scares me.

A theme was emerging. No one could be trusted—people set you up and then fire you. No matter what people say ("We're 90% sure we can cure the cancer") things will end badly. If this were a psychological issue and if I felt that she were integrated at a neocortical level with the freedom to feel, evaluate, and respond, that is, with some freedom over affect and its consequences, I would have asked her about her distrust of doctors, steering the session toward the transference. However, since in the formulation I had concluded that this woman's affect was controlled at both the biogenetic and primitively conditioned levels, I decided that I did not want to intensify the transference because I had hypothesized that such an intensification would introduce less freedom into her thinking by arousing more primitive fear and state dependent memory. I therefore decided to explore the issue of distrust with her, but in the extratransference. I asked,

Therapist: You anticipate being shot down?
Patient: Yeah. That's what they do. It's why the company is so successful. They'll do whatever they have to do to cut costs. The good die on the rack [it was a clothing company]—unless they're willing to

work for free. Once they feel you want more, they
fire you. That's what's happening to Dawn.

Therapist: There aren't any people to trust?

Patient: Exactly. I mean Dawn is generous and talented.
              And now, they'll just hurt her. It's inevitable.

I felt that what she was saying was that it was inevitable that
one got hurt whenever one allowed oneself to need another
human being. I could have confronted her with the inconsistency that she was confiding in me, an authority figure and a
doctor but I felt from the content of the session and from the
transference–countertransference data (her reliance on me)
that I might better use the transference differently. I said nothing. She went on.

Patient: Joe called to invite me to dinner with a group
              from work, you know a nothing get together.
              Thank God I had an excuse not to go. It'd be
              painful to be there. I mean Sam would be there
              [a man on whom she had a crush]. I feel exposed
              to him already. I'm not going. I don't want to feel
              that way. I don't want him to know that he has
              any power over me in any way [transference].
        (I decided to push the issue of safety further.)

Therapist: It would be dangerous to trust anyone?

Patient: I don't want to be surprised. I mean at various
              points in the past, I've been hurt; I don't want to
              be surprised. I want to know before, be ready. I
              want to know what might be coming.

Therapist: Knowing that Sam likes you but is involved with
              someone else, and that his reaction really isn't so
              much about you but is about the makeup of his
              life, all that knowledge doesn't seem to help you.

Patient: No. It's conscious. I agree with you there. But
              even if I try, these things will just get me. It will
              get me. I can't risk being around people who hurt
              me like that.

Therapist: Knowing his situation doesn't help?

Patient: No.

Responses were inevitable. Freedom was minimal. And thus to go back to the beginning, "The doctor said he was 90% sure that she would be cured by radiation—I'm not sure what that's supposed to mean." It had become clear what that meant.

The patient was afraid to trust, unable to believe anything that anyone might say. Thought offered no help. Affect, in part biogenetically driven, and in part through conditioned response, ruled. In terms of locating this data neuropsycholgically its origins were genetic in terms of inherited affective illness and in lower order pathways through conditioned response. Conscious and yet inevitable are qualities of emotion routed below the level of the neocortex. I hypothesized that she would project that distrust both psychologically and biologically in her object relations and in her perceptions. So I felt certain that these projections would be directed into the transference, and indeed this hypothesis had been borne out in the past whenever I had remarked on the contradiction that she was confessing to me that there was no one to whom she could confess. What is wrong with confronting a contradiction in the transference? Nothing, so long as one has data that support the conclusion that the patient is able to think about the confrontation. I had more and more data in the formulation and in the session to support the hypothesis that she had very little freedom, very little safety, and that she would not be able to use much reason to help her think about issues in the transference or in the extratransference.

But what does one do when the data support the hypothesis that lower order pathways are dominant in their control of affect, and therefore when there is limited access to neocortical reason? One answer is that one uses the transference with its access to primitive affect in an attempt to slowly decondition primitive affect. I attempted to accomplish this in two general ways. First I anticipated her use of projection; I told her that I was quite convinced that when in crisis she would see me as one of those people who would offer her false assurances ("90% sure of cure"); in essence that she would see me as someone who would lie to her. I made this prediction so that when she turned against me in the transference (when the displaced negative transference returned), she might possibly remember the prediction as a way of holding onto the thought that some of the force of the negative transference might have more to do with the power of subneocortical affect and with state dependent memory than with me. I was trying to warn her neocortex that there would come a time when lower order pathways through psychobiological projection would attempt to destroy all of the memory (history) of our work. Thus I was predicting what would happen in an attempt to bolster neocortical control.

Second, I tried to find ways to use the transference to blunt the impact of her projection both in the transference and in the "real world." That is, I suggested how she might use the treatment as a template against which lower order reality could be compared. I tried to anticipate with the patient those situations where primitive affect might be expected. I reviewed specific issues that she had to face and gave specific but limited suggestions as to what she might anticipate. I offered advice concerning decisions where I felt they would impact directly on affect. I encouraged her to call me as she approached a feared interpersonal situation in order to help her delay the time between stimulus and response. I did all this up to a point determined by my assessment of her psychological sophistication, her genetic state, her biological conditioning.

Was I fostering dependence? Yes. Did this represent transference gratification? Yes. Can this encourage splitting and displacement? Yes. Therefore one must be careful lest one outstep data and hypotheses, and the needs and strengths of the patient. To be successful this approach requires working on the edge of safe transference.

Another example, this from the treatment of the lawyer whose speech was difficult to interrupt, whose mother had been a Holocaust survivor, and whose father worked in the diamond trade. He entered the session, the third week of February, and asked, "So how was your Valentine's?" He paused; I began to say something when he cut me off and began a long description of his weekend, his visit to his parents' home, his father's new car, a new client at work. One hypothesis I held about this man was that he feared attachment and thus that he feared his own curiosity about me. But I had data to support that he had been able to think about this, and therefore I felt more confident that I could push him closer to the transference and be heard. I said to him, "You ask me a question, and then when I begin to answer, you pick up the pace of your speech making it impossible for me to speak." He paused and said,

Patient: I was walking over here thinking about Valentine's Day. I was thinking should I ask you about that? It was just a thought I was having. I didn't really—I don't really care that much what the answer is.

Therapist: Perhaps. But you ask the question and then seem to become anxious [affect]. Your speech becomes a little pressured [mental status], you change the topic [defense mechanism]. It didn't seem so much that you didn't want to know as you were a little frightened to want to know.

Patient: I don't. I mean it's not conscious. It just happens. I wanted to escape from the question. I don't want to know. I mean maybe I do. But I don't. It would have been easier for me if we just didn't deal with it at all. I was just being polite. Well, no. There was more I don't know. When I was with my parents and my father was showing me his new car. I didn't care. I hate cars. Then he goes into this long thing about what car I should buy. Gotta be American.

He continued a long description about cars, the relative value of Buick versus Ford, obsessional details about the weekend. I felt that this was resistance and that the anxiety that was fueling it had to do with the transference. So I said to him, "You wander away from your question about me." He thought for a moment.

Patient: I'd rather have things be tidy than cling. It introduces an element of unpredictability and chaos.

> You're right. It's difficult for me to hold onto in-
> formation about another person. My own bound-
> aries, my own sense of who I am, they're just not
> defined enough and so I just move away.

He was describing issues that I had hypothesized—that as he started to feel more involved, curious, and involved with another human being (transference), he would become anxious (affect), reflecting a subneocortically conditioned, state dependent memory and response (history). When this occurred, his thinking would become more primitive and defended, reflecting this hypothetical shift from higher order to lower order pathways. But unlike the patient in the previous example, he was able to tolerate the anxiety of the transference and think about it. He said, "You're right. I ask a question and then I realize that I don't want to hear anymore. I mean it's not conscious. It just happens. It's this basic fear thing."

The use of the transference is determined by several factors brought together in the formulation. If one discovers from data and testing of data that there is relative responsivity of affect to input and reason, then the transference can be used to demonstrate inconsistency, contradiction, illogic either as these pertain to thought or to affect. However, if the data support the hypothesis that the affect is not free, and that there is subneocortical dominance and a conditioned response to transference interpretation, then the transference should be used to decondition affect, to diminish lower order projection, and to help restore neocortical control over affect. If there is a mix, as there is in most treatments, then one must move back and forth depending on the data and affect in each session.

One should anticipate there will be times, many times, when working with transference in this way, that one steps too far. In order to begin a new medication, I had instructed a patient, the woman who worked as a pharmaceutical representative for the company that manufactured nicotine patches, to stop taking fluoxetine (Prozac). I had explained that as she had been on a low dose and as the drug had a long half-life, I anticipated few withdrawal symptoms if she just stopped. The next week she came to the session enraged with me. She was having trouble sleeping, was convinced of my incompetence, and was almost certain that I "didn't give a shit." Further she refused to accept any recommendations I had as to how to better deal with the insomnia that she was experiencing. As I had gone to great lengths to blunt some of this woman's primitive fears, I felt myself wanting to accuse her of ingratitude. I thought for a moment of ending the treatment. These powerful reactions should serve as a reminder that when one is working on the edge of transference, there are landmines. When they go off, be especially mindful of explosions in the countertransference.

The uses of the transference I have described are to a certain degree cognitive behavioral interventions aimed at increasing the sense of safety by desensitizing and deconditioning lower order psychobiological projections. But this is not cognitive–behavioral therapy; it is a treatment that to be effective must first identify data and affect, and then fashion one's responses through the transference depending on one's hypothesis of the central nervous system balance. One uses the transference to get to this level of affect, and then more often than not uses these same transference elements to communicate. It is a primitive communication. One cannot call forth these "half-tamed demons" (Freud, 1905, p. 109), and then expect them to speak proper English (or German). The communication, like the demons themselves, is more basic, and involves moving between genuine availability, gratification, and limits, between genuine support and interpretation. To move in this terrain requires a clear sense of where one is going and what one expects to find.

Working with specific data, forming specific hypotheses, having a sense of what part of the brain one is talking to, one can formulate when to use language to reason with a patient, and when to comfort, to advise, to share, to gratify, to limit. What is crucial is that one be able to mold one's responses through the transference.

The transference can be used to increase the bounds of safety and understanding, and to increase the patient's ultimate independence from primitive affect. Ideally this extends neocortical dominance, and leads to an increased reliance on language and interpretation. But to get to the point where logic can be applied directly to the practice of psychotherapy requires that most treatments go through a phase where primitive affects are first controlled, soothed, contained, conditioned, and only interpreted as evidence of higher level affect and neocortical control emerge. With most patients it takes time before one can say, "Now I know your motive," as Freud had said to Dora (1905, p. 109). It takes time to get to the point where one can have confidence that not only what one is about to say is correct, but that the patient will neurobiologically be able to listen and think about what one has said. Such a verbal, symbolic interpretation is a goal reached by some, but by no means all treatments. The route there begins with data and hypotheses; they provide the bearings. Transference is the vehicle. Affect gives the direction. The formulation is the map.

References

Amaral, D., Price, J., Pitkanen A., & Carmichael, S. (1992). Anatomical organization of the primate amygdaloid complex. In J. P. Aggleton (Ed.), *The amygdala* (pp. 1–66). New York: Wiley-Liss.

Amini, F., Lewis, T., Lannon, R., Louie, A., Baumbacher, G., McGuinness, T., & Schiff, E. Z. (1996). Affect, attachment, memory. *Psychiatry, 59,* 213–237.

Andreasen, N. C. (1994). Changing concepts of schizophrenia and the ahistorical fallacy. *American Journal of Psychiatry, 151,* 1405–1406.

Beckett, S. (1961). *Happy days.* New York: Grove.

Bollas, C. (1987). *The shadow of the object.* New York: Columbia University Press.

Bowlby, J. (1969). *Attachment.* New York: Basic.

Bremner, J. D., Randall, P., Scott, T., Bronen, R., Seibyl, J., Southwick, S., Delaney, R., McCarthy, G., Charney, D., & Innis, R. (1995). MRI-based measurement of hippocampal volume in patients with combat related posttraumatic stress disorder. *American Journal of Psychiatry 152,* 973–981.

Breuer, J., & Freud, S. (1893–1895). Studies on hysteria. In J. Strachey (Ed.), *The standard edition of the complete psychological works of Sigmund Freud.* (Vol. 2, pp. 1–309). London: Hogarth Press, 1955.

Carroll, L. (1947). *Alice's Adventures in Wonderland.* New York: Books. (Original work published 1865.)

Cooper, A. M. (1985). Will neurobiology influence psychoanalysis? *American Journal of Psychiatry, 142,* 1395–1402.

Darwin, C. (1872). *The expression of the emotions in man and animals.* New York: Appleton.

Emde, R. N. (1991). Positive emotions for psychoanalytic theory. *Journal of the American Psychoanalytic Association, 39s,* 5–44.

Freud, A. (1966). *The ego and the mechanisms of defense.* New York: International Universities Press.

Freud, S. (1894). The psycho-neuroses of defence. In J. Strachey (Ed.), *The standard edition of the complete psychological works of Sigmund Freud* (Vol. 3, pp. 41–61). London: Hogarth Press, 1962.

Freud, S. (1895). Project for a scientific psychology. In J. Strachey (Ed.), *The standard edition of the complete psychological works of Sigmund Freud* (Vol. 1, pp. 281–291). London: Hogarth Press, 1966.

Freud, S. (1896). Heredity and the aetiology of the neuroses. In J. Strachey (Ed.), *The standard edition of the complete psychological works of Sigmund Freud* (Vol. 3, pp. 141–156). London: Hogarth Press, 1962.

Freud, S. (1900). The interpretation of dreams. In J. Strachey (Ed.), *The standard edition of the complete psychological works of Sigmund Freud* (Vol. 5). London: Hogarth Press, 1953.

Freud, S. (1901). Psychopathology of everyday life. In J. Strachey (Ed.), The standard edition of the complete psychological works of Sigmund Freud (Vol. 6). London: Hogarth Press, 1960.

Freud, S. (1905). Fragment of an analysis of a case of hysteria. In J. Strachey (Ed.), *The standard edition of the complete psychological works of Sigmund Freud* (Vol. 7, pp. 1–122). London: Hogarth Press, 1953.

Freud, S. (1912). The dynamics of transference. In J. Strachey (Ed.), *The standard edition of the complete psychological works of Sigmund Freud* (Vol. 12, pp. 97–108). London: Hogarth Press, 1958.

Freud, S. (1913). On beginning the treatment (Further recommendations on the technique of psycho-analysis, I). In J. Strachey (Ed.), *The standard edition of the complete psychological works of Sigmund Freud* (Vol. 12, pp. 121–144). London: Hogarth Press, 1958.

Freud, S. (1914a). On the history of the psycho-analytic movement. In J. Strachey (Ed.), *The standard edition of the complete psychological works of Sigmund Freud* (Vol. 14, pp. 1–66). London: Hogarth Press, 1957.

Freud, S. (1914b). Remembering, repeating and working-through (Further recommendations on the technique of psycho-analysis, II). In J. Strachey (Ed.), *The standard edition of the complete psychological works of Sigmund Freud* (Vol. 12, pp. 145–156). London: Hogarth Press, 1958.

Freud, S. (1915a). Instincts and their vicissitudes. In J. Strachey (Ed.), *The standard edition of the complete psychological works of Sigmund Freud* (Vol. 14, pp. 109–140). London: Hogarth Press, 1957.

Freud, S. (1915b). Observations on transference-love (Further recommendations on the technique of psycho-analysis, III). In J. Strachey

(Ed.), *The standard edition of the complete psychological works of Sigmund Freud* (Vol. 12, pp. 157–171). London: Hogarth Press, 1958.

Freud, S. (1916–1917). Introductory lectures on psycho-analysis. In J. Strachey (Ed.), *The standard edition of the complete psychological works of Sigmund Freud* (Vol. 15). London: Hogarth Press, 1961.

Freud, S. (1920). The psychogenesis of a case of homosexuality in a woman. In J. Strachey (Ed.), *The standard edition of the complete psychological works of Sigmund Freud* (Vol. 18, pp. 145–172). London: Hogarth Press, 1955.

Freud, S. (1926a). Inhibitions, symptoms and anxiety. In J. Strachey (Ed.), *The standard edition of the complete psychological works of Sigmund Freud* (Vol. 20, pp. 75–172). London: Hogarth Press, 1959.

Freud, S. (1926b). The question of lay analysis. In J. Strachey (Ed.), *The standard edition of the complete psychological works of Sigmund Freud* (Vol. 20, pp. 177–250). London: Hogarth Press, 1959.

Freud, S. (1930). Civilization and its discontents. In J. Strachey (Ed.), *The standard edition of the complete psychological works of Sigmund Freud* (Vol. 21, pp. 57–145). London: Hogarth Press, 1961.

Freud, S. (1940). An outline of psycho-analysis. In J. Strachey (Ed.), *The standard edition of the complete psychological works of Sigmund Freud* (Vol. 23, pp. 139–207). London: Hogarth Press, 1964.

Friel, B. (1994). *Molly Sweeney.* New York: Plume.

Gabbard, G. (1994). Psychotherapists who transgress sexual boundaries. *Bulletin of the Menninger Clinic, 58,* 124–135.

Glassman, A. H. (1993). Cigarette smoking: Implications for psychiatric illness. *American Journal of Psychiatry, 150,* 546–558.

Glück, L. (1990). The Untrustworthy Speaker. In *Ararat.* Hopewell, NJ: Ecco Press.

Gray, S. (1992). *Monster in a box.* New York: Vintage.

Greenberg, J., & Mitchell, S. (1983). *Object relations in psychoanalytic theory.* Cambridge, MA: Harvard University Press.

Guare, J. (1990). *Six degrees of separation.* New York: Dramatists Play Service.

Hebb, D. O. (1949). *The organization of behavior.* New York: Wiley.

Herman, J. L. (1992). *Trauma and recovery.* New York: Basic.

Holtzman, W. (1996). *Sabina.* New York: Primary Stages.

Kandel, E. (1979). Psychotherapy and the single synapse. *New England Journal of Medicine, 301,* 1029–1037.

Kandel, E. (1983). From metapsychology to molecular biology. *American Journal of Psychiatry, 140,* 1277–1293.

Kandel, E., & Schwartz, J. (1982). Molecular biology of learning. *Science, 218,* 433–443.

Kandel, E., Schwartz, J., & Jessell, T. (1995). *Essentials of neural science and behavior.* Norwalk, CT: Appleton & Lange.

Kandel, E., & Spencer, W. A. (1968). Cellular neurophysiological approaches in the study of learning. *Physiological Review, 48,* 65–134.

Kernberg, O. (1991). The psychopathology of hatred. *Journal of the American Psychoanalytic Association, 39s,* 209–238.

Killingmo, B. (1989). Conflict and deficit. *International Journal of Psycho-Analysis, 70,* 65–79.

Krystal, H. (1984). Psychoanalytic views on human emotional damage. In B. van der Kolk (Ed.), *Posttraumatic stress disorder, psychological and biological sequelae* (pp. 1–28). Washington, DC: APA Press.

Kuller, S., Nichols, J., & Martin, R. (1984). *From neuron to brain.* Sunderland, MA: Sinauer.

Kupfermann, I. (1981a). Motivation. In E. Kandel & J. Schwartz (Eds.), *Principles of neural science* (pp. 450–460). New York: Elsevier/North-Holland.

Kupfermann, I. (1981b). Learning. In E. Kandel and J. Schwartz (Eds.), *Principles of neural science* (pp. 570–579). New York: Elsevier/North-Holland.

Kushner, T. (1992). *Angels in America.* New York: Theater Communications Group.

Langer, L. (1991). *Holocaust testimonies.* New Haven, CT: Yale University Press.

Lawrence, J., & Lee, R. (1960). *Inherit the wind.* New York: Bantam.

Lear, J. (1990). *Love and its place in nature.* New York: Farrar, Straus, & Giroux.

LeDoux, J. E. (1992). Emotion as memory. In S. A. Christianson (Ed.), *The Handbook of Emotion and Memory* (pp. 269–288). Hillsdale, NJ: Lawrence Erlbaum.

LeDoux, J. E. (1993a). Emotional memory systems in the brain. *Behavioral Brain Research, 58,* 69–79.

LeDoux, J. E. (1993b). Emotional memory: Research of systems and synapses. *Annals of New York Academy of Sciences, 702,* 149–159.

LeDoux, J. E. (1994). Emotion memory and the brain. *Scientific American, 270,* 50–57.

LeDoux, J. E. (1995). Emotion: Clues from the brain. *Annual Review of Psychology, 46,* 209–235.

LeDoux, J. E. (1996). *The emotional brain.* New York: Simon & Schuster.

LeDoux, J. E., Romanski, L., & Xagoraris, A. (1989). Indelibility of subcortical emotional memories. *Journal of Cognitive Neuroscience, 1,* 238–243.

Lorenz, K. Z. (1965). *Evolution and modification of behavior.* Chicago: University of Chicago Press.

Marshall, J. R. (1997). The course and inpact of panic disorder. *Journal of Clinical Psychiatry, 58,* 36–42.

Martin, J. H. (1989). *Neuroanatomy text and atlas.* New York: Elsevier.

Masson, J. M. (Ed.). (1985). *The complete letters of Sigmund Freud to Wilhelm Fliess 1887–1904.* Cambridge, MA: Belknap/Harvard University Press.

Miller, I., & Keitner, G. (1996). Combined medication and psychotherapy in the treatment of chronic mood disorders. *Psychiatric Clinics of North America, 19,* 151–171.

Mitchell, D., Osbourne, E. W., & O'Boyle, M. W. (1985). Habituation under stress: Shocked mice show non-associative learning in a T-maze. *Behavior and Neural Biology, 43,* 212–217.

Nieuwenhuys, R., Voogd, J., & van Huijzen, C. (1981). *The human nervous system: A synopsis and atlas.* New York: Springer Verlag.

Oates, J. C. (1991). *The rise of life on earth.* New York: New Directions.

Olds, S. (1980). *Satan says.* Pittsburgh: University of Pittsburgh Press, 1995.

Pavlov, I. P. (1927). *Conditioned reflexes.* New York: Dover.

Richardson, R., Jr. (1995). *Emerson, the mind on fire.* Los Angeles: University of California Press.

Rogan, M., & LeDoux, J. E. (1996). Emotion: Systems, cells, synaptic plasticity. *Cell, 85,* 469–475.

Schwartz, A. (1987). Drives, affects, behavior—and learning: Approaches to a psychobiology of emotion and to an integration of psychoanalytic and neurobiologic thought. *Journal of the American Psychoanalytic Association, 35,* 467–506.

Shakespeare, W. (1952). *The complete works.* New York: Harcourt Brace & World.

Sophocles (1985). *The Theban plays.* New York: Penguin.

Stone, M. (1991). Incest in the borderline patient. In R. Kluft (Ed.), *Incest-related syndromes of adult psychopathology* (pp. 183–204). Washington, DC: American Psychiatric Press.

Thase, M. E. (1996). The role of Axis II comorbidity in the management of patients with treatment-resistant depression. *Psychiatric Clinics of North America, 19,* 287–309.

Uhry, A. (1986). *Driving Miss Daisy.* New York: Theater Communications Group.

van der Kolk, B. (1996a). The complexity of adaptation to trauma. In B. van der Kolk, A. McFarlane, & L. Weisaeth (Eds.), *Traumatic stress* (pp. 182–213). New York: Guilford Press.

van der Kolk, B. (1996b). The body keeps score. In B. van der Kolk, A. McFarlane, & L. Weisaeth (Eds.), *Traumatic stress* (pp. 214–241). New York: Guilford Press.

van der Kolk, B. (1996c). Trauma and memory. In B. van der Kolk, A. McFarlane, & L. Weisaeth (Eds.), *Traumatic Stress* (pp. 279–302). New York: Guilford Press.

van der Kolk, B., Hoestetler, A., Herron, N., & Fisler, R. (1994). Trauma and the development of borderline personality disorder. *Psychiatric Clinics of North America, 17,* 715–729.

Vertes, R., & Miller, N. (1976). Brainstem neurons that fire selectively to a conditioned stimulus for shock. *Brain Research, 128,* 146–152.

Weiss, J., & Kilts, C. D. (1995). Animal models of depression and schizophrenia. In A. F. Schatzberg & N. Nemeroff (Eds.), *Textbook of psychopharmacology* (pp. 81–124). Washington: American Psychitric Press.

Wilde, O. (1989). *The complete works.* New York: Harper & Row.

Williams, T. (1945). *The glass menagerie.* New York: Penguin.

Winnicott, D. W. (1971). *Playing and reality.* New York: Routledge.

Author Index

Subject Index